INDEPENDENTS' DAY

BROOK TURNER is a freelance journalist who has written for the *Good Weekend* and *The Monthly*, and edited a number of magazines including *The Australian Financial Review Magazine*.

'Brook Turner has written a handbook for a revolution. It's the fascinating story of how frustrated citizens rose up to humble the mighty Liberal party and create a new force in Australian politics in the 2022 federal election.'

PETER HARTCHER, political editor of
The Sydney Morning Herald* and *The Age

'A forensic, intimate and detailed account about how a bunch of outsiders—all but one of them women—blew the 2022 federal election wide open.'

JANE CARO AM, Walkley Award–winning columnist

'Brook Turner has meticulously examined the process of making an authentic Australian Democracy Sausage, and it turns out to be just what we were hungry for.*'
*grass roots

CATHY WILCOX, cartoonist

Dear Joe Richard

I in no way did justice to your daughter, who has done [...] hate [...] things. Cannot [...] the next edition

INDEPENDENTS' DAY

The inside story of the community independents
and volunteers who changed Australian politics forever

BROOK TURNER

ALLEN&UNWIN
SYDNEY · MELBOURNE · AUCKLAND · LONDON

Susie Byce

Dena Shield

Tina Jackson

Louise Hislop

First published in 2022

Allen & Unwin
Cammeraygal Country
83 Alexander Street
Crows Nest NSW 2065
Australia
Phone: (61 2) 8425 0100
Email: info@allenandunwin.com
Web: www.allenandunwin.com

*Allen & Unwin acknowledges the Traditional Owners of the Country on which we
live and work. We pay our respects to all Aboriginal and Torres Strait Islander
Elders, past and present.*

A catalogue record for this
book is available from the
National Library of Australia

ISBN 978 1 76106 797 6

Set in 13/17.5 pt Granjon LT by Midland Typesetters, Australia
Printed in Australia by McPherson's Printing Group

10 9 8 7 6 5 4 3 2 1

The paper in this book is FSC® certified.
FSC® promotes environmentally responsible,
socially beneficial and economically viable
management of the world's forests.

To John, Pam, Ken and Gin, as always

CONTENTS

1

TWO WORLDS

It's 8 March 2022 and Lyndell Droga is sitting in the living room of her house in the Sydney suburb of Woollahra. It's after eight, but the makings of her and husband Daniel's dinner still languish in butcher's paper by the sink. After eleven hours at the office, the new chair of the Allegra Spender campaign for the Sydney seat of Wentworth is making room for one last interview before her day ends.

On the table in front of her, a glass of wine—a pleasure she and the candidate are yet to share—sits untouched. Serious art covers the walls: Michael Cook's glowering post-colonial pastiche *Civilized #13* is by the door; a vast Imants Tillers, a disintegrating surface of symbols and auguries, blankets the main wall.

The art is of a piece with the house. A classical Mediterranean villa from Sydney's inter-war period, it's of a similar vintage to the 1920s mansion where Spender's mother, the late fashion designer Carla Zampatti, lived—just a stone's throw up the hill on Edgecliff Road.

Throw that stone a little further and you'd hit where Edgecliff Road meets the suburb's main drag, New South Head Road.

The red-brick 1940s façade that occupies that corner has housed the electoral office of Wentworth's two most recent Liberal representatives, Malcolm Turnbull and Dave Sharma. Diagonally opposite, Spender's new campaign headquarters occupies an Art Deco bank that was once home to the local Video Ezy.

A golden mile of entrenched Liberal privilege, you'd think. Except that Droga—like Spender, whose father was a shadow minister under opposition leaders Andrew Peacock and John Howard, and whose grandfather was a minister under Prime Minister Robert Menzies—is hell-bent on revolution.

It's exactly one year—to the day, it turns out—since Droga devoted herself to trying to find a candidate to unseat Sharma. Woollahra's built infrastructure is testament to how furiously times change in Australia's wealthiest electorate. What she and others are looking to do is usher in a new era: the age of the non-aligned, socially progressive, economically responsible, centrist independent.

And there's no question that the media-shy Droga has been central to the push. After co-founding Wentworth Independents with sustainability strategists Maria Atkinson and Blair Palese, she identified Spender, whom she had never met, as their ideal candidate and spent months convincing her to run. Since Spender announced her candidacy in November 2021, Droga has been her discreet shadow, accompanying her to events and closing as many of them as possible with a call to action—please volunteer, please donate, please tell your friends—co-running a campaign that has quickly become a litmus test of the times.

Droga and I have already spent an hour discussing the twists and turns along that road when we arrive at the two-million-dollar question: what chance a campaign, into which she and her husband have already sunk $50,000, with a promise to double that if needed, actually stands come election day? 'Oh, who knows? I don't know!' she exclaims with mock exasperation, sitting back in her chair, eyes to the ceiling.

By her own admission someone who tends to see the glass as not so much half-empty as smashed, she is encouraged by the insurrectionary energy within the campaign. Buoyed, too, by the shock 19 per cent swing secured by independent Larissa Penn in the by-election the previous month in the Sydney seat of Willoughby vacated by former NSW premier Gladys Berejiklian, a swing Penn has attributed to local anger missed by commentators and government alike.

But Droga is also acutely aware of the received wisdom that independents stand a snowflake's chance on their march to Canberra. 'I do know there's a massive appetite for change, particularly among women,' she says. 'Standing at Edgecliff Station at 7 a.m. last Thursday, handing out flyers, these young professional women heading for town, they're saying, "Don't worry, she's already got my vote."'

As for the broader movement: 'Campaigns are springing up like weeds all around the country, but the movement's in its infancy,' she says. 'It'll be very hard to go to Canberra, given the margins. Yes, the response is phenomenal, and yes, we all get on board. But we are living in our little echo chambers. We don't know what's going to hit us when the election is called; we don't know what they've got in store for us.'

Droga is hardly alone in tempering optimism with scepticism. A few weeks later, Kate Chaney, a more recent recruit as the independent candidate in the Western Australian seat of Curtin, says almost the same thing when asked about her prospects. Internally commissioned polls suggest it will be a close fight, she says. 'I reckon there's still a large chance'—she adds, trailing off before breaking into a broad grin—'that I won't win!'

'You've got to be realistic about this,' Chaney continues. 'Doorknocking is a really good way to keep it real. Inside your echo chamber you think everybody cares. Get out there and you realise most people just hate politics. They don't want to vote for anyone, or they've always voted Liberal or Labor and they're not planning on changing.'

~~~~~

A week after I talk to Droga, NSW senator Andrew Bragg and I discuss the same topic in his Sydney CBD office. Bragg is the government's point man on the non-aligned independents in general, and Warringah on Sydney's northern beaches in particular. In December 2020, the party opened a local office, 'Liberal House', there, the first step in what was at the time expected to be a long and aggressive campaign to win the seat back from the incumbent independent, Zali Steggall. More recently, Bragg authorised the zalihasfailed.com website (its homepage asks: 'Did you know, Steggall voted with Labor 64 per cent of the time?' beneath a drop-down menu inviting readers to 'Discover Zali's failures'). He also asked the Australian Electoral Commission to ensure the independents are complying with funding-disclosure requirements.

Those efforts have been bolstered by Bragg's colleagues—everyone from Treasurer Josh Frydenberg to Mackellar MP Jason Falinski—stating constantly, almost regardless of topic, that the burgeoning community-backed candidates are 'fake independents'. In April, former prime minister John Howard will ratchet that rhetoric up a couple of notches, labelling the independents 'a bunch of anti-Liberal groupies' looking to 'hurt the Liberal Party' rather than 'represent the middle ground'.

'There are a lot of horrible people in politics,' Bragg says, eyeing me hard as he sits down at a boardroom-sized table in a meeting room decorated with a framed flyer for the Marriage Equality Campaign (of which he was national director) and a framed Uluru Statement from the Heart (which he also supports). 'Look, mate, I just think they're a bunch of protestors,' the self-described 'social liberal' says. 'They've got three-word slogans and they've got a handful of policies. I'm a policy person, first and foremost . . . and when I look, their cupboard looks bare. They operate like a party—they coordinate their activities, they coordinate their resourcing, they coordinate their reporting, and their regulatory obligations.'

What follows is a simple narrative governed by a simple imperative: *Cherchez l'homme*. In this case, the man we're looking for is Simon Holmes à Court, who founded the Climate 200 funding group before the 2019 election, raising almost $450,000 to back environmentally minded candidates, and is doing the same on a far grander scale this time around. 'The guy behind this [is] a pretty unsavoury type,' Bragg says. 'He wants to be a national public figure, influencing the nation's policies, but he's not prepared to put his name on the ballot paper . . . And I think that's weak.' While the senator doesn't spell it out, that logic makes the almost exclusively female candidates fronting independent campaigns around the country not so much groupies as Stepford Wives. A chorus of Trilbys to Holmes à Court's Svengali.

As for what might be motivating Holmes à Court, 'His issue is he's also hung out with these anti-Semite people,' Bragg says, flagging what will become a plank of the defence strategy in seats with significant Jewish constituencies or incumbents, such as Wentworth in Sydney, and Goldstein and Kooyong in Melbourne. 'I won't say anything more about this on the record right now because I gave a speech using privilege, which you can use,' he suggests, directing me to allegations he has made in parliament, where he has immunity from defamation.

Look beyond the malcontents of the independents movement, he suggests, and all is well. The 'Liberal Party's brand is strong,' he says. 'We do a good job of representing broad diverse interests.' The member for Bradfield on Sydney's upper north shore, Communications Minister Paul Fletcher sings a similar song when I run into him the day after speaking to Droga. 'I think we will be okay,' he says. 'The Liberal Party is a broad church.' It's the government logic of the moment: this too shall pass; the centre will hold.

〰〰〰

There were excellent reasons for Droga's and others' uncertainty in March 2022, a time at which two parallel universes seemed to coexist in Australia without ever breaching each other's bubble. On one side was the status quo, exemplified by Andrew Bragg and his Coalition colleagues. On the other was the roiling energy of the independents movement, a multi-fronted maelstrom of volunteers, candidates and campaign people. By early February 2022, they were working around the clock, seven days a week, improvising as they went.

Their inspiration was a clutch of independent victories over the previous decade: Cathy McGowan and Helen Haines in the rural Victorian seat of Indi from 2013 to 2019; Kerryn Phelps in Wentworth in 2018; and Zali Steggall's celebrated 2019 Warringah victory.

Key strategists, organisers and logisticians of this evolving movement were veterans of those earlier campaigns. They sat at the centre of the Venn diagram that made up the independents movement, coordinating, sharing their expertise, lessons, contacts. They had been there before. Had a clearer view of the path ahead.

For the most part, however, the participants were political novices, working on instinct, word-of-mouth, hardly daring to believe that what they were doing might work.

Each campaign was its own unique constellation of 'Voices of' and independents groups, volunteers, campaign staff and vehicles. What united them, however, was an almost perverse optimism, what one Mackellar volunteer dubbed 'active hope'. Among the top leadership of each campaign, that hope was qualified. But, closer to the base, it was raw and unalloyed.

Many of the seats they were contesting were wealthy, traditionally blue-ribbon Liberal seats, such as Wentworth or Curtin. Or Kooyong in Melbourne, where paediatric neurologist Dr Monique Ryan was taking on federal treasurer Josh Frydenberg. Or Goldstein, where former ABC journalist Zoe Daniel was fronting Liberal Tim Wilson.

But many were not. In the highly diverse 17,000 square kilometre NSW seat of Hume, which includes parts of the outer Sydney south-western suburbs of Liverpool and Penrith, the fashionable Southern Highlands and the small rural town of Boorowa, digital consultant Matt Murfitt and pilot Alex Murphy had founded Voices of Hume and Vote Angus Out, which then chose Penny Ackery as their candidate. Both had taken career breaks to dedicate themselves to unseating Angus Taylor, the federal Minister for Industry, Energy and Emissions Reduction.

In Groom in Queensland's Darling Downs, former social worker Suzie Holt and agricultural consultant Meredith King had done the same thing to work together as candidate and campaign manager. In the northern NSW National Party stronghold of Cowper, Cancer Council board member and former director of nursing and midwifery at the Coffs Harbour Health Campus, Carolyn ('Caz') Heise, was fronting Caz4Cowper. And in the sprawling 15,000 square kilometre Victorian agricultural electorate of Nicholls, Shepparton businessman Rob Priestly had taken a leave of absence from the family's commercial laundry business to take on the Liberal and National parties.

All up, Climate 200 would end up backing 23 campaigns (excluding the rural candidates who did not seek, or declined, funding) from a war chest that ultimately topped $13 million, more than four times Holmes à Court's most optimistic expectation when he relaunched Climate 200 in mid-2021. All up, the $250,000 he and his wife, Katrina, contributed ended up representing less than 2 per cent of that total, raised from more than 11,000 donors.

In the months leading up to the 21 May 2022 election, however, your reality was largely determined by which universe you inhabited. Particularly given each seemed to be fed largely by its own media. On one side, News Corp was the voice of the status quo. As the weeks went by, its outlets ran stories accusing the Daniel and Spender camps of being anti-Israel, echoing

Andrew Bragg's line. They attacked Ryan for her supposed Labor sympathies, and her campaign director, academic Ann Capling. There was a stream of articles critical of Holmes à Court, who became the face of a movement that never had one face.

On 18 March, *The Australian* ran a front-page article revealing that four Sydney independent candidates—'possibly more'—were using the services of Populares, a Sydney-based communications company founded by a trio of Labor and GetUp! veterans: Anthony Reed, Mark Connelly and Ed Coper. 'An investigation by the *Weekend Australian* into political connections at Populares raises questions about whether the campaigns of these and other independent candidates for the May election are—unwittingly or not—being coordinated centrally and by supporters of Labor and GetUp!,' the article said. *Cherchez les hommes*, indeed.

'I am not sure News Corporation bothers to deny its bias these days,' author and academic Margaret Simons wrote in the *Sydney Morning Herald* in mid-May. 'Some of the content in News Corporation tabloids has read like political advertising for the Coalition.' Would the 2022 election prove to be 'the election in which the impotence of its skewed reporting is exposed,' Simons wondered. Post-election, former news.com.au political editor Malcolm Farr labelled the 'savaging of independent candidates by News Corp . . . brutal and relentless'. But in the lead-up it was that 'savaging' that helped frame the debate about them.

Other mainstream outlets struggled with the opposite question: how—and how much—they should cover a movement made up of individual campaigns and candidates. In a letter to subscribers on 10 December 2021, *Age* editor Gay Alcorn was frank. 'One of the biggest discussions we had that week was about how we cover the "Voices of" movement, the independents challenging moderate Liberals at next year's election,' she wrote. 'Australia is a democracy, and it is a good thing when people decide to stand for election. But *The Age* doesn't give extensive coverage to every person who runs for political office.'

While her readers were flocking to stories on candidates, 'what we have to assess—and it's not always easy—is how significant minor parties or independents may be, whether they represent something shifting in the community', not least given independents did 'not have a great record of success in Australia'. Alcorn concluded that *The Age* would 'not cheer on independents, nor treat them with disdain'.

Alcorn's reservations about the independents' chances at the polls reflected the prevailing wisdom at the time. Books have been written on the hurdles independents faced, notably Andréa Cullen's *The Independent Effect*. Right up until election day, non-partisan experts and commentators expressed their doubts that the indies could prevail in significant numbers. Few, though, were as categorical as News Corp's Joe Hildebrand, who, three days out from election day, declared that they might fail to win a single seat, with 'private polling' showing 'them failing to even make it to second place in North Sydney'. 'Campaign insiders' had told Hildebrand that Frydenberg was 'looking good in Kooyong', and that there was a 'strong chance' Tim Wilson could hang on in Goldstein.

For their part, the indies relied on the modes and spaces of disruption rather than the legacy media: old-fashioned word of mouth, town hall meetings, social media, online forums, events and workshops. Community-backed independents had, after all, been born online as a mass, multi-electorate phenomenon. And turbocharged by Covid and the limitations on movement and mass gathering the epidemic had imposed. As Covid became a collective moment of reflection (and dissatisfaction), social media, group chats and video-conferencing services had become the meeting rooms, parish pumps and town squares of a world suddenly, stunningly paused.

The two parallel worlds occasionally bumped up against each other in real time as campaigns began to blossom in mid-February. As Leigh Sales hosted ABC TV's *7.30* program on the evening of 14 February, for instance, unpacking the news of the day, her predecessor was anchoring an online forum for Cathy McGowan's Community Independents Project. Kerry O'Brien was interviewing two former Australian prime ministers, Liberal Malcolm Turnbull and Labor's Kevin Rudd, on the question of whether the Australian media's election coverage was weakening democracy, with a particular focus on News Corp.

Watching the latter, you wondered whether you were witnessing the last, zombie life of an old paradigm—past players reliving past campaigns—or the birth of a new one. Even those who were most used to navigating this tricky new terrain were unsure how hard to hope. As Populares' Anthony Reed stated, 'You can never be sure. I mean, even though we run by decent margins [in terms of polling], they're still really close, within 5 per cent.'

All of which makes the scale of what ultimately took place on 21 May 2022 the more revelatory. A revolution had been hiding in plain sight, visible only to those with eyes to see.

2

WAITING FOR GODOT

Like most revolutions, the independents' 2022 victory only looks as though it came out of nowhere. The conditions that enabled it had been coalescing for more than a decade, even if its final catalysts seemed to appear as suddenly as a bank of waves.

The Grattan Institute's 2018 *A Crisis of Trust* report painted a picture of Australia before the 2019 federal election. The share of the vote won by minor parties and independents had been increasing for a decade, reaching its highest point post-war in 2016, when more than a quarter of Australians voted other than Liberal–National Party Coalition (LNP), Australian Labor Party (ALP) or Greens in the Senate, and more than an eighth in the House of Representatives.

By 2019, the House of Representatives vote for minor parties and independents had hit a new record of almost 25 per cent, or one in four voters. It was driven by what former Grattan Institute chief executive John Daley, a professorial fellow at The University of Melbourne, termed an 'anyone-other-than' movement. 'It's against the government; anything other than the existing major parties,' Daley said in 2021, adding that 'unlike the Greens or One Nation, which have traditionally achieved Senate seats, the independents have a shot at winning lower-house seats because of preferences'. Cathy McGowan had won Indi in 2013, after all, and Rebekha Sharkie won Mayo in Adelaide in 2016.

In the end, the Greens defied Daley's expectations in 2022, winning three extra lower house seats in inner Brisbane, which they added to leader Adam Bandt's seat of Melbourne (and the six seats that give them a total of twelve, and the balance of power, in the Senate) in a 'Greenslide' that was every bit as historic as its teal sibling. 'The Greens picked up some seats essentially from the left of the ALP in electorates that were about as far left as they could be, probably aided by the fact that teals weren't running there and those seats had been under water twice in recent months,' Daley concluded after the election.

But if the 2022 results were unexpected, change wasn't. Lachlan Harris and Andrew Charlton had co-authored a piece titled 'A Pox on Both Your Houses' for *The Monthly* in the wake of the 2016 election, examining the growing repudiation of both major parties by Australian voters. The rise of the minor parties and independents represented, they wrote, a seismic structural shift in Australian politics that they thought even then threatened to create 'the largest crossbench in more than 70 years'.

Three years later, the marginal vote at the 2019 election was within a hair's breadth of what Harris regarded as the historically magical number of 25 per cent. 'The minor party vote has gone over 25 per cent only three times since Federation,' Harris told me in late September 2021. In 1901, the recently formed ALP won fourteen seats in an election dominated by Edmund Barton's Protectionists and George Reid's Free Traders. During the

Great Depression, Lang Labor split from the ALP and gained nine seats at the 1936 election. And during the wartime turbulence among the conservative parties, the Country Party found itself for a time no longer part of a coalition but instead a substantial minor party. On each of these occasions, 'one of the major parties has [eventually] either collapsed, fused with another party, or split', Harris said.

All of which made the rising independent/minor-party vote in 2019 'a big flashing light on the dashboard of democracy saying voters want something different, and something's going to change', he said. 'It's an indicator of a desire for change; the pressure that causes the tectonic plates to shift ... when one-quarter of voters aren't voting for the majors, the political system itself adjusts.'

'I mean look, let's call a spade a spade,' he told me. 'The Liberal Party and the Labor Party aren't doing such a great job that you'd say, "These guys deserve to run the country unchallenged for the next 100 years." They need a good kick up the arse, quite frankly, and it might be more than that. It might be a sayonara. It feels very organic and piecemeal at the moment, but that's how it starts. People think, "Oh, political change means there's going to be a new Labor Party, or a new Liberal Party." I don't think so. What we've had is not what's coming.'

But if change was becoming inevitable, Harris was far less sure that community-backed independents would be the force that harnessed that pressure in 2022. When I spoke to him, only North Sydney's Kylea Tink of the eventual 2022 winners had announced her candidature. It was still possible at that time that the election might be held in 2021, making the runway for the independents' take-off almost impossibly short. Simon Holmes à Court had only recently relaunched Climate 200; the scale of funding it would shortly attract would shock even its founder.

Then there were all the usual structural caveats, not least that independents might do a lot better under another system. 'Compulsory voting and preferential voting combine to mean that, in order to win a lower house seat, you have to get a very large number of votes, first preference, or second preference, or third preference,' Harris said. 'And that's just expensive. It requires scale, it requires a lot of campaigning capacity.'

When we spoke again in April 2022, though, Harris had tacked to what was by then a discernible change in the wind. 'I drove over to Warringah on election day in 2019,' he recalled. 'I went as a political tourist, to get the vibe, and there was just no doubt. I've never seen a seat more activated, more aggressively, politically activated for an independent than I did that day. You are beginning to see the beginnings of that in Wentworth, where I live. If that sort of momentum was to be sustained, I think they'll have some pretty significant victories.'

On election night, he sent a single, four-word text at 9.30 p.m.: 'The tectonic plates shifted.' John Daley was just as surprised. 'I probably should have read my own analysis,' he quipped. The mathematics of the moment had proved inexorable.

〜〜〜〜〜

As for the causes of the rank dissatisfaction that enabled the independents to blossom on 21 May, they are myriad and longstanding.

Another Grattan Institute report often cited on the independents' trail, including by policy wonks Allegra Spender and Kate Chaney, was Daley's 2021 *Gridlock* report, which warned that Australia's governance had gone backwards after a golden era of policy reform in the 1980s and 1990s, with successive governments failing to progress reforms recommended for decades.

It's no coincidence that integrity came before issues such as climate and equality among Climate 200's priorities. While it was often taken as shorthand for the establishment of a federal anti-corruption body, so as to put an end to the pork-barrelling that had been such a prominent feature of the last years of the Morrison government, its importance was far broader and more fundamental. 'It's the biggest issue, because it's about the breakdown of democracy,' Holmes à Court told me. 'If parliament worked the way people think it should work, or if it were truly democratic, then issues with climate or equality would be easier to solve.'

Those pork-barrelling controversies had, though, dramatised what might otherwise have been an abstract issue for voters, from the federal government's car-park rorts and 'Sportsgate' to NSW premier Gladys Berejiklian's nonchalant testimony to her state's corruption commission, ICAC, that no one should be surprised that millions of taxpayers' dollars had been directed to Daryl Maguire's NSW seat because 'at the end of the day, whether we like it or not, that's democracy'. Integrity became the sleeper issue of the campaign.

The private member's bill to establish an Australian federal integrity commission that Helen Haines introduced into the House of Representatives in October 2020 was the direct result. The member for Indi is clear: she didn't introduce her bill out of idealism, she did it because voters in the seat she held by a relatively slim margin demanded it. 'When Cathy retired and I was invited to be the next candidate at that deliberative forum that we had in Benalla in January 2019 that selected me, it was very clear that I needed to prosecute this issue and finally bring home an integrity commission,' Haines told me. 'All through 2019, through town hall meetings and kitchen-table conversations, and goodness knows what else, people were very clear to me that we needed this.

'And whenever I was in the media talking about integrity, I would be overwhelmed with messages from all over the nation. Integrity was an issue that everyday people wherever I went—whether they were the president of the local footy club or someone on the street or kids in a classroom—really got. They really don't like it when they feel like they're getting ripped off by politicians, and they could smell a rat. The issue of integrity really, really resonated. And the independents were the ones that really pushed it big time.'

Governance gridlock, the difficulty in achieving legislative action on important issues—from gender and marriage equality to Uluru, from climate to the economy—had put the system of party patronage and loyalty under the microscope as never before. While the Liberal Party was busy highlighting the voting record of the likes of Steggall, the independents began to return the favour, making the voting records of government representatives such as Trent Zimmerman, Sharma, Falinski and Frydenberg a key issue, highlighted by the key message that a vote for a moderate Liberal member was a vote for Scott Morrison and his deputy, Barnaby Joyce.

'There's so much patronage tied up in parties, in staying with your party,' says John Daley. 'That was one of the points of my *Gridlock* report: to a significant extent, membership of a political party is about getting yourself elected, and then sharing in the spoils of office. It doesn't really quite so much matter what you plan to do to the country. What matters is that your party is part of a tribe, and therefore [you] qualify to share in the spoils.'

What threw this picture into sharp relief was a triple bill of crises: bushfires, Covid and floods. It has become a truism that Covid magnified the shortcomings of an already ailing status quo. To Adrian Pabst, professor of politics at the UK's Kent University, what Covid highlighted was nothing less than the lengthy interregnum in which the world had been stranded since neoliberalism's very public failure during the 2008 Global Financial Crisis.

'As the post-viral economic cataclysm unfolds, the liberal West looks like the undead, not coming back to life but equally refusing to die,' Pabst wrote in his 2021 book *Postliberal Politics: The Coming Era of Renewal*, prophesying that 'a space is opening up for an alternative that . . . offers an ethical compass with which to navigate our times: postliberalism'. While that alternative was yet to emerge in any viable form in the UK or elsewhere, its tenets were clear: 'Postliberalism rests on a recognition that society is not founded upon an impersonal social contract between individuals, as for liberal thought since Hobbes and Locke, but emerges from a reciprocal covenant between the generations,' Pabst wrote. 'Liberty is not freedom from obligations or freedom for selfish interests but a freedom of care for oneself and for others. Individual fulfilment based on personal autonomy has to be balanced with mutual flourishing.'

What was true for the rest of the world was triply true for Australia, where plague would be sandwiched between the other biblical cataclysms of fire and flood. Australians traditionally expect governments to provide services and support; what they got, within months of Scott Morrison's May 2019 election, was one example after another of how hollowed-out government had become as a result of the endless privatisations, 'efficiency dividends' and other cost-cutting that have been neoliberalism's articles of faith.

In November 2020, Cathy McGowan published her autobiography. Titled *Cathy Goes to Canberra*, it was the story of how her electorate of Indi had pioneered the community-backed independent model. Upon its publication, she was immediately swamped by requests for advice. Rather than deal with them piecemeal, McGowan ran a two-day Zoom conference, 'Getting Elected', in February 2021. 'I thought we'd have about 50 people, because I'd had about 50 phone calls from all over Australia and it was a short time-frame,' she said in September 2021. 'Instead we got more than 300 people from 81 electorates. We thought, "Shit, we've really tapped a nerve here."'

Independent Andrew Wilkie, too, sees a fundamental difference in the tide of independents that arrived in 2022. 'Back when I was first elected [in 2010], every crossbencher had their own unique story,' he tells me in August 2022. 'We know Bob Katter's long story, how he's carved out a role for himself quite uniquely in North Queensland. Adam Bandt was the only Green for a long time, suggesting it wasn't a Green-slide, it was really Adam's unique strengths and some unusual preference flows when he first got elected. Rebekha Sharkie was elected off the back of Nick Xenophon and the Xenophon team . . . even Zali Steggall [in 2019] was very much about the good people of Warringah wanting to replace Tony Abbott. What happened this time around is that there was much more of a groundswell for change across multiple seats. Whereas I don't think you could apply that description to all us oldies.'

In 2021, McGowan put the initial stirrings of that seismic shift in political engagement down to how closely the object lesson of Covid had followed the object lesson of the 2019–20 fires. 'With the bushfires, everyone could see that the government wasn't the answer, that fire brigades weren't the answer, that just trusting the system to solve your problems wasn't working,' she said. 'For a number of years, people haven't had to rely on each other, because the system was basically working. And then we got Covid, and Covid absolutely fundamentally showed us that you need your community around you.'

In that context, the 2022 floods were just the coup de grâce. Any doubts about climate change, any residual faith in the efficacy of government, were washed away as the citizens of the northern NSW city of Lismore were left to save themselves, and then struggled, like the citizens of south-east Queensland, to survive the months that followed.

And when threats become existential, who better than an existentialist to diagnose them? Professor Pabst quotes Albert Camus' novel *The Plague* to explain how singularly unifying and galvanising Covid—the biggest global crisis since World War II—became. 'There were no longer any individual destinies but a collective history that was the plague, and feelings shared by all,' Camus wrote in his 1947 classic, which drew inspiration from a nineteenth-century cholera epidemic in Algeria. 'The greatest of these were feelings of separation and exile, with all that that involved of fear and rebellion.'

And where did those feelings of separation and exile, of fear and rebellion, go to be shared when Covid hit, the music stopped and Australia was stranded in an interregnum within an interregnum? They went online.

To Kristen Lock, founder of the action group she named 'North Sydney's Independent'—which in September 2021 became the first of the local groups to announce a candidate, Kylea Tink—the combination of technology, time and undivided attention proved 'the yeast in flour, the thing that enabled it to rise'.

North Sydney's Independent had just hit its stride when the first Covid lockdown hit. 'It was terribly challenging, we had just got going. We were going to do democracy walks every weekend, we'd just done our first politics in the pub, "meet and do" stuff,' she recalls. Looking back, however, it seems a 'fluke. What first looked like it was going to slow us down and put out our community fire, ended up spreading that fire so much further and faster. It meant everyone had got their head around Zoom, even the grey army—if it had been a year before, they might have fumbled, gone, "What Zoom? What internet?"— so we could hold Zoom functions. And people could attend really easily without having to drive, be somewhere, risk getting Covid. It was low risk in every way. It's quite socially confronting to brave a room of strangers. Whereas if you're just clicking on a Zoom meeting and sitting quietly in the audience, you don't even need to have your camera on.

'We just went so much further than it would've gone if we had had to do the same thing physically, in person. I mean, the physical was really important and came later, and it's very satisfying, socially, to meet people. But in terms of entry, it made it really easy for people.'

Again, it is an anecdote that taps into a much larger and older story: the wholesale disruption that technology has wrought. Like the recording industry, for instance, where emerging technology began to destroy existing barriers to entry at the turn of the 21st century, and artists suddenly discovered they no longer needed record companies to release their work. The same process would upend everything from the film and TV industries, to tourism and the accommodation sector.

In a sense, politics, the party machine, was one of the last areas to be challenged by that disruption. 'Almost every other industry has been dis-intermediated, balkanised,' Lachlan Harris observed in 2021. 'People have found their own identity, and those new information flows mean it's easier to find communities you identify with; the era of informational monopolies and duopolies, of us all listening to the same music, watching the same 7 p.m. TV show, are gone.'

And as those barriers to entry and dissemination fell, the possibility of launching your own campaign, rather than having to submit to preselection, the serfdom of the party system, was now a real possibility. As Cathy McGowan, who was nudging 60 with no political campaign experience when she ran in Indi in 2013, says: 'Working through the parties was never going to work for someone like me. The competition is just too strong. So the game was to actually work through getting elected so that I could do what I needed to. Clearly, getting onto the crossbench was the easiest way for me to get a seat at the table, which is parliament.'

Not that that was suddenly magically easier. As US singer-songwriter Aimee Mann once told me, the freedom to release music in the noughties really only amounted to 'a lot more ways of making not very much'. Similarly, working 'through getting elected'—like taking your song viral—was far easier said than done.

The heft of Climate 200 would help to level the playing field in terms of campaign spending and expertise. As would the know-how that had been built in Indi, Wentworth and Warringah from 2013 onwards. The 2022 campaigns were digitally primed as never before, as Populares co-founder Ed Coper would trumpet in the pages of the *Sydney Morning Herald* a few weeks after the election. But that digital scale and reach were continually reinforced by in-person events—old-fashioned doorknocking and real-life get-togethers.

Because no matter how important the digital was in targeting and massifying, there was no alternative to the human-scale power of individuals and communities. From the candidates themselves to their armies of volunteers, that would be the lesson—individuals matter, community and communities matter. 'It is critical that you have people and you have them in significant numbers, because they're the soldiers,' says veteran independent Tony Windsor. 'They're the ones that are talking over the fence to the neighbour. They're the ones in the pub spruiking. You've got 2000 microphones wandering around, and they're the ones that put on a T-shirt or put out a sign, and it creates this aura of "Oh, these people are fair dinkum." Then you just add some money to that.'

Or, as accountant Damien Hodgkinson, a veteran of independent campaigns from 2016 to 2022, puts it: 'The biggest differences this time were Climate 200, which supercharged the donor base ... but, more importantly, those large, grassroots volunteer networks that [go back to] Cathy McGowan. They were middle class and upper-middle class people from professional backgrounds who suddenly said, "This is important to me and I'm going to go out and participate." I don't know whether part of that was a post-Covid need for connection. Or the fact that during Covid we had to start thinking about more than ourselves. But there was a cultural shift that happened.'

It happened for the same reason as it always does. In the end, there is only one trick left when threats become existential and every trick has been tried: the end of all tricks. As Camus' protagonist, Dr Rieux, says in *The Plague*: 'It may seem a ridiculous idea, but the only way to fight the plague is with decency.'

3

MOTHER COURAGE

There is a particular irony to attempts to characterise the so-called 'teals' as the stooges of Simon Holmes à Court, or the dupes of communications outfit Populares' male founders. Because, however you look at it, the community-backed independents movement has been one founded predominantly by, through and with women.

It was propelled towards its target at the 2022 election, too, by an unprecedented collision of scandals that threw the lack of progress on gender equality in Australia into deep relief. According to the World Economic Forum's *Global Gender Gap Report* in March 2021, Australian women's economic participation had plummeted from 12th in the world in 2006 to 70th in 2021; from 57th to 99th on health and survival; and from 32nd to 54th on political empowerment.

And the controversies that dramatised that decline came thick and fast in early 2021. In late January, Grace Tame, whose harrowing account of being groomed and raped at fifteen by her 58-year-old teacher had helped change the law in her home state of Tasmania, was chosen as Australian of the Year. Less than a month later, Brittany Higgins alleged that she had been raped in Parliament House in the lead-up to the 2019 election. Less than three weeks later, Attorney-General Christian Porter confirmed he was the person who had been named in a historic rape allegation. And in between, an Instagram poll initiated by 24-year-old Chanel Contos generated not only 5000 sexual assault accounts within a fortnight but also an online petition that garnered 44,000 signatures in a month.

That fury was turbocharged by Scott Morrison's spectacularly ham-fisted response, including the revelation that only paternity and patriarchy had finally helped him understand Higgins' allegations: 'Jenny and I spoke last night. And she said to me, "You have to think about this as a father first."' As Morrison and Tame posed for photos after her searing January 2021 acceptance speech, too, the new Australian of the Year reported the PM said to her: 'Well, gee, I bet it felt good to get that out.'

In fact, the response was more culpable than clumsy given the government's inaction in the wake of Higgins' allegations and the refusal of Morrison or the Minister for Women, Marise Payne, to publicly meet with the March 4 Justice protestors who surrounded Parliament House on 15 March 2021. Against that backdrop, the video that emerged days later of a male staffer masturbating on the desk of a female Liberal MP just seemed the ultimate damning snapshot of what the corridors of power offered women. More confirmation than shock.

As for the men supposedly duping and directing 2022's female candidates, they are crystal clear on both who was really calling the shots in those campaigns and the mood feeding into them. 'These candidates are all highly successful women who had had enough and were brave enough to step into something that they had never done before,' said Populares founder, Anthony Reed, who worked across five campaigns and had input into others. 'They were there because they're super-smart and highly accomplished. They surrounded themselves with good advice because that's what you do when you've been successful. But it was them making the decisions. That's what the Liberal Party don't get: they called the shots. I could say, "My advice to you is this," but they chose to take it or not.'

Holmes à Court was equally categorical in a mid-February 2022 speech he gave to the National Press Club. That speech began by acknowledging 'the pathfinder and inspiration to the community independents movement', Cathy McGowan, and former Democrats leader Meg Lees. 'Women around the country are red-hot with anger,' Holmes à Court continued. 'They're furious that we have made so little progress over recent decades, and that the current leadership team treats women as if they are some political problem to be managed.'

'You have to wonder whether the poor representation of women in parliament isn't partly to blame for the culture that we find ourselves in,' he said. 'Just 20 per cent of Coalition members in the lower house are women: 25 years ago, it was 21 per cent. Ruth McGowan, one of Cathy's nine sisters, runs monthly boot-camps for women who have decided to run for parliament. Ruth tells me that since Ms Tame and Ms Higgins and so many others stepped forward last year, demand for her training is off the charts. Professional women are standing up, they're putting their hands up and standing up to be independents. As Dr Monique Ryan, the independent candidate for Kooyong, said recently: "When a woman in her fifties sees a problem, she says to herself, just give it to me, I'll fix it."'

The outpouring of anger had been close to white-hot a week before Holmes à Court's speech, when Higgins and Tame had shared the podium in a joint Press Club appearance. Tame revealed a 'threatening phone call' she'd received from 'a senior member of a government-funded organisation' on the evening before the 2021 Australian of the Year Awards, in which he had asked her to give her word that she 'would not say anything damning about the prime minister' in her acceptance speech.

Underlining the historic dimension of the moment, Higgins had worn suffragette white for both her Press Club appearance and for the March 4 Justice speech she delivered a month later. Former Australia Post CEO Christine Holgate had similarly chosen a white suit a year earlier for the Senate committee hearing at which she outlined how she had been humiliated and bullied by Scott Morrison; this followed a Wear White 2 Unite campaign organised by licensed post offices (tagline 'Christine Holgate was bullied. It can happen to anyone. It can happen to you.')

It's difficult to exaggerate how hard and fast the fury generated by these events flushed through the 2022 independent campaigns. Lyndell Droga traces her decision to devote herself to unseating Dave Sharma—joining other professional women in their fifties, such as Blair Palese and Maria Atkinson—to a single moment on International Women's Day, 8 March, in 2021.

It was a breather between lockdowns, a week before the March 4 Justice hit Canberra. Talk of the protest—and of Higgins, Tame, Contos and Porter—had been swirling for weeks, when Droga caught sight of Dave Sharma handing out flowers to women in the street on International Women's Day.

'We were like "What's happening?"' Droga recalls of the women's dumbfounded response to what seemed like a moment out of a 1980s Impulse deodorant commercial. 'I'm the mother of two daughters. Chanel Contos is actually from this electorate,' she says. 'There are women and men marching on Canberra, the government won't even leave the building to come and meet them, and Dave Sharma's in Sydney handing out flowers.'

The march, arranged to protest the lack of government action on the Higgins and Porter allegations, would itself prove to be a major catalyst. After taking part, NSW Cancer Council director Caz Heise, for one, decided to throw her hat into the ring in Cowper. A 51-year-old mother of two adult children (with her paramedic wife), Heise had been recovering from a life-threatening cancer diagnosis when Covid hit in 2019. As she weighed up what to do with the rest of her life, that brutal interruption had given her time to consider not only her own health, but also that of the nation. 'I went down to the rally on the lawns of Parliament House with a friend and some very handpainted banners,' Heise recalled when we spoke in July 2022. 'Then we did a tour of Parliament House and I kept thinking: "Okay, I've beaten cancer against the odds. I'm well, I'm healthy, I'm qualified and I'm very passionate about the Earth and the misogynistic, unequal [power imbalance] that still prevails." I thought, "If I can beat cancer, I'm going to stand up and shout from the rooftops about what really matters, and I may as well do it in a way that could create real change."'

It's worth remembering, too, just how heightened Australians' flight-or-fight response had become at the time. From fires and floods to racial injustice, sexual assault and Covid, all kinds of danger seemed to go from notional to existential in real time. We had spent the early 2020 lockdowns unable to escape the Black Lives Matter protests in the US that followed George Floyd's murder. His dying words, 'I can't breathe', became shorthand for just how visceral threats of all kinds had become.

Denise Shrivell, one of the founders of North Sydney's Independent who would end up running Jane Caro's 2022 Senate campaign, recalls the night of the March 4 Justice as a particularly crucial moment. In that clean air between lockdowns, after a powerful day of action, people who had only met on Twitter and Zoom were able to get together in the flesh to compare notes, discuss next steps. 'We all ended up at [boutique Canberra hotel] the QT. Everyone was there, Tina Jackson, [Voices of Goldstein co-founder] Sue Barrett, Jane [Caro], Margo Kingston [founder of the No Fibs citizen journalism website], Licia Heath of Women for Election, and Kate Hook and Linda Seymour [who would run as community-backed independents in Calare and Hughes, respectively].'

'I absolutely draw a direct line from the March 4 Justice to the success of the teals,' Jane Caro agrees, looking back at the events of the previous year in August 2022. 'The whole march [had this] sense of camaraderie; that something was brewing. People said afterwards, "Well, what's happening? Where's that gone? Oh, it was just one [event]." No: a whole lot of women decided to stand for election; to stand up and say, "No, your parliament is not taking us seriously, so we're going to invade your parliament. We're going to make you take us seriously. We're going to make you listen to what we have to say."'

Nor is it a coincidence that the pivotal role Sue Barrett played in helping to organise the March 4 Justice in turn played into a pivotal role as campaign manager for Zoe Daniel's Goldstein campaign. Barrett runs an eponymous seven-person consultancy, advising organisations on sales and customer experience (tagline 'Everybody lives by selling something') with her husband, Jobst Schmalenbach, an IT expert.

When the Brittany Higgins allegations hit in mid-February 2021, Barrett hooked into her natural habitat, the Twittersphere, retweeting an article she had written about #MeToo public enemy number one, Harvey Weinstein. As plans to surround Parliament House with 4000 protestors began to crystallise in late February, she volunteered to do the messaging while Schmalenbach worked on the website. She did so, she says, 'Because to me we had to treat it as a human issue, for anyone who cared about fairness, equality and mistreatment, not just a women's issue. Anyone reading the messaging had to be able see themselves in it. If we got men there, we'd done a good job.

'It was fascinating to me as a strategist because we went from zero to 110,000 people in 200 locations around the country in less than fourteen days,' she says. 'Suddenly we weren't just doing an event in Canberra. It had gone national. The website took over 800,000 hits from Australia alone on Saturday 13 March, 40,000 from the US and 30,000 from Europe. On the Monday it got over one million hits. We had at least 25 per cent men turn up to that event [they included Simon Holmes à Court], and a lot of women who'd never been to a protest in their life.'

Barrett had told Voices of Goldstein, 'I'm just doing this for a moment, I'll be back soon.' When she did return, 'The people I was working with on VoG went, "Oh my god, that's amazing,"' she says. 'It helped demonstrate my model: that messaging is everything. Having a connection, a sense of purpose and agency.'

~~~~~

It is a mistake, however, to look at the independents movement too long or too hard through any one lens. Yes, gender and equality, like climate and integrity, were galvanising forces across campaigns and candidates in 2022. But another characteristic of the movement underpinned those issues and unified the campaigns even more fundamentally.

To Cathy McGowan, the predominance of women in the independents movement is the inevitable corollary of the fact that the community-backed independents movement is what it says on the tin. 'I always rail against being defined by gender,' she says. 'Yes, there were a whole lot of women, but one of the really fundamental reasons why is because it was community-based. It's the community that attracts the women—and the blokes, the good blokes, because there was a huge number of good blokes.' As for the predominance of women candidates: 'I think it's because the community said, "You're the right person at the right time." There were two or three really good blokes that ran as well and, in another time and another place, the communities would choose blokes.'

Tending and engendering a sense of community—and forging alternative networks when the established power networks weren't open to them—is something with which women have traditionally been identified, for reasons good and ill. As McGowan herself says: 'I'm informed by women's ways of working. I mean that's my whole basis.'

It's no accident, for instance, that McGowan's autobiography, *Cathy Goes to Canberra*, has the subtitle *Doing Politics Differently*. Those words would become a rallying call on the independent trail. Nor is it a coincidence that so many of those involved in 2022's campaigns were linked by predominantly women-led networks, from climate to professional groups, from book clubs to Twitter feeds. The latter was how the electorate of Groom's independent candidate, Suzie Holt, for instance, first connected with the woman who would become the manager of her campaign, Meredith King. It was also how Sue Barrett was introduced to another Voices of Goldstein founder, Katerina Gaita, by a friend, Denise Shrivell, with whom Barrett had been discussing—on Twitter—how to get independent candidates up in their electorates (but whom she would only meet for the first time at the march). Most of these networks were about as far from traditional boys' clubs, or the formal networks that rule political parties, as could be imagined. But their power was evident everywhere and at every level in 2022.

When independent Mackellar candidate Dr Sophie Scamps, for instance, held a public forum at Collaroy Surf Club on 2 April, she was interviewed by a special guest, TV news veteran Felicity Davey, whom she knew from watching their daughters play sport. The guy who set up and emceed the event, and who only introduced himself as 'Ed', turned out to be 'Fast Ed' Halmagyi, the chef from Channel 7's *Better Homes and Gardens*, who has known Scamps since childhood ('my sister was her best friend').

Scamps' wrangler on that day was Louise Hislop, a founder of Voices of Warringah who had ended up co-managing Zali Steggall's 2019 campaign and had then planned to take it easy after its success. Within months she was dragooned into the Mackellar race by a friend she has known since kindergarten, Leonie Scarlett, whom Hislop had inspired to found Voices of Mackellar. Initially agreeing to attend a weekly strategy meeting with Voices of Mackellar, Hislop became a seven-day-a-week core campaigner. Meanwhile, an initially reluctant Zoe Daniel was finally secured as the Voices of Goldstein candidate in a months-long pincer movement by her close friend, documentary maker Angela Pippos, and Sue Barrett.

There were big-end-of-town networks, too, but they were no less personal. In Wentworth, Allegra Spender's campaign was backed by a who's who of corporate women, from Women's Electoral Lobby co-founder Wendy McCarthy to Reserve Bank board member and Clean Energy Finance Corporation chair Jillian Broadbent. Both starred in a front-page splash story in the *Australian Financial Review* after Spender's late-November 2021 campaign launch. Both had been close friends of her mother, Carla Zampatti, and had known Spender for years.

As had another connoisseur of power, Rowena Danziger, former headmistress of Spender's alma mater, Ascham School, which occupies pretty well a whole block on Edgecliff's main drag, opposite the Sharma/Turnbull electoral office and beside Spender's campaign headquarters. An alumna of boards ranging from Opera Australia and the Art Gallery of NSW to Crown Resorts and Crown Melbourne, where she was a personal appointee of Kerry and James Packer, Danziger publicly threw her own support behind her former head girl and dux, as did many of the school's old girls.

Those networks may have reflected a very particular kind of identity politics in a very particular community, but they were just as authentic and effective. As McGowan says in her autobiography: 'The thing about being a community-based politician [is that] personal networks are everything, but you can't fake those connections or have an ulterior motive. It takes years to establish and nurture; and genuine motivation and integrity are key.'

Such relationships proved to be the connective tissue of the 2022 campaigns, and just as invisible from the outside. Which is why those targeted by the campaigns found them so existentially threatening and felt the need to counter by making their own threats. When a senior journalist at a major news outlet hosted an early panel of independent candidates in 2021, for instance, the local member called their boss, demanding to know why.

The early word, as Wentworth Independents and others tried to find candidates in the second half of 2021, was that no one would put their hands up because of the very personal heat they knew would follow. One of the female businesspeople who supported Spender reported being told she would never get another Coalition contract or appointment again. In February 2022, Senator Andrew Bragg raised questions with the ABC in Senate estimates about anti-Coalition tweets posted by TV personality Julia Zemiro, who was not directly employed by the ABC but hosts *Julia Zemiro's Home Delivery* and had emceed independent candidate launches and events.

It's easy to see why independent candidates would seem like kryptonite to a government so self-referential and divorced from its constituents that the prime minister imposed hand-picked candidates on key seats, including the almost uniquely polarising Katherine Deves in Warringah, just a month before the election, as a result of factional battles within his party. Similarly, the Opposition parachuted its deputy Senate leader, Kristina Keneally, a resident of Sydney's northern beaches, into the safe lower house seat of Fowler in Sydney's south-west, which includes Liverpool and Cabramatta, to sidestep its own factional battles. In so doing, it turned its back on young female lawyer and daughter of Vietnamese refugees Tu Le, in one of Australia's most diverse electorates.

But finding the right candidate—even being that right candidate—was just the beginning of doing politics differently, according to the woman who coined the phrase.

~~~~~

Two days after Scamps' 2 April public forum at Collaroy's ramshackle surf club, a very different crowd piled into the upstairs bar of North Bondi's architect-designed equivalent on a still, clear night to hear veteran ABC journalist Kerry O'Brien and Cathy McGowan in conversation with another ABC alumnus, Quentin Dempster.

The topic of the evening was 'Truth + Trust' and it was a very leafy-east crowd: CEOs and other professional types, off-duty journalists mingling with retirees, and as many men as women, including a posse of Young Laborites who'd come to check out the woman behind the event, Allegra Spender, about whom they'd heard good things.

By halfway through, though, it was McGowan who was laying them in the aisles. Dempster had just asked her how she first won Indi from the widely disliked right-wing Liberal incumbent, Sophie Mirabella, back in 2013. McGowan paused for dramatic effect. 'It was all a mistake,' she said finally, as the crowd cracked up. 'We didn't think we were going to win. Making the seat marginal was the ambition, so we sort of made it up.'

McGowan's niece and nephew, Leah Ginnivan and Ben McGowan, had at that time both been in Melbourne working and studying. As McGowan explained in her autobiography: 'When many of our young people from the north-east [of Victoria] move to Melbourne, they set up households and even micro-neighbourhoods in the inner suburbs, where they form little expat communities. Naturally, the talk will turn to home, bemoaning life in the country.' The pair first floated the idea of her running for parliament during a late-night, wine-enhanced phone call in May 2012: 'Cathy, we've been having dinner together and we think we need to make Indi a marginal seat. We reckon you should run as an independent candidate.'

'We knew the incumbent [Mirabella] had certain characteristics,' their aunt told the Bondi audience, to more laughter. 'And we knew ... our competitive advantage was not being them; so we decided we'd be values-driven, we'd be positive. Not because we had any grand notion of what that meant. We just knew it would appeal to the community. [I said that] if I got elected I'd consult, with no intention of doing it; we weren't going to win. But we knew the theory of what we should be doing, as a group of community workers and people who knew best practice, because we had done it in other ways.'

A one-time Liberal staffer, McGowan was a local farmer who ran her own regional-development consultancy at that time. As did another local farmer, Alana Johnson, who became convenor of Voices for Indi. Johnson had found herself at university in 1974 thanks to the introduction of free education by Gough Whitlam. 'Thousands of us young rural women landed in Melbourne in the midst of the second-wave women's liberation movement,' she told me. 'Many became the first tertiary graduates in their families.' They returned to their towns and farms determined 'not to have the invisible and predetermined lives of our mothers and grandmothers. We became change-makers, and in the 1980s and 1990s we fundamentally altered how rural Australia works.'

Both McGowan and Johnson had honed their skills as graduates of the Australian Rural Leadership Program. Their work as consultants had also made them very aware of the federal government's neglect of rural and regional issues in general, and in Indi particularly. The hopelessness that pervaded the area as a result had created widespread antipathy to their then local member, Mirabella.

Johnson's time as a director of the Victorian Women's Trust (VWT), which she later chaired, had taught her about kitchen-table conversations. Small discussions among ten or so people about community issues and representation, they had been designed by VWT executive director Mary Crooks and would become a major feature of the independents model. Those conversations usually resulted in a report that could be used as the basis for a campaign. In the late 1990s, it became the cornerstone of the Purple Sage project, which galvanised about 6000 rural Victorians (three-quarters of the project's 100 leaders were women) against Jeff Kennett. That politicisation was so effective, according to Johnson, that Kennett would later blame the VWT for his 1999 defeat.

All up, Voices for Indi conducted 50 conversations in March and April 2013, involving 440 people aged eighteen to 75 across 40 postcodes. 'Our intention with the kitchen-table conversations wasn't really to get the issues, it was to create engagement,' McGowan told her Bondi audience. 'But the issues came out anyway: lack of mobile phone coverage; no internet; very bad public transport; failure to recognise Indigenous people. Very practical things that people in the electorate said they wanted something done about. So I bravely said, "Well, if I get elected, I'll work on that.""

She was as surprised as anyone when she was elected by 431 votes. Having promised consultative, values-based representation, 'We said "now we'd better do it",' McGowan said. 'But the thing that came with it was 500 people who had all been out there engaged in kitchen-table conversations. It wasn't just the candidate, it was the community who said, "We want to be the change.""

For McGowan, that lesson ran deeper than Voices for Indi, or her work across political divides as a rural-development consultant. She had grown up towards the middle of thirteen children in a large Catholic family in rural Australia in the 1950s and 1960s, when sectarian fault lines divided communities. In the 1950s, her father had been involved in social organisations that led to the foundation of the Democratic Labor Party, including the National Catholic Rural Movement, before becoming an active member of the Liberal Party and the Farmers' Federation.

'The shock of being bullied by older state school kids, just because we were Catholic, stays with me to this day,' McGowan wrote in her autobiography. What her parents taught her to fight with, however, was strategy. 'I can see all these years later that I was getting some good training for being a crossbench MP, both at home and on the school bus.'

Negotiating factions in a family in which almost two decades separated the eldest and youngest was another lesson. As the youngest of the oldest groups, she had to learn 'how to manage up', while also forming alliances with her juniors. 'Growing up in that farmhouse was a degree course in leadership and conflict resolution,' she wrote, resulting in skills that became so 'deeply ingrained ... I've often found myself bewildered that other people haven't developed [them].'

That they hadn't been developed was, however, immediately apparent when McGowan arrived in Canberra for the first time in 2013. 'It was a big, long corridor; people didn't talk to each other,' she told the Bondi audience. 'Abbott was in. Labor had just been [defeated]. It was a wounded community. Gaping. Traumatised.'

How, Dempster asked her, had she gone about navigating that polarisation, factionalism? 'We didn't,' she replied. 'I have to be a bit humble about this. I'd got there not expecting to win. We had promised a values-based campaign, so I had to be my best self. I had to work out how to get things done, because I didn't really know much about that. And then I got incredibly busy being the member for Indi. What happened was I decided I didn't have enough time in my day to pay attention to the Liberal and National Party and Labor. I had to read the papers and know what was going on, but I was too busy checking legislation every day, working out how to vote, attending to my constituents ... If there was any capacity in my brain, it went to my community.'

Rather than letting their path be determined by old fault lines, McGowan and her staff played to their strengths. 'I'm a country woman, a very clever and sophisticated country woman,' she said. 'I knew that my competitive advantage was that I could create a community in parliament, rather than thinking about all that other stuff.'

The 2013 crossbench members—including Clive Palmer, Adam Bandt and Bob Katter—were stranded together at the unfashionable end of that long corridor. The Palmer United Party staff had trouble knowing what was happening inside parliament because their leader wouldn't let them use the intranet. 'He said, "The Chinese have bugged Parliament House." And you might laugh but three years later he was proved right,' McGowan told her audience. 'Throughout, his parliamentary address was clivepalmer@yahoo.com. He never ever used the parliamentary website.' So McGowan's office provided Palmer's with 'all the running issues every few days. We became very good colleagues. Not about politics, but in terms of the relationship.'

She also decided to invite 'a small number of people to come for homemade fruit cake in my office,' she recalled. 'Our office became the social hub of parliament. Not necessarily the politicians, but the library staff. The cleaners, who would say, "Have you heard . . .?" I'd go down to the hairdresser in Parliament House, Martine [Kendall], who did everyone's hair. I'd say, "Martine, what's going to happen?" and she'd say, "This and this and this."'

Morning tea was such a hit that when 'we got to winter 2014, me and my staff thought, "Why don't we do it a bit bigger?" So we had a midwinter soiree and invited people we knew—journalists, lobbyists, some of the people we liked. We put on cheese, Rutherglen muscat and homemade fruit cake . . . Adam Bandt said they'd bring inner-Melbourne delights, which were all vegan . . . Clive brought macaroons—boxes and boxes of them—and Bob Katter brought a platter of meat. About 50 people came. It was a hoot.'

The midwinter soiree in turn morphed into the 'Very Crossbench Christmas Party'. 'When I finished up in 2019, 500 people came to that party. And you know who came? The PM and opposition leader and both deputy leaders, and all the staff we wanted to talk to. More business was done at that Very Crossbench Christmas Party than at any other party in Parliament House.

'I'm telling you that because it's me working to my strengths,' McGowan concluded. I'm a community-builder. I can invite people and they'll come because I'm not going to make them feel embarrassed. I'm not going to do horrible things to them. And it's a neutral place to come to do work. That's why I didn't have to worry about the politics of the main teams; it wasn't actually my agenda, which was to be an effective, values-driven member of parliament who her community could respect, like and vote for again. But, better than that, I could be what they wanted me to be.'

It's telling that in her account, what she achieved for Indi in her first term is relegated almost to parentheses, in favour of how she achieved it. 'When I ran the second campaign in 2016, I actually had to demonstrate that I was effective; that was important. We'd got 50 new mobile phone towers; we got commitments to fix the trains.'

The ultimate proof of the efficacy of her approach, though, was that 'they voted for Helen Haines [who successfully ran for the seat after McGowan retired in 2019] because we had demonstrated that all that was possible . . . You can just start being kind and honest to your constituency. You just start turning up and have some really good arguments about policy, without getting personal, and, if you do that, people will engage.'

Sitting in that Bondi audience, it was hard not to admire what was a bravura performance, the fullest and funniest that I saw on the election trail. Not that long ago it was the accepted wisdom that Barnaby Joyce was the country's best retail politician, but watching McGowan in full flight, you suspected the title always belonged to her.

The former member for Indi would later report that she looked out across the sea of CEOs and professionals in the audience and realised that the government was sunk. As a review of one of the high-profile city campaigns would conclude post-election, 2022 was the year 'the country came to the city'.

But if anyone in the audience at McGowan's conversation with Kerry O'Brien and Quentin Dempster was expecting to meet that warm, funny aunt after the show was over, they would be disappointed. Covid mask back in place, McGowan was all business. 'Give me feedback, give me feedback,' she urged the guy in front of me, waving away the compliment he'd just offered. This is, after all, the woman who coined the term 'verbal karate' to describe the martial art of winning people over, conversation by conversation. She was always looking to hone her technique, improve her cut-through.

And never more so than in early April 2022. Crunch time. Community-backed independent campaigns had flowered all around the country, spreading further than anyone had foreseen. But an as yet uncalled election had to be held by 21 May, just weeks away, and, like any good farmer, McGowan was intent on tending her crop ahead of that harvest.

Her North Bondi Surf Club appearance was the beginning of a lightning, two-week trip around key electorates to make sure campaigns were on track, hold workshops for campaign staff, gee up volunteers and front events like this one. That itinerary would take her from Groom in Queensland to Page

(Grafton) and Cowper (Coffs Harbour) in northern New South Wales, Bradfield on Sydney's north shore and Calare in central western New South Wales. She visited Indi's neighbouring electorate, Nicholls, centred on Shepparton; and Mallee, centred on Mildura and Swan Hill.

The mask remained in place throughout. 'I don't want to get Covid, that's for sure. That would really stuff me up,' she told me when she hit Nicholls. Nothing could interrupt her momentum. Because Indi didn't slow after McGowan won, or won again. Or even after she was succeeded by Helen Haines. It continued its grassroots engagement, one of the principles named in Voices for Indi's original report arising from the kitchen-table conversations. That grass simply got greener, farther-flung.

'When Indi was successful in 2013, we were inundated by communities right around the nation saying, "How can we do the same thing?"' says Haines, who with her husband, Phil, was involved with Voices for Indi from the start. 'There was a very public, open, transparent sharing of information, including a town hall workshop that people from Warringah and other electorates as well attended. Warringah really took it seriously after coming to Indi [and] continued to have many, many conversations with the Voices for Indi and campaign people, and then, of course, developed their own way of doing things based on similar philosophies and similar on-the-ground organising methodologies.' The first of those sessions was a weekend workshop event, #Indishares how-we-did-it, in early 2014. Two more Indi Shares workshops followed in 2015 and 2018.

Within Voices for Indi at the very beginning there had been some disagreement about how much outreach they should do, as opposed to focusing on McGowan's re-election and, later, that of Haines. That question—how much attention should be paid to the immediate battle, how much to waging the larger war?—would also split at least one other campaign in 2022.

In Indi, one of the original Voices for Indi founders, Denis Ginnivan, father of Leah Ginnivan and husband of McGowan's sister, Helen, opted to focus on outreach. His name would crop up regularly as an early adviser, even prime mover, in 2022 campaigns.

Louise Hislop, for instance, first encountered Ginnivan and Phil Haines when they talked to lawyer Kathryn Ridge about her independent campaign for the NSW state seat of Manly in the 2017 by-election caused by then premier Mike Baird's retirement, which Hislop worked on.

She then attended the 2018 Indi Shares event, which led to Voices of Warringah. 'It was great,' she says. 'Cathy did one of the sessions, Denis and Phil ran the day, including a session on kitchen-table conversations. They talked about the whole community-movement thing, how it brought everyone together and made it okay to talk about politics, and the day-to-day workings of building a movement. It changed everything. I just realised what you had to do.'

4

GROUND ZERO

Saturday, 18 May 2019 was a signal day in the revolution that was to bring a record crop of community-backed independents into the Australian parliament in 2022. The day of the 2019 election marked the moment a movement sparked six years earlier in rural Victoria made it to the Big Smoke—and came to stay.

Well, not the Big Smoke perhaps, but close by, in the federal seat of Warringah, just across the harbour from Sydney's CBD, stretching from Mosman and Manly to Curl Curl in the north and Killarney Heights in the west.

Former Rudd staffer Lachlan Harris remembers the energy that was palpable on that day, the whiff of victory in the air. Louise Hislop recalls a quite different lead-up in an electorate that, since its creation almost a century earlier, had always been held by the Liberals or their predecessors, the original United Australia Party. 'People look back and think, "Well, of course, she was always going to win," but that wasn't the general feeling throughout the campaign,' she says. 'There was no sense this was a foregone conclusion, ever.'

By the evening of 18 May, however, the victory couldn't have been more emphatic. Zali Steggall had not only defeated the former prime minister, Tony Abbott, 57 per cent to 43 per cent on a two-candidate preferred basis, with a swing of almost 19 per cent, but also garnered a whopping 43.5 per cent of the primary vote. Abbott had received just 39 per cent of that vote, down from 51.7 per cent three years earlier. Better still, Steggall had done all this in an election in which Scott Morrison's Coalition was returned to office with a slight swing.

It's early April 2022 and I am talking to Steggall in the airless meeting room of her campaign office, which is sandwiched between a Botox clinic and a hair salon on Mosman's Military Road. The May election is yet to be called but Scott Morrison has just imposed an unknown Katherine Deves on Warringah as a 'captain's pick', though rumour has it that Balgowlah's Liberal House, ten minutes' drive away, has already shut up shop permanently.

Clive Palmer's United Australia Party has taken up residence in an office a few doors down, stripes bizarrely decaled onto the window, like a tiger's back, or jail cell. Inside the UAP office, the party's standard sign 'We Can Never Trust the Liberals, Labor or Greens Again' has been replaced by 'We Can Never Trust the Liberals, Labor or Zali Again'. As I peer in, a middle-aged man walks by. 'They're dream'n,' he mutters to no one in particular.

While her 2019 victory has long since passed into folklore, what Steggall did immediately after it is as interesting again. Rather than savouring the win, she doubled down: 'That election day in 2019 was immediately day one,' she says three years later. 'It was the start of . . . not just the next election campaign— it'd be a bit exhausting if everything was just with an eye to re-election—but delivering, showing why this works.'

The immediate reaction to her win back then only strengthened Steggall's resolve: 'What was surreal was the response—"It's a fluke; it's a knee-jerk reaction to Tony"—literally the day after the election,' she recalls. In support of that proposition, commentators cited Kerryn Phelps's failure in 2019 to hold Wentworth, which she had won seven months earlier at the by-election triggered by Malcolm Turnbull's retirement. And Maxine McKew's failure to keep Bennelong for the ALP after unseating John Howard in the 2007 Ruddslide. 'One-hit wonder,' Steggall says, summing up the logic of those who doubted her. 'You'll never hold it.'

Like Cathy McGowan before her, Steggall knew she had to prove the model if it was to survive: 'Independent Warringah couldn't just be about me. It had to be about more than just the personality of the current member,' she says. 'That's what was so historic with Indi passing to a new independent. If I'm not able to get re-elected, then the major parties have a strong argument that [voters] can turn to an independent when an incumbent is unpopular, but it's a wasted vote, because ultimately the seat returns to a party.'

As for what she had achieved during her first term, Steggall points to the climate change bill she tabled just months after being elected. That bill had received widespread support, including from the Business Council of Australia and Australian Industry Group, even though the government blocked it. 'We really pushed the case for net zero by 2050,' she says.

'And we got everyone to accept it. Prior to the last election, no one was talking net zero by 2050.'

When I speak to Liberal senator Andrew Bragg in March, he, too, cites Steggall's climate bill, but as proof of the ineffectiveness of the indies. 'You can't govern from the crossbench,' he says, when asked why the bill wasn't even debated. 'The people of Warringah are unable to get policy outcomes achieved, because they haven't got a member of the government. In the case of their current member for Warringah, that member will be empty-handed when it comes to the next election . . . we're the government, and we have a process that we need to go through for developing the proper plan to show Australia how the emissions reductions will be achieved.'

Whatever the impact of Steggall's climate bill (on which, more later), there can be little doubt about the final point Steggall made when I spoke to her in April 2022: 'If you look at how many independents are running professional well-resourced campaigns, I think we've proved that we're not a flash in the pan,' she said.

At the time, it sounded like a statement of the obvious, given the number of community-backed independent campaigns that had launched by April. But the role Steggall and her team had played in that process turns out to have been far more extensive than just the inspiration of a signal win.

While there are good reasons for saying that the model of the contemporary urban-community independent campaign was actually minted across the water in Wentworth in 2018, it was refined and crystalised in Warringah a year later. And since

2019, Warringah, and the cast of characters responsible for that win, have very consciously taken it to the world.

Outside the meeting room where we spoke, Tina Jackson, Steggall's 2022 campaign co-manager, sat at one of the junior-burger desks behind reception. Her title hugely undersells Jackson's contribution to the wider movement. A veteran of Zali 1.0, the former National Trust CEO had pivoted in 2019 from saving crumbling edifices to tearing them down, before co-founding the Community Independents Project with Cathy McGowan, Alana Johnson and Jill Briggs in the wake of McGowan's February 2021 'Getting Elected' conference.

With McGowan, Jackson is the community independents movement's great connector. Steggall's other campaign manager, Kirsty Gold, has a desk in the same low-key pod. If the movement can be said to have a den mother, it is Gold. 'Kirsty and Tina' come up constantly when people talk about who they turned to for advice on setting up campaigns and finding candidates, from lists of campaign must-haves to the democracy walks, which were held in many electorates.

'Kirsty and Tina are the multipliers in this equation,' says former political staffer and Manly local Ranya Alkadamani, who worked on independent campaigns in 2019 and 2022. 'You have to remember that there's no party machine behind these campaigns. It's the grunt work of local volunteers, usually with no political experience, that makes this happen. Those communities need people with experience to give them the confidence to know they can do it and to point them to the resources and tools they need to deliver.'

To Cathy McGowan, Jackson and Gold's role has been as significant as any. 'What Tina and Kirsty did in Sydney, bringing that group together and supporting each other, is as important [as Climate 200]—not more important, but hugely important.'

If Gold is the movement's den mother, then the den in question is the award-winning, architect-designed pile she and her husband, Archer Capital CEO Peter Gold, inhabit over-looking Balmoral. 'The big thing after 2019 was for us to replicate the Warringah story around Australia, and help anyone who wanted to be helped,' explains another insider from the 2019 battle. 'Kirsty had a lot of meetings at her house. She always flies under the radar, but she's incredibly generous. She and Tina had people from everywhere meeting there every six weeks or so for a long time. There'd be 20 to 30 people, almost all women, and they'd come from everywhere: Mackellar and North Sydney; Wentworth; Hume; people would fly up from Victoria, like the Kooyong women.'

Lyndell Droga remembers an early meeting, when Wentworth Independents was still just a glimmer in its founders' eyes, at which McGowan told them it often took 'a group of women to get a woman to believe that she can do something'. Droga adds: 'That's what is so irritating about being told repeatedly by the media that it's all one movement under Simon [Holmes à Court]. That room was 90 per cent women. We're very grateful for support, but we're not directed by Climate 200 or anyone else.'

'The term "doctors' wives" was coined during the 2004 federal election,' Jacqueline Maley wrote in the *Sydney Morning Herald* on 2 May 2019, 'to describe a purported demographic of middle-class women turning against John Howard because of his stance on moral issues such as the Iraq War and asylum seekers.' The bulwark against Tony Abbott in Warringah was, Maley wrote, 'more a case of "bankers' wives"'.

Those women included Anna Josephson, wife of Rickard Gardell, the founder of private equity firm Pacific Equity Partners. Josephson, who hosted fundraisers and volunteered, described herself in a *Sydney Morning Herald* article at the time as 'pretty typical of Zali supporters, at least, where we are on the lower North Shore and Mosman—long-term Liberal voters who, over the last couple of years, have started to feel very disenfranchised, feeling that our local member does not represent who we are'.

Straight-up and funny, Josephson is no stereotype of a banker's—or anyone else's—wife when we speak via Zoom in July 2022. 'You could feel the mood building in the electorate. Even around Mosman, which is where I'm from, people were really starting to get fed up with him,' she recalls of 2018. 'We had a social group that used to run, swim and have breakfast every Wednesday, and we used to complain a lot [about] Tony Abbott. We maintained a pace that allowed us to complain while we ran. One morning at breakfast, after running and complaining, a friend of mine, Julie Giannesini, said: "Seriously, maybe we should stop talking and do something. Are you with me, Anna?"'

Giannesini 'got in touch with a lot of those already existing grassroots movements and a few people that seemed to be active on the environmental side,' including Louise Hislop and Mark Kelly, founder of Vote Tony Out. 'Kirsty, me, Louise and Julie had this initial meeting. We didn't really know each other, and we said, "Let's see if we can do this: connect to everyone else and form a group and try to find an independent candidate and create a vehicle to be able to run a campaign." And that's sort of what ended up happening.'

Warringah was a different beast to Indi six years earlier. As Kirsty Gold said in early 2022: 'We always joked we were grassroots Warringah-style, because we're professional, we're educated, we have funds and connections. The sum of the parts was a grassroots movement; but done very professionally, because politics is an A-grade sport. A blood sport. You need a coach who knows what they're doing and can tell you how to play the game.'

That's not where Gold had seen herself even a few years earlier. 'If you'd asked me, I would have said I voted between doing the shopping and dropping kids at sport. I was completely politically disengaged,' she said in early 2022. She had been, she said, a 'traditional Liberal voter, but a Malcolm Turnbull Liberal' who had 'never voted Labor'. What politicised her was climate change: 'I watched Al Gore's climate movie [*An Inconvenient Truth*] in 2006 and thought, "Oh, my goodness. We're blowing up the world." That was my wake-up call. But I had a two-year-old and a baby. I thought, "I can't do anything about this."'

Her call to action came with Gore's aptly titled *An Inconvenient Sequel: Truth to Power* in 2017. 'It said, "It's not too late. You can do something." So my New Year's resolution in 2018 was to get rid of Tony Abbott.' If that sounds almost casual, it wasn't. 'My husband has always said you have to focus your efforts where you can have the most impact and influence. How you can get real about what you can do.'

Nor did that politicisation arise simply from a movie. 'My climate activism, or advocacy, is around politics. It's also around philanthropy, climate investments,' she said.

She doesn't mention it, but it was the Golds, together with Josephson and her husband, and Rob Purves, a former

Worldwide Fund for Nature president and founding member of the Wentworth Group of Concerned Scientists, who set up and seed-funded Warringah Independent Ltd in 2018. The new company meant the campaign could start raising and spending money. While the founders were willing to go further, they only ended up putting in a little over $55,000 apiece, with the Steggall campaign, the best funded of the 2019 independent campaigns, raising more than $1.1 million from almost 1400 donors.

In June 2022, a month after the election, Kirsty Gold hosted a lunch. It was not only for the victors, but also for those who had toiled just as tirelessly without an immediate result. 'Who told you about that?' she shot back when I inquired about it. 'It was for everyone to be able to come back together and share their stories. To talk about what had happened, how amazing it had been and what they had achieved,' she eventually explained. 'There was so much blood, sweat and tears from so many, often for a couple of years, that it was amazing to be able to share that joy and celebrate together. And that's what we did in Warringah. We shared with others, but they did all the hard work and they created their own results.'

While they're ubiquitous within the movement, Gold and Jackson studiously avoid the media. Few would relish the kind of headline the Drogas generated in November 2021 ('Short-seller and his wife going after Morrison') or the rich-boy-dabbles-in-democracy coverage that dogged Holmes à Court. For their part, some in the media, turned down for interviews by some of the movement's less public figures, question why those backing public political campaigns should expect to avoid scrutiny.

~~~~~

As for Warringah's inspiration: 'Indi was important in that it informed the kitchen-table model, the "Voices of" movement,' says Louise Hislop, a founder of Voices of Warringah, which held 100 such conversations between September 2018 and April 2019. 'It gave me the belief that it could be done, because I mean Sophie Mirabella was quite aligned with Tony Abbott. But rural and urban are very different, so I didn't take too much comfort. When Kerryn Phelps won in an electorate we can literally see from part of our electorate across the harbour, though, that gave everyone the belief that we could do it.'

Between 2018 and 2019, the lessons from Phelps in Wentworth turned three-dimensional, encompassing not only her shock 2018 win but also her narrow loss to Dave Sharma seven months later, in the process making the seat marginal. All eyes were on Sharma's 1.3 per cent winning margin in 2019, Droga says, when they came to consider founding Wentworth Independents to contest the seat a third time in 2022: 'If it had been a lost cause, if the margin had been 20 per cent, we wouldn't have done it. It wouldn't have been worth it. It was knowing it was so close.'

Many of the key components of the contemporary urban independent campaign were forged in the 2018 Wentworth by-election campaign, itself a classic tale of politicisation and improvisation. Not to mention unintended consequences, given that the victor was, as McGowan had been five years earlier, as surprised as anyone when she huffed, puffed and blew down the safest of Liberal Party houses.

'Wentworth had been a Liberal–Conservative stronghold for its entire [120-year] history,' Kerryn Phelps told me in June 2022. 'We needed a greater than 18 per cent swing on a two-person-preferred basis to be able to win. So when I decided to stand, I was making a point about the leadership upheavals in the Liberal Party, the lurch of the Coalition to the far right, which I found very disturbing, and the lack of action on climate change and treatment of refugees. But I didn't do it with an expectation of winning. When we achieved a swing of almost 20 per cent, people just shook their heads and said, "What just happened?"'

Phelps's 2018 campaign had grown out of a planned tilt at the lord mayoralty of Sydney. She had been elected as a councillor in 2016 on Lord Mayor Clover Moore's ticket, and become deputy mayor. But after the two fell out, Phelps's mayoral bid was being planned by a 'small committee of eight or ten people. We'd been discussing things like design and colour, and policies and how you might manage a campaign; educating ourselves a little bit about what a campaign in a local government electorate might look like,' she recalls.

Phelps was well known at the time as a doctor who had practised in Wentworth for almost twenty years. She had also been the first woman to head the Australian Medical Association and a prominent campaigner in the lead-up to the same-sex postal survey less than a year earlier, in November 2017. It's hard to overestimate that survey's significance as an ignition point in the growth of the community-backed independents movement.

The political travails and delays that preceded the survey, and the licence it afforded homophobia in Australia, are widely cited as a watershed by those involved in the 2022 campaigns, from Warringah and Wentworth in New South Wales to the ACT, and Groom in Queensland. Candidates and campaigns would also look to their own electorate's vote in the national survey as a litmus test for their electoral chances—not least in

Warringah, home to the leading 'No' campaigner, Tony Abbott, where three-quarters of the electorate voted for marriage equality.

In terms of her 2018 run, Phelps says, 'Indi wasn't on my radar, nor was it on the radar of my organising team' at the time, although 'Cathy came to Sydney after I'd announced my candidacy to just have a chat and tell me a little bit about how campaigning might work, and how being an MP might work.' Nonetheless, Phelps ended up doing a crash course in Indi-style community consultation during her lightning-fast, six-week by-election campaign.

Between the dumping of Turnbull as prime minister, the marriage-equality debate and the ongoing issues of climate change, health care and refugee policy, the political temperature was rising so fast that frogs were boiling everywhere at the time. 'People knew what values and principles I stood for,' Phelps says. 'I couldn't go anywhere without somebody stopping me in the street or sending me a text or calling me and saying, "Kerryn, there's a by-election happening. Why don't you stand?"

'That's when I took it back to my group and said, "What do we all think?" I actually excused myself from the meeting where they discussed whether they would be prepared to shift to a federal campaign, on the understanding that the likelihood is that we wouldn't win, but that we would run a campaign based on principle and values. They were all in, though. That's how it started. None of us had any campaign experience.'

What made 2018 so pivotal, Phelps says, was that 'politically, the attention of the entire country was on this one little part of the eastern suburbs of Sydney. It was the only election in the country at that time. It wasn't like there were 151 electorates around the country with their own individual thing going on. Once I announced, people just came from everywhere. One guy drove from Lightning Ridge to stand on New South Head Road for days helping out. Another couple called us from their car on the way from Brisbane to say, "We're coming down to help." And anyone who had a bit of an axe to grind, a policy that they wanted to promote, or an issue that they felt was important, stood as a candidate for a micro-party or as an independent.'

It was an early crack in the dam wall that would fully fracture four years later. Phelps ran, too, on many of the same policy positions in 2018 that preoccupied the independent candidates in 2022—from integrity to climate, equality to refugees. 'I was visited by the [National Integrity Committee] of retired judges, so the integrity commission was one of my policies at the 2018 by-election. And the Kids Off Nauru campaign basically set up camp in Wentworth in 2018. All of the refugee advocates visited me and we developed policy around all children being removed from detention and an end to indefinite offshore detention. It was a values-based, principles-based, policy-based by-election that harnessed a mood of dissatisfaction on a whole range of issues. I represented for enough people in the community of Went-worth who were looking for a different way of doing politics, and we also talked about the "sensible centre".'

Timing would prove her undoing, however. Elected on 20 October 2018, Phelps didn't hit parliament until 26 November. 'In between, we had to set up for the legislative calendar, find somewhere to stay, employ staff, get across what was happen-ing in legislation, what I needed to do, write a maiden speech. Then we had the time in parliament negotiating and passing the Medevac legislation [which meant sick people in offshore detention could be airlifted to the mainland for urgent medical treatment] and nobody knew when the election was going to be run.'

Wendy McCarthy, who chaired the 2018 and 2019 Wentworth campaigns, vividly recalls Phelps's maiden speech, in which the new parliamentarian called for urgent action on climate change and for the 'human experience' to inform political decision-making, warning that Australians had had 'enough of the way party politics [was] being practised'.

'I was sitting in the gallery with my nephew, a Canberra lawyer, whom I'd asked to be my guest,' McCarthy recalls. 'And as Kerryn was about to speak, Morrison led the Liberal Party out of the chamber. He didn't want to hear a word she had to say . . . It was shocking. My nephew's jaw dropped and he said, "I'm no ingenue, but are they always this rude?"' The gesture was all the more striking given that Morrison was at the time leading a minority government that needed Phelps's support. Three and a half years later, women everywhere would return the favour, walking out on Morrison en masse.

By the time the federal election was called on 11 April 2019, however, another game was being played on another pitch. 'Some of the people who had helped us out with things like scrutineering, who were from Warringah, had gone back to help [the Steggall campaign], as had Anthony Reed,' Phelps recalls. 'Some of the donors, too, were then putting their money elsewhere, because we weren't the only show in town. There were 151 electorates, so we were purely relying on our staff and our local volunteers at that point, and they'd been under the pump for months. We were all pretty tired, but we found the energy to go again in April–May [2019] and we went really, really close.'

The nearness of that miss would be a lingering, galvanising regret for Simon Holmes à Court, who first founded Climate 200 just before the May 2019 election with support from 35 donors, including tech billionaire Mike Cannon-Brookes. Climate 200 contributed $437,000 to twelve independents' campaigns at that election. 'If 1200 people had preferenced differently, Kerry Phelps would still be the member for Wentworth,' Holmes à Court told me in September 2021, a few months before Allegra Spender announced her candidature.

'We were kicking ourselves afterwards that we had under-invested in Kerryn's campaign,' he said. 'It was only seven months after the by-election. Her fundraisers were exhausted, her donors were exhausted, her team was exhausted, and the national spotlight was off her. If she had [had] a few tens of thousands [of dollars] more early on, to beef up her campaign, I think she would have retained the seat.'

Holmes à Court was speaking at the time about what had motivated him to resurrect Climate 200 in late 2021 to try to level the playing field for independents once more. Tellingly, he had retained two people to run a review of Climate 200's first iteration before he decided to go again.

One of them was Byron Fay, a former Paris Agreement negotiator who, fresh from working on a Joe Biden–aligned political action committee during the 2020 US election, would become Climate 200's CEO. The other was Anthony Reed.

A key, if sometimes polarising, figure in the independents movement, Reed came up through Young Labor, which he joined at fifteen, before working with the unions and as chief of staff for former NSW Labor minister Phil Costa. He had worked with Labor-aligned PR agencies before being brought into Phelps's 2018 campaign by McCarthy along with Darrin Barnett, Julia Gillard's former press secretary. He was, says Josephson, crucial to the 2019 victory. 'I would say we would not have been able to do it without him. His perspective and his knowledge and his expertise were critical.'

Reed remained on the Climate 200 advisory council after he and Fay completed their review, only stepping back in January 2022 to focus on the campaigns that had retained him. His base camp during the election became Wentworth, where he co-managed the campaign with Droga, while also giving strategic advice to Mackellar, North Sydney and Warringah. As such, he would promulgate more broadly the model that had been developed during Kerryn Phelps's 2018 by-election campaign and honed in Warringah. 'My experience of working with Kerryn in that campaign crystallised the ideas that I had,' he says. 'During the campaign, I was approached by a bunch of people who were really excited about having a go at Warringah. The success we had really gave me the confidence to move into Warringah, [where I] basically convinced them to fund the start-up costs of Warringah Independent.'

Reed wasn't alone. Speaking to *The Saturday Paper*'s chief political correspondent, Karen Middleton, in March 2019, Damien Hodgkinson cited Phelps's 2018 campaign as seminal. A former KPMG partner and Sydney Gay and Lesbian Mardi Gras director, Hodgkinson had been part of the group planning Phelps's mayoral bid, to which she had recruited him for his skills in community campaigning and volunteer marshalling.

When Malcolm Turnbull resigned from parliament, Kerryn Phelps was on the phone.

'I was on holiday . . . and I get a phone call saying, "I think we're going to pivot a little bit,"' Hodgkinson recalled. A year later, after teaming up with political strategists, including Reed, Hodgkinson was 'set to be a pivotal backroom figure in the coming election', Middleton wrote. He ultimately consulted to eight of the 2019 independent campaigns, including those of Kerryn Phelps, Zali Steggall (Hodgkinson established Warringah Independent) and Julia Banks. For those candidates, he was instrumental in 'setting up campaign infrastructure, including donor and volunteer databases, and advising on logistics, administration and other back-of-house necessities'.

While Anthony Reed managed the Wentworth 2018 campaign, it didn't come down to any one person, Phelps says. 'It was a team effort and I was the team leader. You need to look at how things were structured and how they worked. I had input on policy. I had input on operations. In the end, as the candidate in 2018 and 2019, I determined the messaging that went out and what we were going to do. What I sought from Anthony was the operational side of things. He organised the corflutes. He organised for the teams to go out and put them up. We had volunteers who were prepared to organise volunteers for polling and pre-polling booths . . . All the how-to, operational stuff, Anthony organised in 2018. I think what he saw was how our team coalesced, how we all worked together, all those other elements of a campaign.'

As Kerryn Phelps's chairperson in both 2018 and 2019, Wendy McCarthy watched the independents model change speed in real time. 'I went and talked to the Zali people early on—Kirsty and a couple of others,' she recalls. 'That was a very different game. Ours was right out of the grassroots of the community. They were all uber rich but with a passion for doing things right. A lot of Kerryn's team went to work for Zali because they had that experience. It didn't mean they deserted us, but they were doing both and were moving into a mode of really professionalising their role in setting up independents.

'Then you saw Simon Holmes à Court getting a war chest together. It's a really interesting time in terms of the machinations and manoeuvrings of people who are really, I know it's corny, but fiscally conservative and socially progressive. Care very deeply about climate change and their children's futures, and who just weren't finding that anyone was having that conversation with them in this country.'

But it wasn't just the few. What those A-grade skills harnessed and helped direct was a widespread and very local mood for change that had been building for half a decade. Voices of Warringah was the first really visible local group. But by the time Louise Hislop became its president, she was already a veteran of numerous local ginger groups. Over five years she had headed the Australian Progressives Warringah hub, doorknocked with the grassroots #StopAdani movement and attended the weekly People of Warringah meetings founded by same-sex marriage campaigner Nathan Thomas.

Later, an anonymous, youth-led Instagram account called Think Twice Warringah would document the anti-Abbott posters blossoming across the electorate. When Hislop wrote about her early experiences for Margo Kingston's No Fibs

Independents Day website, she described how Warringah had gone from 'an electorate that never talked about politics' to one where you couldn't pay for petrol without the service station owner telling you Abbott had to go.

Mark Kelly, owner of international surfboard distributor Global Surf Industries, was part of that awakening. Kelly cites Abbott's decision to absent himself from the marriage-equality bill vote that resulted from the $100 million survey as the last straw that led him to establish the Vote Tony Out Facebook page in 2018. 'I'm just a normal guy, but over the last couple of years something's woken me up,' he told me in 2021. 'I just started talking to people. A lot of people had an opinion, but they'd never talked about it. I think that's the whole Vote Tony Out thing. We sort of made it okay to talk about politics.'

Cathy McGowan describes kitchen-table conversations, and the community-backed independents movement more broadly, as a mechanism for giving people permission to think, speak and vote differently. Vote Tony Out was a prime example. One of its first posts to hit the media in 2018 came from a Mosman dentist, David Eyles. 'We have never been involved in a movement or a political party,' it read. 'We are just trying to get on with life. But enough is enough. We feel compelled to speak up. Wake up Warringah! Let's get out of the habit of just voting for whomever the Liberal Party throws at us.' Reporting the post, the *Sydney Morning Herald* noted that Eyles had 'last popped up in the news when his Queenscliff home broke local records after it sold for over $12 million . . . not your typical anti-Liberal firebrand'.

By the election, Mark Kelly's closed, by-invitation Vote Tony Out Facebook group had grown to 2000. An Instagram account featuring locals wearing the teal T-shirt peaked at 20,000 followers. Coloured T-shirts as a brand weren't new. 'Election night in a hall in Wangaratta, with orange every-where,' McGowan starts her autobiography, speaking of the Indi version. 'Orange balloons. Orange streamers. Orange shirts. Orange was our colour.'

But the database the Vote Tony Out T-shirts created was as important as the walking billboards who wore them. Kelly used the T-shirts very much as a marketing and engagement tool, hand-delivering the first 1600 because 'I wanted people to see I was just a normal guy and I wanted to talk to them about why they were joining.'

Drawing on his marketing background, Kelly carried out multiple surveys of the 6000-strong database Vote Tony Out built across its touch points. 'Ninety-five per cent of them had never done anything politically before,' he says. 'They'd never been engaged, never joined or donated to a political movement. So basically, without spending a dollar, we were able to rely on peer-to-peer communication, people talking to their friends.'

All the groups were interconnected. 'I got one of the first ten Vote Tony Out T-shirts from Mark,' says Kirsty Gold. 'Tina and I walked up and down Balmoral Beach in them twice a week for six months. We're all out of the same factory, with different brands. And because Mark had set up Vote Tony Out, and Louise had Voices of Warringah, they were our public face; the rest of us didn't need to be public-facing.'

It was through the Vote Tony Out T-shirts that Zali Steggall first entered the picture. 'A friend of mine is a very good friend of Mark Kelly's,' Steggall said in 2021. 'I'd seen her photo with a T-shirt, and I ordered a whole bunch for Christmas presents for my family. I bought them for my parents. I didn't buy them for my in-laws because, ironically, they were old friends of John Howard and Tony Abbott.'

Through that mutual friend, Kelly ended up spending New Year's Eve with Steggall and her husband, Tim Irving, at her parents' house above Manly Oval. 'Tim and Zali were peppering me with questions about the movement: how many people were in the campaign; whether we had a candidate,' Kelly says. 'I told them that there was a company called Warringah Independent that had funding and had organisation and had a campaign manager all ready to go.'

Steggall agreed to do an Instagram post in the T-shirt on New Year's Day 2019. Three days later, she rang to discuss running. Three weeks later, her candidacy was announced.

But those urging change in Warringah had already had a candidate for six months when Steggall called. Looking for someone with a profile, the group had approached scientist, environmentalist and writer Tim Flannery in mid-2018. Flannery had agreed to be Warringah's backup candidate. He had also moved to Sydney with his family, becoming a distinguished visiting fellow at the Australian Museum, where earlier in his career he'd worked for fifteen years.

Flannery's standing as a climate warrior was unquestionable. In terms of the very precise silhouette of Warringah's ideal candidate that had begun to emerge, however, he was high-profile rather than right-profile. With Flannery's blessing, the search had continued. 'There was a group of us who spent six months canvassing lists of names in the electorate and speaking to people,' one of the Warringah recruiters said. 'We joked we needed a chief executive woman who was a local mother who'd won a gold medal.'

It sounds casual, but it wasn't. Steve Kulmar is the founder of the consultancy Retail Oasis, which occupies an office above Humphreys newsagency on Manly Corso with a view of the beach. He remembers attending a meeting at Manly Surf Club in early 2018, at which Kirsty Gold had talked about trying to pull together the 'Voices of' groups in a way that would effectively drive a change of representation in the Warringah electorate.

Inspired, Kulmar volunteered his firm's data-research services pro bono. By October 2018, that had yielded very precise candidate criteria. The person they approached needed to be female, because men were seen as less compassionate, and her name needed to be as memorable as Tony's. Given the northern beaches' strong behavioural bias to sport, she needed to be some kind of athlete, and preferably to have represented Australia at an international level, as that would make it harder for Abbott to attack her. She also needed to be articulate, intelligent, respected within the community, and to have lived locally for a long time.

Into that frame walked Zali Steggall. Her first name was so memorable she barely needed a second, except that it reminded locals that her father had been a local solicitor for 30 years and was a member of that bastion of Liberal Party support, Manly rugby club. Not only was Steggall a sportswoman, she was an Olympic skiing medallist. And a barrister. The candidate from central casting, you might say, in a part of the world where 'you needed to have been wheeled in a pram down the Corso to qualify as local—and she was', as *Guardian* journalist Anne Davies noted, quoting an attendee at Steggall's campaign launch.

'If enthusiasm and grassroots support are the keys to a successful political campaign,' Davies wrote, 'Zali Steggall got off to a flying start in her quest to wrest Warringah from former prime minister Tony Abbott.' Steggall's January 2019 launch had been 'hastily arranged,' Davies noted, but still more than 400 supporters had turned up in 'striking turquoise "Vote Zali Steggall" T-shirts . . . under a Moreton Bay fig in a park in Balgowlah'.

'That morning only about twenty of us knew that was going to happen,' recalls Mark Kelly. At 7.30 a.m. Kelly had sent a text to 600 people who were on the Vote Tony Out database and lived in suburbs around the park: 'Vote Tony Out is endorsing Zali Steggall for Warringah. We're having a media launch at 11.00 a.m., we'd love you to come half an hour earlier.' At 10.30 a.m., '400 people turned up. The media is thinking it's going to be Zali on a soapbox, doing interviews. But they get there and there's a fucking circus. Everyone's there in their Zali for Warringah T-shirts. And all of a sudden, it was "This is a two-horse race."'

Not that Steggall didn't make use of her soapbox. Calling time on Abbott's 'destructive and divisive' quarter-century in federal politics, she said he had been a handbrake on progress on many fronts in Australia. 'I know what I am getting into but I am not a wallflower,' she said. 'I am tough. I learnt from sport that you have to put the work in and can't just turn up on the day hoping for the result. I will do the work for this, just as I did the work for sport and law.'

Permitted to stand down, having stood ready, Tim Flannery recorded a video message endorsing Steggall, and went back to his day job before anyone even knew he'd been a contender.

~~~~~

Of all the characteristics that made her so Warringah-ready in 2019, it is curiously the barrister in Steggall that comes to the fore when we speak three years later, in April 2022. A barrister has an overriding duty to the court to always act with independence in the interests of the administration of justice. 'You do your best for your client, but you can never overstep the mark of misleading the court,' Steggall explains. 'It's a really important distinction because, without it, where's the line?'

It made her think long and hard about her inaugural term in the 46th Parliament. 'I think there's a real problem,' she says. 'When you're sworn into parliament, all you have to do is swear an oath or an affirmation of allegiance to the queen. It's not [to] the Australian constitution, and it's not to the Australian parliament or the Australian people. There should be an oath to uphold trust in the Australian parliament. Or the institution of government. There must be that higher duty.'

Particularly given 'our constitution doesn't say anything about political parties', Steggall continues, referring instead to 'members of parliament to represent communities. Obviously, groupings will form, but is a member there to represent their community or their party? Is their duty to the system? There's a conflict of interest that is at the root of the problem.'

In that context, the contemporary independents are back to the future, Steggall says. 'We're getting back to the true intent of the constitution and the formation of parliament, which is to represent people.'

5

THE MATHEMATICS OF DESIRE

If the expertise brought to Zali Steggall's 2019 Warringah campaign was A-grade, by the time the next election rolled around three years later, those skills had evolved, multiplied and hugely expanded in terms of reach and sophistication.

The conventional wisdom before the 2022 election was that Prime Minister Scott Morrison was an ace campaigner, whose 'miracle' May 2019 win could in part be attributed to the daggy-dad persona he had carefully cultivated after succeeding Malcolm Turnbull in August 2018. It would be a further irony of the 2022 election that the man whom the satirical online rag *The Betoota Advocate* had dubbed 'Scotty from Marketing' in 2018 was so consummately outplayed by better marketers, many of them political novices.

Nor was it only marketers. Strategists and advisers, campaigners and organisers would all outmanoeuvre a government that had at its disposal not only all the resources and advantages of incumbency, but also a party machine that had once seemed an almost insurmountable barrier to entry for non-aligned players.

The community-backed independents were able to achieve this because, however artless their campaigns may have appeared from the outside—founded often on an optimism bordering on naivety, fed by enthusiasm rather than realism—there was, in fact, much more to them, in terms of both the depth and breadth of that community backing and the professional skills they could marshal. Which often turned out to be the same thing.

And just as the seemingly new independents movement had in truth been developing for a decade, the marketing skills they deployed had evolved over many years, often in other campaigns or careers, before finding their mark in 2022's federal election.

~~~~~

Steve Kulmar, the founder of Retail Oasis, is a case in point.

The company had hammered out the ten-point profile into which Zali Steggall had walked in early 2019 from demographic and psychographic analysis. To do so, they had drawn on a range of publicly available data sources: Australian Electoral Office research; Australian Bureau of Statistics data, predominantly the Household Expenditure Survey; Australia's largest consumer data source, Roy Morgan, which includes 60,000 interviews with consumers; and Roy Morgan's demographic tool, Helix Personas (tagline 'Town by town, street by street, Helix Personas paints the picture of a nation that is constantly being reshaped by social change').

Retail Oasis's commercial clients, ranging from the Commonwealth Bank and Afterpay to jeweller Michael Hill and online fashion and sports retailer The Iconic, use its analysis to inform decisions on everything from advertising to where they should open and close stores. The difference in this case, of course, was that the product being retailed to voters was a candidate to represent—effectively to mirror—them.

It was the psychographic data that had confirmed that Warringah had the strongest behavioural bias to sport of any electorate in the country, though only its extent was a surprise in an electorate networked with beaches and walking tracks. An electorate, too, where more than a hundred swimmers meet at 7 a.m. each day at Manly Surf Club to swim to Shelly Beach with the Bold and Beautiful swim group. It's no coincidence that Kulmar is a member of B&B, which became a hotbed of pro-independent, anti-Abbott sentiment, not least on Instagram, while also including Liberal supporters and alumni, including Bruce Baird. Nor that Josephson and Giannesini first decided to act after a run-and-grumble.

That psychographic and geographic data also allowed the campaign to tailor messages more precisely to electoral outlets in 2019. 'The Manly Village Public School booth was much more strongly progressive around a number of key subject areas, and the economic and financial issues were less import-ant,' Steve Kulmar says. 'Whereas at the Mosman Public School's booth, the financial and economic messages were still important.'

Most significantly, the data had confirmed the campaign's starting hunch that Abbott was vulnerable. 'A whole lot of key drivers, things like awareness and interest and concerns around climate, around sexuality, around integrity, around a whole lot of subjects came up in [the Roy Morgan] research,' says Kulmar. 'Interestingly, once you moved into affluent suburb areas, you began to see these trends embedded over a longer period of time. So, in 2019 we discovered that really Abbott's core, rusted-on level of support was not that great and identified that there was a substantial opportunity to turn Warringah into an independent electorate.'

~~~~~

The teal-shaded marketing launched in Warringah in 2019 would have a fair claim to have spawned the single most successful brand campaign in Australia in recent years. Numerous independent campaigns featured some shade of the blue–green spectrum in 2022. Even so-called moderate Liberals such as Dave Sharma attempted to camouflage themselves in the colour, hoping to blend in long enough to survive.

It was so omnipresent, in fact, that it became—for better or worse—shorthand for an entire movement. And one person had more to do with creating it than anyone else. Dof Dickinson had first been introduced to those plotting revolution in Warringah in late 2018 by Diana Ryall, the former managing director of Apple Australia, and the first woman to lead an IT company here.

As head of creative services at Brains agency, which has offices in Sydney and Amsterdam, and specialises in global campaigns, Dickinson had been creative director on Apple computer's account before working for clients ranging from Microsoft to Telstra. Warringah was looking for 'someone who had the capacity to run a big campaign, even though it was just a small electorate,' Dickinson told me, speaking from London, where she has recently been based, in July 2022. 'They wanted it to be professional, because we were going to win on professionalism.'

Dickinson attended an initial late-2018 kick-off meeting that also involved Kulmar and another agency that subsequently dropped out. Warringah 'was high-risk for an agency to take on,' she says. 'Many of our clients are actually staunch Liberal supporters. Some agencies felt that this wasn't what they wanted to do. And also, it didn't look initially like we would necessarily win. We had a lot of numbers to achieve. I can't remember the exact swing that we had to achieve, but I think Abbott had never pulled less than 40 per cent.'

Mitigating that risk, Dickinson was not only a woman but also local. 'We were so passionate about making the change,' she says. 'We couldn't see another three years of climate denialism, that treatment of women. It made people's blood boil. Many of us were, potentially, ex-Liberal Party voters who had become so disillusioned with the party that we had to make a change.'

Engaged in November 2018, Dickinson cancelled Christmas to review the data and the focus-group results, creating a messaging stack 'that spanned an overarching value proposition for Zali and the campaign tagline "What are you waiting for?"'

It was a passion project, rather than an earner. 'We were paid for one video and we did ten. We were supposed to do one brochure, we did five,' she says, echoing Damien Hodgkinson's comments on what had quickly become a second strand of his business, providing back-office expertise to campaigns. 'We cover costs in terms of the staff and time involved and there's probably a small profit margin but it's nothing like the other work we do,' Hodgkinson said.

Kulmar's analysis meant the Steggall 2019 campaign had the sort of detailed, expensive work pro bono that focused the task considerably. 'The Helix Personas showed us that more than 19 per cent of the electorate would never vote anything but Liberal, so we just didn't target them,' Dickinson said.

'It's a classic advertising strategy: don't spend money trying to convince people; convince the people you can. We could win another 36 per cent, and 13.6 per cent of those we knew would be easy. Then there was a 15.3 per cent audience of apathetic voters we knew we could turn to enthusiastic voters.'

They knew because Warringah was almost magically homogeneous. 'Basically, we only had two personas; that is unheard of, for someone like me, who's used to dealing with markets that are complex. But when we did the research, we were talking to rich people and their kids: Leading Lifestyles and Metrotechs,' Dickinson said, referring to the top two of the major Helix groupings in terms of education and income. 'Leading Lifestyles are people who have the best lifestyle in Australia. And Metrotechs are young people who are technology oriented but also have a great lifestyle. And we could see them on a street-by-street level. Steve [Kulmar] had access to that data, being a retail agency. That is how Warringah was able to reach these levels of professionalism, through people being incredibly generous.'

When it came to Steggall, 'I was going to market her like a product,' Dickinson says. 'Because I came from that advertising background, I was going to do my demographic research. I was going to find out what people wanted, research that messaging, check the audience aligned with it. And towards the end of the campaign, we segmented that messaging. So if you lived near the [then-proposed northern beaches] tunnel, which was an issue on the first campaign, you would see a message about that. If you were older and you had money, then you would see the franking credits message. Different people saw different things in their Facebook feed.'

It was, she says three years later, 'a primary reason why we are more powerful than the Liberal Party. They can only come up with basically one message and pump it out across Australia. They don't have time to break down one electorate into layers like we did, and then go after them much more precisely. They don't have the energy to do it, I don't think, and they don't, or didn't, seem to have the smarts. So they would just come out with something like "Stop the boats" [or the government's 2022 rallying cry, "for a stronger economy"] and then just tell everybody that's the message. We got much more subtle with our messaging.'

As for the teal identity: 'it's very simple: it's "we're not blue, we're not green, we're somewhere in between",' Dickinson says. 'We wanted to be the sensible centre. It's not ugly, it's not threatening, it's a very clean brand that you want to be associated with . . . [and] teal was new; you didn't see major brands with it, so it got cut through. We decided to go for white, teal and turquoise as the three brand colours to really have this crisp, fresh feel to it. And it was also slightly reflective of the ocean.'

The beach, which would become the clean, climate-reinforcing backdrop for 2022 campaigns from Steggall to Spender to Scamps to Sharma, was an almost accidental star in 2019. 'Liberal Party photographs still tended to have someone in a suit and tie with the flag behind them on a dark background,' Dickinson recalls. 'I said: "No jacket; T-shirt; look like everyone's best friend; outdoors, wind in your hair, big smile." Zali didn't have much time. She was still working as a barrister . . . we had to get her up at six in the morning and onto the beach to film the video, and I wanted to film her in golden hour, sunset, so she looked great. She was tired and I drove up to the place we were supposed to shoot and I said to the photographer, "It's not right." But there was a beautiful low tide on Manly Beach, so we came back and took that iconic shot.'

Another key independent campaign ingredient, positivity—remaining above the politics-as-usual fray—can be traced back to Indi in 2013. Further: to Ted Mack and the generations of independents that preceded the recent crop. But it was also a retail-marketing imperative in Warringah in 2019. 'Big brands know that you don't win by saying something else is rubbish,' Dickinson says. 'What you need to do in advertising is move the playing field to where you can win. We never wasted time slagging off the opposition. We just said, "Look, isn't this great," because we were basically asking people to get divorced in that electorate and introducing a new woman. It's like, you've used Apple all your life and now I'm going to tell you to use a Microsoft computer. It's a big ask for people to walk away from what is often a family [tradition of voting Liberal]. But the good thing about Liberal voters is they're generally intelligent. You can say: "You know, they're not respecting Liberal values anymore. Look how far they've moved to the right." And most people were feeling that anyway. We picked up on a zeitgeist. There's no doubt that the feeling in the electorate was there.'

Positivity would become the golden rule that 2022 campaigns would credit as crucial to their success, however difficult a naturally rambunctious candidate such as Dr Monique Ryan would sometimes find it to observe.

Dickinson would go on to work on Steggall's seminal Climate Action Now campaign, her 2022 campaign and Climate 200. Brains worked pro bono on the latter's pitch document and was later retained to write the generic 'why vote independent' messaging that went out across electorates. The agency also tested taglines via the Swayable platform, with the winners turned into short, animated ads on social media. While other campaigns contacted Dickinson, Brains considered its dance card full.

~~~~~

The Allegra Spender campaign originally hoped to find an ad agency in the electorate but was unable to find one that could or would take the account for all the reasons Dickinson cites, even after the Warringah victory. In the end, Wentworth retained both Dickinson and Kulmar, figuring they, too, would live or die by the professionalism of their campaign.

Steve Kulmar had received a call from Kirsty Gold, who 'had been getting queries from Wentworth, from Mackellar, North Sydney and other places, and asked if I would be prepared to meet with them,' he says. He met with all three, helping 'them with high-level work on how Mackellar differed from Warringah; how North Sydney and Wentworth were different again.' Wentworth became Retail Oasis's first for-fee political client.

Their analysis suggested subtle but significant differences between the electorates. Even more homogeneous than Warringah, Wentworth also skewed towards slightly older and better off financially, as well as having the largest Jewish population of any federal electorate. The Covid lockdowns also meant that, while climate change remained a major issue, economic management and honesty in government came to the fore as important concerns. But then they always were anyway in Wentworth.

Brains came up with the campaign's slogan: 'A Better Climate for Wentworth'. The idea was first to plant the dual meaning of 'climate' in the electorate's mind and then to elaborate it into more targeted messages, such as 'A better climate for business' or 'A better climate for kids', so as to attract not only Liberal but also traditionally Labor and Green voters. Messaging in individual suburbs would be tailored to that suburb's 'dominant persona'—whether its residents tended to be traditional swing voters or have a particular party affiliation; whether they wanted their vote to address major issues impacting Australia and Wentworth, or to help their personal situation.

In the end, though, the homogeneity of the electorate made the sub-messages superfluous. The single 'Better Climate for Wentworth' message did, however, according to insiders, facilitate the government attack line that Spender was a one-issue climate candidate, which the campaign then had to combat in other ways.

Wentworth's brand colour, too, would be different, in line with differences between the electorates: a pale, safe, small-l Liberal blue with a harbour-and-surf chaser, rather than Warringah's environment-first teal, turquoise and white. It wasn't just demographic differences that determined the subtleties of shading. Everyone from Droga to Allegra's fashion-designer sister, Bianca Spender, had a view on what colour said 'Wentworth' and would cut through.

As in Warringah, work was undertaken to profile the ideal candidate. 'We looked at both Dave Sharma and Malcolm Turnbull, and Kerryn Phelps, and assigned them archetypes,' explains Retail Oasis director Trent Rigby. 'We were then able to look at those voters we most wanted to attract and build an archetype: very detailed criteria for the type of leader that they would respond well to and the best means to communicate with them (e.g. a distinct tone of voice and guiding core values).' That turned out to be a Joan of Arc–type character, young and female and brave enough to stand up to the powers that be. At 44, Allegra Spender was the youngest of 2022's female independents.

Not that that was how or why Spender was chosen. The market-research work done in Wentworth was confirmatory rather than revelatory, says Lyndell Droga. Their ideal candidate was in their sights before any archetype came to hand. Retail Oasis's advice only reinforced choices made out of common sense and local knowledge, she says.

Dickinson, too, had a picture of her candidate that turned out to be transcended by Spender herself. 'I didn't have any say in the search of the candidate, but once I saw her, I just wanted to make her [New Zealand PM] Jacinda Ardern,' she jokes. 'I had a very clear image in my mind: she was stylish, she was urban chic, those were the words we used for her. But we just didn't know her well enough at that time. It's hilarious because it's actually [Bianca] who is urban chic. Allegra is a gym junkie and she's full of fun and doesn't really care about fashion at all. She would always borrow clothes from the fashion house to come to the photo shoot.'

By definition, marketing is a numbers game, calculating how many of what kind of people can be reached by what means. But it was only one of the numbers games that underpinned independent campaigns in 2019 and 2022.

In 2019, Anthony Reed's approach had been informed by the gap between Warringah's 75 per cent vote in favour of marriage equality in the national survey and Tony Abbott's public opposition to it. His eureka moment during the 2018 Phelps campaign, which he then took to all the campaigns with which he was involved in 2019 and 2022, was based on a simple equation: 'What became clear to me was that if I could find the right candidate, and build the right campaign, I could effectively move over all those people that were disaffected with Abbott,' he recalls. 'You really only had to build on another 5 per cent or 6 per cent of people who viscerally disliked him, to win. So I needed to build a campaign around a candidate that was a safe place for the Liberal people to park their vote, but also one that appealed to Greens and Labor voters as well; everything may not have been their cup of tea, but if it ticked two out of three boxes . . .'

By micro-targeting voters in urban seats with an unprecedented volume of advertising, the digital advertising strategy of the teal campaigns had created a direct line to voters that made TV ads superfluous, Ed Coper, co-founder of Populares, later wrote in his piece on the 'Secrets from the teals' digital war room' for the *Sydney Morning Herald*. That strategy had borrowed from both corporate marketing and cutting-edge US political campaigns, allowing them to not only target voters more exactly but also digitally test and refine messages as they went.

The key attack line that Populares' Anthony Reed minted— 'Vote [Sharma, Zimmerman, Falinski, Frydenberg, etc.], Get Barnaby Joyce'—had seemed brutally effective in the wake of the 2021 Glasgow Climate Change Conference. When they tested it in late 2021, however, they 'uncovered the insight that Scott Morrison was even more toxic in these seats than Joyce,' Coper wrote. 'That became the narrative platform for these campaigns.'

Those kinds of marketing—and particularly retail marketing—skills were brought to the fore in many of 2022's most high-profile campaigns. But even when they weren't, the mathematics of aspiration, the equation by which a potential candidate became a real contender, was always front of mind. Cathy McGowan administered preliminary doses of reality to aspiring candidates: 'People say, "Look at me, look at me, I'm running," and I say, "Who's your community base? How are you organising?"' she told me in September 2021. 'If they say, "It's just me doing it," I say, "Well, it's not going to happen. How many votes do you need?" If they don't know, I tell them to go and work that out—who's going to change their vote to them, and how they are going to convince them to do it—then come back and talk to me.'

Subsequent doses of McGowan reality, administered across independent campaigns, included how many individual conversations your team needed to have with how many voters, over how long a period, in order to convert people and achieve the magic vote number required for victory. Or the simple maths of corflutes, T-shirts and volunteers (basically, she who has the most will in the end win).

The career of Melbourne marketing guru Peter Court has been fairly illustrious. In the late 1990s, he took over international ad agency Ogilvy & Mather's Melbourne office and became its managing director. He then went on to found Streetscope research, and co-found leading marketing-operations platform IntelligenceBank, of which he remains executive chairman.

In July 2021, IntelligenceBank—which has more than 400 clients across 55 countries, including ANZ, NAB, Suncorp,

Bupa, KFC and Hertz—announced a $50 million investment from the US to speed its expansion there before moving into Asia and Europe. Add in the farm at Mansfield in Victoria, where Court was spending an increasing amount of time building a new house, and you would think he had plenty on hand to keep an executive chairman happy.

Instead, Court spent the latter part of 2021 and early 2022 working on Zoe Daniel's campaign for the Melbourne seat of Goldstein. 'We would have daily morning meetings, with between eight and twelve people around the table,' he recalls. 'There'd be very senior journalists, people who had run major field forces for Telstra and other major corporations, volunteer-recruitment experts, electoral demographic modelling experts, digital marketing experts, fundraising specialists.'

Those people included Sue Barrett as campaign manager; veteran ABC journalist Jim Middleton; community activist and demographics expert Alex Fein; and Katerina Gaita, founder and CEO of Climate for Change, who was in charge of volunteer teams and field operations. And of course—first among equals—the candidate herself.

Court had originally been persuaded by Keith Badger, a close friend from yet another social swimming club, Melbourne's Icebergers, to come down from his farm and, somewhat reluctantly, meet Daniel in October 2021. 'There are some people you meet who have something about them, a charisma that is compelling. I would guess they wouldn't understand what it is, or why,' Court recalled. 'I remember I was sitting at that table, talking to her and thinking, "I can see you on the floor of the House making a big difference to the way politics is managed in Australia, and I want to help you get there."

'Zoe is one of the smartest people I've met, and her experience internationally is likely broader than the vast majority of people in parliament. Her experience as the ABC's US Bureau chief in Washington, and her book *Greetings from Trumpland* about the election that put Trump into the White House, demonstrated for me her deep understanding of the dangers of populism and misinformation, and erosion of trust and integrity in leadership. It was clear to me that if anyone was going to stimulate action in Australia after a decade . . . an independent Zoe Daniel was our best bet for the climate, for integrity, gender equality and most of all for Australia's future prosperity.

'I said to them, "Look, I can give you until Christmas," because I just had so much on my plate, with IntelligenceBank, cattle-embryo programs, plus building a new farmhouse . . . But when Christmas arrived, I was . . . obsessed with the prospect of success. Intellectually, this project was becoming one of the most stimulating and fulfilling things I'd ever done.'

Court, whose going rate as a consultant was $3000 a day, became another 40-plus hours a week volunteer, advising on what Sue Barrett shorthands as the 'overall messaging strategy and advertising, and how you break that down into social media and into operational execution and humans on the ground'.

How the Goldstein team arrived at its communications strategy is instructive. 'As someone who founded and ran a research company, you would expect me to say, "Well, we did thousands of focus groups; we did large, quantitative studies,"' Court says. 'We didn't. Because what I had learnt from experience is that research, particularly focus groups, can equally enlighten and confuse. Going more granular, by collecting more and more localised opinions, was not in my view going to give the campaign the clarity it needed. Particularly when our constant feedback from over 1000 field volunteers was unequivocally pointing to a single unifying sentiment, a universal trigger that crossed all demographic, cultural, religious and socioeconomic boundaries.'

And that, for a marketer, is the holy grail. 'I've founded and run advertising agencies,' he says. 'I understand how you break down problems, understand what electorates or markets are thinking. And in political campaigns simplicity is everything, being able to drive a campaign off a single, usually unifying sentiment.'

That single unifying sentiment turned out to be just how fed up the electorate had become with the status quo. 'At the end of the day, everyone—and this didn't just apply to Goldstein, this was across the country—was just pissed off. They'd had enough. Whether you're in the Jewish community in the Goldstein suburb of Caulfield South, or the more manufacturing area of Cheltenham, or suburbs like Beaumaris, everyone shared that one sentiment. You didn't have to have a hundred different arguments, or follow every focus group opinion down every rabbit hole, if you tapped that one.'

That turned into a two-beat messaging strategy, to tap what Court describes as 'a shared frustration, irritation, embarrassment and powerlessness' and motivate 'the 29 per cent of disengaged voters who would not respond unless they could see a clear and immediate material loss or gain'. The first beat was that sticking to your previous voting pattern would get you more of the same, which became the slogan 'More of the same means more of the same'. Launched early on, its aim was to plant the word 'same' in the electorate's mind. '"Same" had to be established as the problem,' Court says. 'It had to carry with it a universal and immediate threat of emotional and material loss. Then, from the moment the election was called, Same needed to become Unsafe.'

Unsafe injected an urgency into the voters' decision process. Safety ranks pretty high on Maslow's hierarchy of human needs; it was the universal proposition crossing all segments, all party loyalties, all demographics, all cultures and religions. After that, discipline was all. 'The base of the campaign never went out and spoke in a thousand ways with a thousand issues. It tapped one sentiment. That discipline and holding that line was critical. Because you are constantly confronted by hundreds of different opinions, and everyone's got an opinion, because everyone's reacting. But a campaign like this . . . has to be completely committed to its understanding of what the driving sentiment is. And that's what the Zoe Daniel campaign was based on.'

Keith Badger doesn't mind admitting that he found the change of pace from corporate to community work challenging. An accountant by training, he had first come to Australia from the UK 30 years earlier to head up the Australian and New Zealand operations for the car-repair company Midas, of which he was to become Asia vice-president. He had subsequently gone back to university in the UK and studied ecological science, before returning to Melbourne, where he began to contact climate groups to see how he could help. 'I found it wasn't a natural fit for me, community organisations, because of the indecision and all the different opinions. I'd been used to the corporate world, where you have responsibility for things. You get on and you do them,' he says.

Despite those misgivings, he became involved in a few of the early meetings for Voices of Goldstein when they were deciding whether they would try to run a candidate. 'I have to be perfectly honest, at first I thought, "I can't see this going very far,"' he says. Which was also how he felt about the leaflet they wanted to drop in letterboxes: 'I looked at it—purple paper and all writing, with no pictures or subheads—and I thought, "Good luck." But we did it and probably got 200 volunteers or so from about 30,000 leaflets that went out.'

In the meantime, Badger had agreed to help set up and become director of a holding company for the campaign, Project IndiGold. On the first weekend, having worked on its constitution, he was going through the database of people who had offered their services as volunteers. He was looking for professionals with the legal and financial skills to sustain IndiGold from a governance perspective as it raised and managed $500,000. Without that minimum sum, they had been told, Voices of Goldstein would be wasting its time.

Much to his surprise, what he found among the volunteers was a Yellow Pages of handy skills, including a leading Melbourne compliance lawyer, a top-tier communications lawyer and 'someone who had been running corporate finance departments around the world and come back to Australia'. Badger continues, 'I rang the first lawyer, who turned out to live nearby, and found he got onto the list because he got that little purple note in his letterbox. I said to him, "I think I'm the one who put it there," and he said, "I don't know anything about politics but we need change. Call me with any legal issues. I'll be your point man on law."'

That high level of professional expertise ran through the personnel of many of the campaigns. Before taking on Josh

Frydenberg in Kooyong, Dr Monique Ryan ran the Neurology Department at Melbourne's Royal Children's Hospital. An internationally recognised specialist in nerve and muscle disorders, she trained at the US's number one paediatric hospital, in Boston. Her campaign manager, Dr Ann Capling, was professor of political science at The University of Melbourne and adjunct professor at the Crawford School of Public Policy at the Australian National University, before becoming a provost at Murdoch University.

After being dux of her school, Allegra Spender completed a Masters in economics at Cambridge University, then worked as a management consultant for McKinsey and as a policy analyst in the UK Treasury. Mackellar candidate Dr Sophie Scamps was a GP and former emergency-room doctor. Her campaign manager, Jacqui Scruby, did combined medical science and law degrees, and worked for a top law firm and as a climate consultant before launching two successful start-ups—the online course '6 Weeks to Plastic Free', which turned into a business, and the Wedding Nest online registry—all while still in her thirties.

Almost regardless of age, a number of those who chose to get involved in community-independent campaigns had entered what Joanna Maxwell, who is writing a book on the subject, calls 'the third stage of work', a point in their life and career where they were financially secure, knew a thing or two, had nothing left to prove and were looking to deploy those skills where they would have maximum impact.

Curtin independent Kate Chaney worked for top law firm Blake Dawson Waldron before moving to the Boston Consulting Group after completing an MBA. She headed business development at Westralia Airports before working at Wesfarmers in roles ranging from Aboriginal affairs manager to sustainability and digital business. Prior to deciding to run, she was director of innovation and strategy at Anglicare WA.

'I've got three kids and I have this opportunity in front of me and, even if it's not going to succeed, if I'm not going to do it, who do I think is?' Chaney said at the start of April. 'I've got a diverse background, good mental health, strong family support. I'm at a point in my life where we can financially afford for me to take four months off to do this. I know some great people who would be fantastic, but they've got mortgages and kids in school. I'm lucky to be in a position where my husband [WA barrister Bill Keane] is very supportive, has a job he's happy in and that pays well. I thought that, if all of these things line up for me and I say, "Sorry, sounds a bit hard," who's going to do it?

But there was something more, almost an unflexed muscle, or unrealised potential, familiar to many women. 'I do feel like I could have gone on to achieve more in any one of the paths that I chose. But I didn't, I changed course,' Chaney continues. 'There were choices involved there, but it also means that I feel like I don't have that early career insecurity and impostor syndrome, where you think, "I can't believe I'm getting away with this."'

That breadth of professionalism meant that while she had zero political or campaign experience, she had all the hard skills that allowed her to improvise. 'I'm pretty data-driven; I do like a framework and a methodology and a plan,' Chaney says. 'So I laid out the "Here's how we're going to develop the campaign strategy. These are the steps. And this is the information I'm going to need at different stages." And I got stuck right into the numbers, and the last election data, and what we could learn from it, and how to segment the population base. Really just [using] my strategy consulting skills, which was a comfort zone to be honest [compared to] media training.

'Then there was the process of "What does the governance structure look like?"' Chaney continues. 'To start with, I had a campaign strategy team, and then an advisory board, and KPIs that we discussed, and inputs so that we could react to external changes and adapt the campaign strategy. That's proven to be a bit unwieldy. I've combined them and then just had a much smaller comms/strategy team that meets more regularly. And so I was very much thinking about how we were going to get this done, but at the same time thinking, "I have no idea if this is how you run a political campaign."'

Her professional experience also meant that, like Zoe Daniel and the Goldstein team, Chaney looked at some of the expensive professional services for which other campaigns opted and decided she could do without them. 'We got some demographic research early on the electorate and I had a couple of conversations, [but] I wasn't impressed,' she says. 'I looked at it and went, "Well, I don't think it really helps us that much. If that's what political research looks like, nah, let's not do any more of that." I have a background in strategy consulting, so I wanted to be quite operationally involved in the governance, setting the strategy, what the process looked like to get there.'

That sort of improvisation had been particularly necessary in earlier independent campaigns. Damien Hodgkinson's accounting prowess was not why Kerryn Phelps had originally recruited him to her 2018 mayoral bid. She was interested in the skills he had developed as chair of the Gay and Lesbian Mardi

Gras. 'Organising an election was not dissimilar to organising a festival,' Hodgkinson says. 'You've got a large volunteer workforce that you have to mobilise, insure, manage, communicate with. You have community communications programs that you have to talk to. It's a similar skillset in terms of the issues that you need to deal with at scale, with everything concentrated around essentially a few days, like a parade.'

But when Hodgkinson started working on what quickly became Phelps's federal bid, 'We looked around and, if you weren't in a major party, there weren't any service providers that actually gave you any assistance on the things you needed in order to be a successful candidate. Things like how to budget and monitor your electoral expenditure from a cashflow-management perspective; how to raise donations; insure volunteers.' The upshot was that Hodgkinson, who makes his living in insolvency, ended up developing a sub-specialty in setting up back-office services to independent campaigns.

If community organisations benefited from corporate upskilling, the reverse was also true. What made those careers, that professional and life experience, more powerful in the 2022 campaigns was the change of context. 'Most of the people who came into senior volunteer roles in Goldstein were at that point where they had considerable professional and life experience, but the beauty of it was that it was a flat structure,' says Keith Badger.

'I had heard about flat organisations for years in the corporate world. But this was the first time I experienced one working well. You get the right people on the bus and then you get them in the right seats on the bus. Those people respect one another for their proven experience. You didn't have to second-guess each other. You'd occasionally have a debate, and then you'd let people get on with it.'

Flat didn't mean amateur. 'From an org-structure perspective, we ran it like a business,' says Goldstein's Sue Barrett. 'We had a proper organisational structure: strategy, finance and governance, product development, sales and marketing, people and culture, and then on-the-ground operations with volunteers.'

The difference was few of them knew each other previously and even fewer had direct campaign experience. And no one knew their deadline until the election was called. 'As Zoe said, we were building the plane after we'd taken off,' says Badger. 'For all that, I have to say I feel really good about what we delivered. We had some other electorates calling us and saying, "Shit, you've got all this going? What advice can you give us?"'

To Mackellar's Jacqui Scruby, the process of building a plane in midair seemed eerily familiar. 'It was like doing a start-up, which I'd done before. Filling out forms, negotiating with council, choosing branding, working out issues, social media, setting up the website.'

The latter she did herself. 'I'd built a website before, enough for it to look half-decent, but not great,' she explains. 'We had people we called who did some tweaks. If you couldn't do it on the template, you'd say, "We really need this, but I can't work out how to do it." But you are running a tight campaign and they charge 200 bucks an hour. You only find them to do the little tiny tweaks you couldn't do yourself.'

More broadly, 'skills just came out of the woodwork' among the campaign's 1200 volunteers. 'We had someone who couldn't give a huge amount of time in terms of being out and about,' she says. 'The app we were using for doorknocking wasn't very functional, and he just came back from doorknocking and built an app. Suddenly we had tech that he had created that could collect data and was really user-friendly.

'The feeling of being in a campaign, and of uniting for this change, and seeing everyday people stand up and take action— honestly it gives me chills talking about it,' Scruby continues. 'It's the way it is meant to be. People are meant to be this excited and engaged about policy and democracy. It is meant to be positive and inspiring. A Liberal staffer said to me, "Oh, how do you do it?" You do it by being positive, being those shiny, happy people that annoy the hell out of everyone, because we genuinely are shiny, happy people. We have our worries and anxieties, but that's why we've stood up. And we're leading the way.'

Involvement is, in other words, a gateway drug. As Peter Court says: 'Things were really rolling, and the last thing I was going to do was stop being involved. I did it completely willingly and with great enthusiasm. And like any gateway drug, it has its costs. My cattle-embryo program up here was only half successful. And the house was put on hold.'

As for IntelligenceBank, the business he had co-founded with his wife and its CEO Tessa Court a decade earlier: 'I had already slowed down my involvement, but it came to almost a standstill over that period,' Court says. 'I didn't intend it to happen that quickly, but I really don't mind. In that respect, it wasn't a bad thing.'

A month after the election, Court saw a newspaper's group photo of the new independents on the floor of parliament in

Canberra. 'Zoe was right up the front and I took a screen grab and sent it to Keith Badger, saying, "This is the vision I had in Zoe's kitchen, this is job done,"' he says.

As for the prime minister who had been removed in the process: 'That's where I don't think you can say, "Look how clever we were,"' he says. 'Scotty Morrison and those guys, they just did it to themselves. All we were doing, really, was tapping into the damage that they were doing to themselves.'

6

SLEEPERS AWAKE

Tony Fairweather usually sleeps like a baby. Particularly after the sort of oxygen overdose he and his wife had subjected themselves to on a running weekend in Pemberton, three and a half hours' drive south from Perth, in early October 2021.

It was a Saturday night. Fairweather had just collapsed into bed after the 7 kilometre trail run when his wife, Fiona McAlwey, handed him her phone. On her Instagram feed was a Climate 200 post featuring Cathy McGowan, Simon Holmes à Court and former Liberal leader John Hewson, seeking support for community-backed independents such as Zali Steggall.

Fairweather had been aware of those earlier independents. He'd also seen the recent news that Kylea Tink, the first of the new 2022 independents to be announced, was running in North Sydney. But for the Western Australian corporate lawyer, who specialises in ASX listings and compliance, October was one of the busiest times of year: annual general meeting season, with all its attendant notices and approvals. His attention had been scattered. Cursory.

On a weekend away, however, the idea of independents had his undivided attention. Fairweather's disenchantment with politics had been growing for a while. 'I've always followed politics, but I'd describe myself as somewhere in the centre, where there's nothing much on offer in Curtin,' he says when we first speak a few months later, in March 2022. 'Neither party represents me and my vote has never counted because of my electorate. I always enjoyed election day, having my vote, filling out the Senate ticket, starting with the worst and working my way up, but that was about it.'

Now his mind turned from frustration to opportunity. 'I knew about Kerryn Phelps and Zali Steggall, and I kept thinking about how Curtin was really the brother or sister electorate over here to Warringah and Wentworth. You know, socially progressive, economically sensible. I looked up the 2019 Curtin election results and [ABC elections expert] Antony Green's analytics on winning a seat against a supposedly safe incumbent. I realised it was feasible. And that was important. If I'd just been frustrated, I wouldn't have got off the couch. There had to be an opportunity there.'

Such was the scale of that opportunity that Fairweather spent most of the night awake. 'My mind was just racing, thinking, "Who do I know? There must be somebody for Curtin,"' he recalls. Finally, he drifted off. 'But when I woke the next morning, I said to my wife, "I've had a revelation."' He was going to try to find a candidate to run in former foreign minister Julie Bishop's old seat, which the Liberal Party had held comfortably since its creation more than 70 years earlier.

~~~~~~

In the same electorate, a few months before, Kate Chaney had been having particular trouble sleeping. 'I tend to wake up at four o'clock in the morning and think about things and listen to podcasts,' she says in April 2022, a few months after Curtin Independent, the campaign vehicle Tony Fairweather would eventually set up, endorsed her as its candidate. Chaney is explaining the steps that led her to give up a comfortable, some would say idyllic, life as the mother of three young children, with a meaningful and fulfilling day job as director of innovation and strategy for Anglicare WA.

In addition to her day job, Chaney had spent the past decade 'on board this non-profit called Next25, which is looking at our future-building system and why we are not making better decisions. Politics is just such a big part of that,' she says. 'I'd got to the point where I thought, "I'm going to a lot of dinner parties and having conversations about everything that's wrong with the world, and that's not going to make anything better. I have to at least learn more about it."'

She embarked 'on a rash of reading [including the Grattan Institute's *Gridlock* report] and listening to politics and economics podcasts very early in the morning. I realised I had to engage, rather than just conjecturing and complaining,' she says. 'I remember looking up membership numbers of political parties and it was something like 0.4 per cent. I thought, "If that doesn't change, how will we see any change?" I hadn't really got my head around the independent movement at that point; I was still thinking two-party system.'

In the dead of night, Chaney, the niece of Fraser government Liberal minister Fred Chaney and grand-daughter of Menzies government minister Fred Chaney Sr, did the unthinkable:

she joined the Labor Party. 'I didn't tell anyone that I'd done it,' she says, 'including my husband. It was two or three weeks later that I casually dropped it in conversation, and he said, "You did what?"

'I said something defensive like, "Well, we've got to actually find out how it works, no point in sitting back." But I didn't. I had a welcoming email from [the Labor Party] and I said, "Looking forward to learning more," or something, and then didn't engage at all.'

Six weeks later, someone at Anglicare suggested they go to a Penny Wong breakfast. Advocacy and government were part of Chaney's portfolio. 'There was nothing wrong with the breakfast, it was perfectly nice,' she says. Penny Wong spoke. But it just felt like it's "us and them; we're the good guys, they're the bad guys". And the people who I knew there were very surprised to see me. I almost felt like . . . "Have I made a mistake? Am I nailing my colours to the mast?" I really railed against that, too. I felt it was ridiculous that you couldn't investigate and experiment with ideas.'

Primed but unsure how to proceed, Chaney decided to bide her time. 'I hadn't realised that, like a Netflix membership, money was coming out of my account each month,' she says. Her ALP membership fee would continue to be deducted until January, when she got around to cancelling it. By which time everything had changed.

~~~~~

The stories behind Kate Chaney's 2022 candidature typify those of many swept into the community-backed independent wave that crashed across our shores in the 2022 election. From volunteers to founders, campaign managers to candidates, it is a movement made up of thousands of personal ignition points— eureka moments that sparked action, trial and error—before connecting with others, becoming collective.

Most of all, it's the story of the networks—formal and informal, fledgling and established—that sped and scaled that connection. They included the labyrinth of Twitter, which Denise Shrivell and others see as an engine of the independents movement. But they also included everything from climate groups to ad hoc professional, school, sporting and familial affiliations. Through them, like-minded people found each other, and common ground, often across political divides.

As Trine Barter, who managed Kylea Tink's North Sydney campaign with another traditional Liberal voter, Suzy Bessell, explains when we speak in early April: 'We are working with people who have voted Liberal their whole life, people who have voted Labor their whole life. They have come together for a central purpose and with the most amazing variety of skills. And I love that.'

Such tales are part of the independents' foundation story. North Sydney's Independent's Kristen Lock, for instance, is a former nurse, Young Liberal and staffer for former Liberal senator Bill Heffernan, whose disaffection with her former party had been mounting in the lead-up to the 2019 election. Not that it ever drove her all the way to apostasy. 'It's a big call for someone who culturally identifies as Liberal to cross,' Lock says. 'I'm Catholic. [Voting Labor] would be like me becoming Protestant. You have to have a really good reason because it's a default. But the centre, for me, was attractive because it took the best of both worlds, was pragmatic and there wasn't this roadblock of loyalties. Our team was such a mix: Labor, Greens, Liberals, independents, former Democrats. A lot of them had left their parties for similar reasons. It was really exciting.'

For Damien Hodgkinson, the eureka moment that spawned his central role in the independents movement was 2017's marriage-equality debate, which he describes as 'probably the most personally damaging experience of my entire life'.

'It's a huge shock when you think you are one thing and find out you're something else,' he says of the way the issue was handled by the government, and the divisive debate that ensued. 'I was white, male, middle class, successful. I hadn't thought about getting married. I thought it was a really bourgeois concept. Suddenly I was told I was a second-class citizen; having to ask my neighbour to give their consent for me to have the same rights as they had was very confronting.'

At the other end of the country, in one of Australia's most conservative electorates, Groom in the Darling Downs, community-backed independent candidate Suzie Holt also cites marriage equality as the issue that politicised her and her husband of 25 years, Toowoomba anaesthetist Miles Brodie. 'What we were witnessing in terms of the divisiveness and polarisation of the debate really made us stand up,' she says. 'Miles and I have a deep sense of social justice and equality.'

Because both were prominent within the local medical community, in an area in which health is a major local employer, 'we could use our voices powerfully to try and affect that change,' says Holt, who manages her husband's practice. 'The other issue is that, as a regional area, we wanted to be innovative, to be able to attract young people to our region. We had to move forward.'

In 2017, Holt posted pictures of the rainbow-ribbon-festooned gate outside their family home, which happens to neighbour that of GP Dr David van Gend, a vocal conservative Christian marriage-equality opponent. They went viral—and this would come back to haunt her five years later, when snaps of her in a rainbow jumper would be reshared to the local community, nearly half of whom had voted against marriage equality. 'We were still challenged during this election on that issue,' Holt says.

For another rural candidate, Shepparton deputy mayor Rob Priestly, climate change was what led him to take a leave of absence from his business to run as an independent candidate in the federal seat of Nicholls. It has, after all, very practical implications in a 14,800 square kilometre electorate that takes in much of the Goulburn Valley in northern Victoria and is at the epicentre of water and water-trading politics. Less than a month after we spoke, the Climate Council would declare the electorate the most at risk in Australia, with riverine flooding projected to make more than a quarter of its houses uninsurable by 2030.

Intensive agriculture had only grown in recent years, Priestly said, as we sat in his improvised electoral office in an unreconstructed bank building on the main street of Shepparton in early April. 'But there are some really significant things coming, in this community specifically but also generally in regional Australia, and one of those is the conclusion of the first part of the Murray–Darling Basin Plan.' The consolidation of the local dairy industry, the corporatisation of agriculture, water trading and the 'abysmally managed' first stage of the Basin Plan had cost the region 'half a billion dollars a year in economic activity', he said. 'And it's not over. If the Basin Plan is enacted to the most damaging set of circumstances, there is another half a billion dollars in economic activity that's at risk.'

Like Cathy McGowan in the neighbouring electorate of Indi, which also takes in the Goulburn Valley, Priestly grew up on a dairy farm. The 'very significant energy demands' of the laundry business he runs with his brother, Phil, which employs 350 people and services towns and cities throughout Victoria, means he has had a long-term interest in energy policy.

'I think urban people are disconnected from those sorts of hard-transition-type questions,' he says. 'People here are closer to the practicalities. Like, my business: it burns a lot of diesel; I use a lot of natural gas. There aren't yet the emergent technologies to deal with those transitions. If you're a cropper, the diesel truck still turns up to your farm. It's not like you haven't chosen to adopt the technology. The technology doesn't exist yet.'

As for Fairweather in Western Australia, it was the scale of the opportunity, as much as the challenge, that prompted him to take on the National Party's Damian Drum, who would subsequently announce his retirement but had been returned in 2019 with a whopping 70 per cent of the two-party vote.

'We're going to grow more food in the next 50 years than [the Goulburn Valley has] ever grown,' Priestly said. 'This region has a unique combination of climate, soil and water. There are huge challenges. It's going to get hotter and drier, but some of the things that we are doing in irrigated agriculture are going to counteract climate changes. This is going to become an island; people are just starting to really put effort into consolidating and investing in this part of the world. It just needs someone to think about the policy framework for a minute.'

Having seen the way the Basin Plan had been handled so far, Priestly was unwilling to leave the rest of its implementation to those currently in charge of it, so he put his life and business on hold. His experience as deputy mayor of Greater Shepparton City Council from late 2021 also helped tip the balance. 'To be honest, having had a look inside local government and understanding how infrastructure gets funded, how randomly this LGA [local government area] gets funded versus others, was another moment of insight. I thought, "If I make this seat marginal, I'm going to do more in those three months of the campaign than I do in the whole next three years of working as a councillor."'

Independent candidate Dr Monique Ryan at first kept to herself that she had thrown her hat into the ring for the Victorian seat of Kooyong, much as Kate Chaney had her ALP move. 'I didn't even tell my husband,' Ryan says.

Out of all the 2022 candidates, most of whom had thriving careers, Ryan's decision is perhaps the hardest to comprehend. In addition to her role as a paediatric specialist at Melbourne's Royal Children's Hospital, where she led the 45-person-strong Neurology Department, she also headed a research team of twelve at the Murdoch Children's Research Institute. No work could be more meaningful.

She loved it, too, as her campaign manager, Ann Capling, discovered when she told Ryan she would have to resign even from the Murdoch role and the candidate burst into tears. Like many of her 2022 peers, Ryan recites a number of issues that led her to register her interest in standing—from the Morrison government's COP26 position to its response 'to the Brittany

Higgins fiasco' and its 'lack of accountability for how they spend public taxes and money'.

She talks, too, about seeing her then-twelve-year-old son Patrick's reaction to a David Attenborough documentary on climate change in early 2021. 'He became visibly, physically distressed by it,' she recalls. 'When you're a parent, you think you should be able to protect your child. But I could offer him no reassurance. I thought, "No, that is the reality of climate change, we should all be that distressed actually."'

But, as for Fairweather, opportunity was a bigger motivation than frustration. And, like Rob Priestly, she had glimpsed not only what was wrong, but how it could be fixed. 'I also did six weeks as the chief of medicine at Royal Children's in 2021,' Ryan says. 'I've been head of department for seven years and it's a tough job. That level of management is challenging, because you're the boss. But, to a certain extent, you are limited in what action you can take on a macro level. Going up a step, into the chief of medicine role, I thought, "Oh, this is much easier because I can actually effect change." I felt like I could get out of the weeds and achieve things.'

One of the decisions that had to be made during that time was 'whether we were going to pull the pin and open a ward dedicated to Covid', she remembers. 'It was going to have quite significant implications in terms of service delivery and beds within the hospital and staffing. But at the time I felt it was necessary; I made that decision and it happened."'

A similar logic lay behind her decision to run. 'I thought, "Look, it's a hugely difficult thing to take on Kooyong and win it. But, if you do . . ." It sounds histrionic, but it's no exaggeration to say that you would change Australian political and social history. Kooyong is one of the great bastions of blue-ribbon Liberalness in this country. For 122 years it has been held by white male conservative politicians. And here we are with the second most senior member of the Liberal government, someone who's been telling people since he was eleven or twelve that he wants to be prime minister one day, who is the heir apparent, who I think has a sense of destiny.'

The chance to disrupt an apparently baked-in paradigm had been Anthony Reed's eureka moment, too, halfway through Kerryn Phelps's 2018 campaign. 'I realised my kids were going to have to live under a Liberal government at least half of their lives,' Reed recalls in early June 2022. 'I just couldn't stomach the idea that it was going to be an ultra-conservative Liberal government, rather than the centrist, moderate Liberal govern-ment we have in New South Wales.'

That realisation was part of what drove him on to Warrin-gah after Wentworth. 'The key person that was driving the Liberal Party to the right was Tony Abbott,' he continues. 'Abbott, Peta Credlin [his long-term chief of staff] and other conservative politicians had used climate for a decade to divide progressives and keep them from gaining power. And there were no consequences for conservatives for their views being completely incompatible with the views of their electorates. I had to change that. If I looked around, GetUp! wasn't going to do it. There was no way you could run a campaign and get Labor or the Greens to win a seat like Wentworth or Warrin-gah. I had the key insights, the experience and I knew how to do it. I had to step up and make it happen.'

~~~~~

In September 2013, and in a rural seat, Cathy McGowan says climate was not on her radar as a major issue for her electorate when she first won Indi, though even then it was crucial to her younger supporters. By the time campaigns blossomed across the cities almost a decade later, however, that had completely changed. And not because Climate 200 ordained it in 2022; Climate 200 itself reflected the broader groundswell underway before it entered the picture.

From Tink to Spender, Daniel to Chaney, all the urban candidates cited as a major tipping point the internecine farce that, for a moment, threatened to dissolve the Coalition in the lead-up to COP26. As Kylea Tink told me in September 2021: 'It's like we've all been thinking, "They'll work it out. They'll sort it out." And then there's a real moment where we realise, "You're not getting it. It's time for us to step in, tidy this up and make this more representative of who we are."'

Similar eureka moments run deep into the campaigns that found and backed those candidates. The co-manager of Tink's North Sydney campaign, Suzy Bessell, for instance, went from bystander to warrior in one fell swoop. In November 2019, she heard Scott Morrison, the man who almost three years earlier had brought a lump of coal into parliament like a pet rock, declare there was no 'credible scientific evidence' linking Australia's emissions to the bushfires then ravaging Australia.

'He said it, then back-pedalled,' recalls Bessell, who had been a senior associate at law firm Corrs Chambers Westgarth and corporate counsel at Optus before moving into business roles at the telco. 'I'd read Ross Garnaut a decade ago. He said that by 2020 we'd be experiencing these kinds of climate crises and, right on time, it's happening.'

For the first time in her life, Bessell wrote to a politician, her local member, Trent Zimmerman, and Morrison himself. 'I said, "I'm really concerned that you're not leaning into the science. You're not standing up and leading us. You should be on the front foot, working out the solution." Then I reached out to Kirsty Gold, who I knew through my kids' school and said, "I know you are active in lobbying on climate. What can I do?"'

What happened next is a classic example of how the climate issue continued to feed and fire the networks that fuelled the 2022 independents' campaigns. Gold pointed Bessell to Zali Steggall's climate bill, then in draft form. 'As a lawyer, I sat down and read [that] and I thought, "This makes perfect sense."' There was a petition, inviting people to sign up and to then prompt your local member to support that bill. So I sent that petition to all my friends and family and outlined why I thought it was a good idea to support it.'

In January 2020, as the bushfires raged, Steggall had called on modern Liberals to support the legislation she would introduce into parliament in November 2020, warning that they ignored the views of constituents 'at their peril'. In March she was launching a national #CLIMATEACTNOW advertising campaign drawing on the fires to rally public support for the bill. By then, Warringah Independent had already set up an online presence, asking people to sign up to support it.

Gold had introduced Bessell to Tina Jackson, who wanted her to coordinate various aspects of a March 2020 rally at which Zali Steggall was going to speak. 'I was like, "Well, I've never done anything like that before. I don't really do Facebook. I'm busy. Surely, you'll find somebody else,"' Bessell recalls. 'But the clock was ticking, and they hadn't found anybody, and

I remember Tina saying, "Look, it's really easy. You just have to do a couple of things."'

Bessell agreed to pitch in, becoming head of the North Sydney branch of #CLIMATEACTNOW. 'I ended up setting up a Facebook group, ordering leaflets, emailing people, co-ordinating them. And two weeks later we were standing outside Zimmerman's office, the day before Covid really started escalating,' she recalls. A year or so later, she would also be the first person to approach Kylea Tink about running in her home seat.

~~~~~

In the lead-up to the election, the Coalition would cite the failure of Zali Steggall to obtain parliamentary support for her climate bill as exemplifying her powerlessness as an independent. Post-election, it looks like the exact opposite. While the government ensured it was never so much as debated in parliament, the bill enabled her to play a role that went far beyond simply inspiring other campaigns by her example. By May 2022, Steggall's warning two years earlier—that moderate Liberals ignored the views of their constituents 'at their peril'—looked prophetic.

Not only did everyone—from the Business Council of Australia to the Responsible Investment Association of Australasia and Australian Industry Group—endorse the bill, but the government's Standing Committee on the Environment and Energy also received 7000 submissions in support of it from all sectors. Meanwhile, #CLIMATEACTNOW galvanised opposition to the government even as the bill languished in committee.

The almost 100,000 sign-ups #CLIMATEACTNOW generated were the tip of a less visible and, for the Coalition, more fatal iceberg. The campaign also encouraged people to start their own #CLIMATEACTNOW groups, as happened in North Sydney and in the electorate of Hughes in southern Sydney, where the founder, urban development consultant Linda Seymour, would go on to become another of 2022's independent candidates.

'The independents put climate, integrity and women on the agenda in ways that neither of the major parties wanted,' Jim Middleton, who consulted to Climate 200 in addition to Zoe Daniel's Goldstein campaign, said of the 2022 election in August. 'Without Helen Haines' [integrity-commission] private member's bill, without Zali's private member's bill, neither of those issues would have been as prominent in the election campaign as they became.'

The experience of working on the Zali Steggall campaign also led Tina Jackson and others to form yet another group, Zero Emissions Sydney North, through which they connected with Our Blue Dot, the climate-action group founded by Dr Sophie Scamps and Anyo Geddes in Mackellar, which would morph into Mackellar Rising and launch a candidacy next door to Warringah.

During the hunt for people to help coordinate groups to support the Steggall bill, Jackson met Kath Naish via Australian Parents for Climate Action. The Quiet Australians Stand Up rally outside Dave Sharma's office on 25 January 2020 was the result. The placard-carrying crowd of upwards of 100 people spanned all ages and stages, and as many men as women. Wrapped around Sharma's office on a tight corner of Edgecliff, it looked like a wave had smashed up against a citadel: a clear and early warning of the tide to come. As Jackson says: 'It was the start of feeling that maybe we could do this.'

Within weeks, however, 'Covid arrived and everyone kind of went to ground, so the #CLIMATEACTNOW impetus lapsed,' she continues. But Covid didn't so much stop activism as drive it online. 'That was when some of these groups decided to start "Voices of"–type groups,' Jackson says. Naish became one of the founding members of Voices of Wentworth, before quitting to join the Spender campaign.

Those Voices groups, too, became critical networking and proving grounds. Not that they were any more uniform than the campaigns some of them would spawn. Each group reflected the particular microclimate of its electorate. Some conducted kitchen-table conversations, produced reports on their findings, circulated them to all candidates, whether major or minor party or independent. Others were dedicated primarily to encouraging grassroots engagement with democracy, and consciousness-raising on political issues in a non-partisan, apolitical way.

Voices of Wentworth, which has been 'engaging with the electorate and reflecting constituents' views on social media and other advocacy activities since mid-2020', according to its founder, Delia Burrage, is a prime example of the latter. It was not aligned with Allegra Spender, and existed before and after her campaign. 'It's understandable that people, particularly the media, like to refer to "Voices of" groups as if they were all doing the same thing with the same goals, but it's simply not the case,' Burrage says. 'Each of them came about because of quite unique circumstances in their particular electorate.'

In Mackellar, Dr Sophie Scamps says she founded Our Blue Dot after her twelve-year-old son and his friend told her, '"You adults have failed us," and I realised I'd better step up and do something.' It morphed into Voices of Mackellar after local member Jason Falinski put out a survey in early 2020. 'There was still smoke in the air,' Scamps recalls. 'People had been through this hugely distressing time and a survey arrives in everyone's letterbox [which said] to tick what issues are important to you. There was a long list of fifteen or twenty issues, and climate change did not appear on that list. There was something near the bottom about protecting our local environment, but nothing about climate change.'

Scamps turned up to a community catch-up that Falinski held shortly afterwards. 'Most people there wanted to talk about climate change and were very upset that he hadn't listed climate change on his survey,' she says. 'At the end of that little meet-up, I think it was only half an hour, I said to Jason—because he got into an altercation with an older gentleman and had to apologise; he was taken aback at how upset people were about this survey—"Jason, you can see people are really upset about climate change and the fires, and we need to hear your voice . . . We don't need to hear any more from Craig Kelly, telling us that it's arsonists . . . or Matt Canavan or Barnaby Joyce or whoever else, telling us it's the Greenies."

'He looked at the ground and he said, "Well, the problem is you can't mention the words climate change in the party room because the Queensland MPs jump up and down." I just thought, "That's that. You cannot represent us. You can see that it's a massive issue for us here."'

Voices of Mackellar had spent hundreds of volunteer hours sitting at kitchen tables with groups of four to ten people and asking what was important to them, what solutions they saw, and turning their feedback into a report. 'But it was never designed to run a candidate. We wanted to keep it as neutral and non-partisan as possible,' Scamps says. 'When we asked about solutions, people would say, "We need an independent, like Zali next door, who can genuinely represent the people who live here." They'd say, "Where's that group? How can we support the independent?" And we'd say, "Well, there currently isn't one," and they'd go away saying, "Well, what was the point of all that then?"'

The upshot was that Scamps and Geddes left Voices of Mackellar and started Mackellar Rising. Jacqui Scruby attended one of its early events: 'It was a very small group and Mark Kelly and Tina Jackson were talking about getting Zali into Warringah. I got so excited and inspired. I had goose bumps.'

Scruby had been on her own trial-and-error odyssey. She and the family had moved to the UK, where her husband launched a start-up. 'I'd grown up thinking, "Okay, if you're going to make a change, where are you best positioned to do it? Individual action, which is important, because that then leads to corporates and government changing? Or do you go direct to government? Or do you go to advising corporates?"'

Up to that point, the answer for Scruby had been advising, via boutique firm Energetics, which advised ASX-listed companies on climate change and energy management. Her first stint with the company had been around the time of Kevin Rudd, the Copenhagen Climate Summit and the scuppered emissions trading scheme.

'I think there was a certain degree of carbon fatigue in the end,' Scruby recalls. 'I had written so many recommendations and reports that weren't picked up by government, and then Copenhagen failed. Where I came back into everything was when I saw the levels of ocean pollution in the Mediterranean. I started doing some things. Our whole family ended up being zero waste. Then everyone asked us how we lived zero waste. So I created an online course called "6 Weeks to Plastic Free".'

Her first start-up was born. 'I'd almost pooh-poohed individual action, but suddenly it felt really good to live your values. Plus everyone seemed to be influenced by it. People were asking me all about it and taking my course.'

Although she had missed the lead-up to the 2019 election, she happened to be back home in Australia for that election night: 'I remember thinking, "Oh my god, this Scott Morrison. How's he got in again?"' The plan had been to keep travelling with the family; then Covid hit, the music stopped and Scruby, her husband and their two kids moved back to Avalon on Sydney's northern beaches, where, shortly after, she met Dr Sophie Scamps through Our Blue Dot.

She subsequently heard Simon Holmes à Court on an online fundraiser in late 2021: 'I'd been going at this for years and never seeing any real action, so when Simon said everything he'd done to this point was hacking at the branches, rather than striking at the root of the problem [which he said he had launched Climate 200 to do], it really resonated.'

Scruby's trajectory was similar to that of Trine Barter, who had spent 23 years living in London and Europe with her American-born venture capitalist husband. Having left in 1997 as 'a proud Australian', she returned 'very disappointed at where this country had gone, and shocked at the lack of climate policy', she says. 'Particularly coming from the UK, where we'd had a Climate Act since 2008 that was extremely effective under a Conservative government.'

While she had had no interest in politics when she left, her husband was 'very, very political. We were involved in Obama's campaign and raising money for him. I was probably more interested in American politics and British and European politics,' she says. 'When we first arrived [back], we were so disappointed in the political system that we searched for a candidate who we believed shared the same values as us. And we discovered Zali, so we supported her campaign and I volunteered, just handing out leaflets, even though we were living in North Sydney.'

It was a meeting with Barter in early 2020 that drew in Renata Kaldor and her husband, Andrew, in the early days, when Kristen Lock was beginning to think about founding North Sydney's Independent. The couple, who had set up the Andrew & Renata Kaldor Centre for International Refugee Law at UNSW Sydney in 2013, would fund a key, and expensive, early survey on attitudes and issues in the electorate. That poll, which predicted the election result, was crucial in reassuring the campaign that it had a chance of attracting the 10,000 votes it needed to come second and win on preferences.

Both of the Kaldors had been long-term Liberal voters until 'John Howard's attitude towards Asian immigration became clear in the early 1990s,' Renata Kaldor says. 'Not only were we Liberal voters, we'd both belonged to the party. One of Andrew's best friends is Nick Greiner. We had been on a campaign when he was trying to become premier [of New South Wales in the 1980s]. That's how we learnt some of our skills. But we were members of a different party,' Kaldor says, speaking of the federal Liberals. 'This is not a party we recognise.'

Kaldor first met Barter, a friend of her daughter's, in 2021, in an effort to convince her not to take on Trent Zimmerman, whom she knew and liked. Instead, the reverse happened. Barter underlined to Kaldor the link between climate change and refugees. 'For us it was always about refugees,' Kaldor says. 'We'd seen what Kerryn Phelps had done [with the Medevac Bill]. We just realised that if we could get enough independents in there and create a third force, we would have a better chance of swaying refugee policy. Because the Liberals and Labor were so close, and still are, on refugee policy.'

By then Barter had met Gold and Jackson, and significantly ramped up her own involvement. 'They were very, very good at reaching out to people who were aligned and saying, "Come to this or come to that,"' Barter says. 'I couldn't go to one of the events, but my husband did and met Kirsty and said, "You need to meet my wife because she's very fired up." Kirsty is an amazing philanthropist in the climate change space. She's part of the Australian Environmental Grantmakers Network, which I joined because of her. I just said to her, "What can I possibly do?" And she said, "It will happen." That's literally what she said, "Something will happen organically."

'So I started a community Facebook group in Hunters Hill about climate change called Hunters Hill Habitat, which grew to about 300 people, plus a smaller local WhatsApp group called "It Never Rains it Pours" to share information about climate change, and then I met Suzy [Bessell] through #CLIMATEACTNOW'

~~~~~

Even where no such issues-based networks existed, others did the work. The day after his 9 October 2021 run and revelation, Tony Fairweather 'checked my enlightenment' with his older sister, Katrina Burton. 'She has been a lifelong Liberal voter, who was by this stage appalled by much of the conduct of the Morrison government, especially its treatment of women and refugees,' he says. 'She has four daughters and a very good heart. I respect her greatly. She didn't think I was crazy, so I was over the first hurdle. My wife, Fiona, also agreed to support me, so I was over the second hurdle.'

The third hurdle was finding a candidate. After the oxygen high passed, Fairweather decided to sound out the one person he had been able to think of on that long night who combined a public profile with a sense of higher calling. Fairweather had worked with WA entrepreneur Anthony ('Maz') Maslin on various ventures, including the July 2018 oversubscribed IPO of Wide Open Agriculture. Maslin had founded the regenerative food and farming company in the wake of the death of he and his wife, Rin Norris's, three children, Mo, Evie and Otis, and their grandfather, Nick Norris, when Malaysia Airlines flight MH17 was shot down over Ukraine in 2014. 'They had decided to make a difference with whatever they did,' Fairweather says of the couple. 'That company really came out of doing something meaningful.' Fairweather had initially hoped Maslin might be willing to stand himself. A week later, Maslin agreed to be involved but wanted to think before committing to a specific role. With that, the Curtin Independent team doubled to two. But the election could be called any minute. The clock was ticking.

By then, Fairweather had collected a swathe of documents, ranging from articles on the rise of community-backed independents to an August 2021 map of the redistributed Curtin, showing it was held on a 13.9 per cent margin. He had also got hold of a piece by Antony Green on the analytics of winning a safe seat, the 2019 election results and the maiden speech by the woman who had won the seat for the Liberals in 2019—lawyer and former Notre Dame University chancellor Celia Hammond.

Being old-school, he kept the documents in hard copy in a manila folder, which is what an old friend, Sarah Silbert, found him reading at a North Fremantle cafe in early November on a break from work. Silbert, too, was a lawyer who worked for AGL. Their children had grown up together. 'She saw the papers and asked what I was doing. I knew she had a good heart, so I said: "Actually, I'm trying to change Australian political history." She was sort of interested. We had a quick chat, and she said to give her a ring.'

'That conversation led to the first of the group's kitchen-table conversations,' he says. 'It was six or seven people, aged 50 to 60, mainly lawyers, all unaligned, never having been members of a political party, all sick of being taken for granted and suddenly understanding this opportunity to do way better, particularly on climate. Early on, for all of us, it was really that mismatch between our sitting member and the electorate, which was generally socially progressive and economically responsible.'

Silbert was immediately engaged, taking a leave of absence from her job to become campaign manager. 'We needed to get the dialogue out there about Curtin Independent, which we'd by then incorporated, and get Maz [Anthony Maslin] out there as our spokesperson, because he has a profile that no one will argue with,' Fairweather says.

In mid-November 2021, Fairweather emailed an optimistic little document, 'The next member for Curtin', to a small group of friends and family that he speculated might 'be the start of a "Voices for Curtin"?', asking them to share it with 'like-minded people'. In that email, he wrote that Curtin had a '"Tony Abbott lite" style' representative who was 'socially conservative and owes her position . . . to "The Clan" [referring to a group that includes conservative Christian MPs and was blamed for the WA Liberals' abysmal showing at the March 2021 state election]. On a 13.9 per cent margin, she is particularly vulnerable to a stellar independent candidate that is socially progressive and economically responsible.'

Maslin duly announced on the front page of the local *Post* newspaper on 11 December that the group was searching for a candidate to take on Hammond. But Christmas was looming. 'We were very late to the party,' Fairweather says. What saved them, again, was networks.

Fairweather's former neighbour in the Perth suburb of Mosman Park was Mike Ottaviano, former CEO of Carnegie Clean Energy. While the two had never discussed politics over the fence, 'I called him for advice, and lo and behold his wife, Mandy, was working full-time on economic policy in the Kylea Tink campaign,' Fairweather wrote in a No Fibs piece.

Through Ottaviano, the newest campaign in Australia connected with the longest-running. 'Mandy led us to the great Kristen Lock and enabled us to tap into a knowledge base far beyond anything we knew,' Fairweather says. 'I'm pretty good at ringing and hassling people, and I rang and hassled Kristen on everything—organisation structure; who to use to incorporate; corflutes, you name it.'

On Lock's advice, Curtin Independent became a hybrid. As a 'Voices of' group, it held kitchen-table conversations; but it also incorporated in December and started looking for a candidate. 'After me and Sarah, Kristen was the third most important person in that process,' Fairweather says.

As had happened in Warringah, it helped that Hammond was polarising. Shortly after being preselected for Curtin, in March 2019, she declared that humanity's contribution to global warming had likely been 'very minimal'; she had also spoken out against 'militant feminism', casual sex and contraception.

Critics had argued from the start that Hammond was too socially conservative to represent Curtin, which had recorded the strongest vote in favour of same-sex marriage in Western Australia. Curtin Independent became a lightning rod for this dissatisfaction, which might have dissipated under normal circumstances.

Justin Kennedy, a lawyer at BHP in Perth, was one of those who contacted the group through its new website, knocked together at speed by Silbert's husband, Michael. 'Justin was very connected and energised,' says Fairweather. That is something of an understatement. Kennedy had been the head of the student union at The University of Western Australia where Celia Hammond, Fairweather and others had studied. He had also been the one who had originally recruited Holmes à Court to AIESEC during the latter's university days. And his generation-spanning network also included a 35-year-old Perth venture capitalist, Charlie Caruso.

A self-described political geek who read Adam Smith for fun, Caruso had previously coordinated global teams for the Australian-founded NGO My Vote. Along the way, her experiments with democracy had convinced her of two things: that the two-party system had outlived its usefulness; and that the only viable alternative was participatory democracy via a grass-roots movement.

She had kept a weather eye on the fortunes of independents from Andrew Wilkie to Cathy McGowan and Helen Haines. But Kerryn Phelps' 2018 victory and 2019 defeat in Wentworth had hit closer to home. All the way over in Perth, Caruso's husband had received homophobic anti-Phelps material by email. Caruso, who was by then helping Margo Kingston produce No Fibs podcasts, including one with Phelps, had contacted the campaign about the messages.

Knowing what Phelps had been subjected to, the narrowness of her 2019 defeat had seemed particularly cruel. 'I was so demoralised watching the 2019 election, and particularly Kerryn's side of it, which was brutal,' Caruso says. 'It took me quite a time to get over that. I had done the numbers in WA and decided the only possible electorate was Curtin and that it was only flippable by a very well-known small-l liberal.'

She had attempted to persuade one such candidate herself, without success. Given nothing was happening in her home town, she made a series of podcasts for Kingston's No Fibs, started a climate charity, and bided her time.

Recruited by Kennedy, Caruso joined the Curtin fight two weeks before Chaney was announced in January, the only person in the team with even indirect (via No Fibs) campaign experience. An initial all-purpose troubleshooting role came to focus on coordinating pre-poll, election day and scrutineering.

Quite a few of 'the core team were lawyers who were at law school around the same time as Celia Hammond,' Tony Fairweather says of the Curtin group. 'UWA was the only law school [in Perth] back then. But while we knew Celia, it wasn't personal. It was just the feeling of being taken for granted by the Morrison government. You happen to be from the same time and place, you're in your fifties, you're thinking you just can't take it any longer and an opportunity presents itself.'

All the candidates express a similar sentiment. Kylea Tink was on a career break in 2021, to be with her son who was doing the HSC, after working in roles such as CEO of breast cancer charity the McGrath Foundation, and of the children's cancer charity Camp Quality. 'It's the right thing at the right time,' she said of her candidacy in early April 2022. 'I'm at an age and stage where I now feel I have a right to stand, because I am confident in what I know. I feel like I've done my time, in terms of living and working. I see this as an opportunity to represent a community, as something I can do fully. If this had come up a decade ago, I wouldn't have done it.'

At 47, Kate Chaney was still climbing that mountain. Running for office 'literally had not crossed my mind', she says. Until, that is, 5 January 2022. 'We were heading off for five days' camping at Rottnest Island and I got two messages from different people saying, "Would you be interested in having a chat with this Curtin Independent crew?"' she recalls. 'They came at the same time and I thought, "How funny that both of those people should have thought of that." And at that time of year, you're open-minded about your life.'

The next day she had a video conference with six people from Curtin Independent from the camping ground. 'It began to dawn on me that this could actually be a thing,' she says. 'Because it did seem to address a lot of the issues that I'd been thinking about. Running as an independent was the only way I felt I could do it with integrity.'

The five days of family holiday 'didn't turn out to have a lot of family in them. I spent a lot of time on the phone, talking to different people, testing the idea. And then it was two weeks from when I got back before I just made the decision.'

Or, as Chaney put it in a Climate 200 podcast in early March: 'To be honest I sort of felt like vomiting, because I thought I might actually have to do this.' Typically, one of the things she did first was to actually verify her independence. 'I started a spreadsheet that had the things that I care about, my position, then "Liberal/Labor". I'd never actually stopped to look at how closely aligned my position was, on the things I cared about, with the different parties. It wasn't a robust piece of analysis, but I did enough of it to think, "I'm actually independent."'

She also consulted her father, former Wesfarmers managing director and chancellor of The University of Western Australia, Michael Chaney, and her uncle Fred. 'I got them together and said, "I want to talk about this seriously," and I took a copy of the *Gridlock* report with me,' Chaney recalls. 'That was instrumental—talking to them and just getting that macro view of how things have shifted between the 80s and now.'

Neither man thought she should do it. 'Fred said, "I advise you not to, because I love you. It's a terrible life, especially for women. It's really hard and you open yourself up to all sorts of attacks,"' Chaney says. 'Fred's view was that it was necessary for our democratic system that independents step up and make some change to the two-party system. He said, "It absolutely needs to be done, but I'm not sure that you should do it."

'They both said, "This is a bad idea." And everyone else who I spoke to said, "You've got to do it,"' Chaney laughs. In the end, everyone else won. On 19 January, Chaney decided she'd throw her hat into the ring. Eight days later, her candidacy was announced.

7

LIGHTNING STRIKES

Into this already richly involved picture walked a man who had stuck his finger in one socket as a kid and was now intent on trying the biggest power point in the country: federal parliament.

Simon Holmes à Court, the second youngest of the four children of Australia's first billionaire, corporate raider Robert Holmes à Court, and his wife, Janet, had tried to unlock an electrical socket with a car key as a two-and-a-half-year-old. More than 45 years later, he still couldn't recall the moment that the current snaked up his arm, flinging him across the room. His mother just found him there, wide-eyed and conscious, his right index finger blasted to the bone.

When we first spoke via Zoom, deep in Melbourne's September 2021 lockdown, Holmes à Court held up the digit that had melted like a candle to show the results of a second, successful skin graft.

Not that the incident deterred him in any way. His mother remembers him enthusing about a 'fantastic' electrical socket that caught his then three-year-old eye, six months later as they walked through Myer. It was the beginning of a lifelong fascination with energy: how things worked and how they could be made to work.

'Even as a really young child, he was constantly tying things together, like a cord from his bed down the stairs and onto the front door so that he could open it,' Janet Holmes à Court said in 2021. 'Robert and I always thought he'd be an engineer.'

Her son's sense of environmental peril was sown only slightly later, when he visited the karri and jarrah forests of Western Australia's south-west. 'As a kid, it really had a big impact on me,' Holmes à Court said. 'From the road, all you saw were these beautiful stands of massive eucalypts. If you took a side-access track and went 200 metres off the road, though, it was clear-felled, hollowed out in the middle. I just remember the environmental devastation, puddles of algae and no regrowth, and the feeling of being cheated; that we were being lied to.'

Like so many paths to the community-backed independents movement in 2022, Holmes à Court's was full of twists and turns, each adding a new wrinkle to what he'd bring to that fight. After neglecting a law degree at The University of Western Australia in favour of student politics in his early twenties, he'd studied artificial intelligence and cognitive science at America's Dartmouth College, before being recruited to work as a software engineer at Netscape in Silicon Valley at the height of the 1990s dotcom boom.

Returning to Australia after that bubble burst, he applied those software and product-development skills to water issues at the eight Northern Territory cattle stations then owned by his family. That culminated in the precision irrigation technology company Observant, which he started in 2002 and sold fifteen years later, while also launching Australia's first community-owned wind farm in Victoria's Central Highlands.

Over the years, he had tried any number of approaches to encourage action on climate. He'd become a regular *Guardian* contributor on the environment and a Twitter stalwart, accumulating 107,000 followers. He also became a member of the Australian Environmental Grantmakers Network, 180 donors who contribute significant funding to the cause. But even that felt like punching the wind. 'Overall, more than $300 million a year goes into the environment from the whole population and what, collectively, has the environment movement achieved?' he said in 2021. 'Howard and Rudd both took emissions trading to the 2007 election [and] we've just gone backwards since . . . the ambition hasn't gone anywhere. We've lost a whole decade there.'

He also regularly cracked his skull against the walls of Parliament House. 'I went on a dozen lobbying trips to Canberra with environmental organisations,' he said. 'I remember saying to a lobbyist I'd just met that I'd just come back from Canberra, and he said, "Oh, you did some Tim Tam diplomacy . . . Let me guess: you went and sat down with Greg Hunt [environment minister 2013–16] and he brought out the Tim Tams and listened to your concerns and made you feel really special, and then he saw you out."

'That was a light-bulb moment for me. I'd assumed the model was that you took a good idea up to Canberra and you presented it to MPs and, because it was a good idea and made perfect sense, and you'd made a social, economic, environmental case, that they'd go, "That's a great idea. Let's do it." But it's not a marketplace of ideas. It's a numbers game.'

He'd also experimented with the change-from-within model, lobbying his local member, Josh Frydenberg, even joining the treasurer's Kooyong 200 Club fundraising group in early 2017. 'I originally went to see him as a constituent, because I decided he would be around for a long time. He's ambitious. He's talented. Kooyong under [Frydenberg's predecessor] Petro Georgiou had been a progressive, positive force within the party. And you read the Liberal Party's core tenets and think, "Yeah, I believe in freedom, and I believe that individuals should be allowed to excel, and I believe in well-regulated markets. I should be a member of that party, shouldn't I?"'

That ended after Holmes à Court wrote a column for *The Guardian* in early 2018 that included a line criticising Frydenberg for trying to keep New South Wales's Liddell Power Station open. 'Less than 24 hours later I got an email from Kooyong 200 saying my membership had been rejected and two years of membership fees and a donation had been returned to my credit card,' he says.

In title and substance, Climate 200 was his reply. Even the font and colour of its initial logo was a riff on Frydenberg's Kooyong 200. The provenance of its name would go largely unexplained in 2022, becoming a sort of residual in-joke that morphed into a story about how its founders initially wondered if they'd attract even 200 donors.

The motivation behind it, on the other hand, could not have been clearer. As Holmes à Court explains: 'Richard Denniss [the Australian Institute's chief economist] probably put it best when he told me the two ways to get a politician to act or change their mind was pain or fear of pain.' If politics was a numbers game, Holmes à Court was going to try to change the numbers in the climate's favour.

His inspiration was Harvard Law School professor and activist Lawrence Lessig, who co-founded a non-partisan grass-roots activist organisation, Rootstrikers, in 2011 to fight political corruption and reduce the role of special-interest donors in elections. The name was a reference to Henry David Thoreau, who wrote in his celebrated collection of essays, *Walden*, that there were 'a thousand hacking at the branches of evil' for every 'one who is striking at the root'. As Jacqui Scruby attests, it would become Holmes à Court's rallying cry.

Along the way, he had also flirted with the idea of a new party, attending early meetings to discuss the one that erstwhile Liberal prime minister Malcolm Fraser had been in the process of founding before his death in March 2015. (Former ALP science minister Barry Jones had suggested calling it the 'Courage Party'.) But that momentum had passed with Fraser.

It was, anyway, too slow a process for a man who describes himself as 'an impatient incrementalist. It's really, really, really hard to start a party and build an identity,' he says. 'You lose years in fighting. And everyone knows what they want to not be, but then you have to find their congruent ideas.'

Conceived a couple of months before the April 2019 election, the first iteration of Climate 200 managed to raise almost $450,000 from 30 donors, including Atlassian billionaire Mike Cannon-Brookes, in a matter of six weeks. This helped fund twelve independent campaigns featuring climate-action policies to try to counter the influence of the fossil fuel lobby. Beneficiaries included Helen Haines in Indi; Kerryn Phelps in Wentworth; former Clean Energy Finance

Corporation CEO Oliver Yates in Kooyong; and Rebekha Sharkie in Mayo.

~~~~~

The margin by which Phelps lost Wentworth—1.3 per cent— was only marginally less than the 2 per cent by which Haines won Indi in 2019 after a 7.3 per cent swing to Liberal challenger Steve Martin. Seen as critical if the Morrison government was to retain power in 2019, Indi had received $243.6 million in infra- structure grants in 2018. According to the *Australian Financial Review*, that represented almost a quarter of the $1.1 billion the Department of Infrastructure, Regional Development and Cities handed out in 2018, and almost half the $569 million the government funnelled into critical battleground seats.

Haines had only been declared victor after a sixth count of Labor preferences. But holding the seat previously held by Cathy McGowan made Haines the first independent in Australian history to succeed another independent in a federal electorate. Climate 200 had been a small cog in that victory, contributing about $30,000 to help fund advertising in the final weeks, but it saw that advertising as critical in getting Haines over the line after a very professional campaign.

In Kooyong, Oliver Yates received just 9 per cent of the primary votes, well below Julian Burnside for the Greens at 21.2 per cent and Labor at 16.8 per cent. But Yates was crucial to the 8.2 per cent swing against Frydenberg in Kooyong, which took the treasurer's primary vote below 50 per cent for the first time. It was the second-largest swing against the Liberals in 2019 (behind the swing against Tony Abbott in Warringah) and, like the Wentworth margin, it would become crucial three years later.

In 2019, Sharkie won by more than 5 per cent in Mayo and Steggall in Warringah by 7.2 per cent. Not that the latter took Climate 200 money. 'I'm not saying I won't,' Steggall tells me in 2022. 'I will if I need to, but I haven't needed to. Warringah is the second most affluent electorate in Australia, so there is a capacity for fundraising that you don't have in a regional seat, like Helen in Indi. But I've supported [Climate 200] in their drive to help other independent campaigns.'

And then, job done, Climate 200 went into hibernation, even before its existence became public when the Australian Electoral Commission released its transparency register of political donations in October 2019. 'I said at the time: "Okay, we showed that there's buy-in to the idea and some evidence of effectiveness. If we did it ten times bigger with a year's run-up, what could we do?"' Holmes à Court said in September 2021.

To find out, he had retained Warringah veteran Anthony Reed and a newcomer, Byron Fay, to conduct a review of Climate 200's first iteration at the start of what might still have been the election year of 2021.

Fay had begun his career at the Rudd government's Department of Climate Change, where he had worked on Paris Agreement negotiations before moving to the UN's Green Climate Fund. By 2021, the then 35-year-old had arrived back in Australia after completing a Master of Public Policy at Oxford University in the UK. That degree had been all about getting into the weeds of where modern political campaigns were won, or not: 'I was very aware of the fact that the progressive side of politics kept losing, and was interested in why,' Fay says. 'It seemed to me that outfits like [Liberal Party–aligned lobbying and polling firm] Crosby Textor had been much better at winning.'

The meteoric rise of Isaac Levido OBE seemed to encapsulate that competitive advantage. A protégé of Sir Lynton Crosby, the man seen as instrumental in Boris Johnson's rise and the UK Conservative Party's successful 2015 and 2017 campaigns, Levido, at just 36, had been credited with playing a crucial role in both Scott Morrison's 2019 miracle win and Boris Johnson's thumping 2019 victory.

Levido had studied at the Australian National University (ANU) a couple of years ahead of Fay, who had completed an Arts/Law degree there. They had even attended the same residential college. 'We'd missed each other; he'd gone off and worked for Lynton Crosby, then the Republicans,' Fay says. 'I knew the data side of things was really important. I went to Oxford determined to try and figure out polling, surveying, things like survey experiments to randomise control trials to figure out if you're having a persuasive effect. I tried to get enmeshed in it as much as I could.'

That led to a job on a Biden-aligned US political action committee called Defeat Disinfo, which specialised in social-media-based persuasion campaigning to counter Donald Trump misinformation in the lead-up to the 2020 US election.

It was through a lens that was accordingly both global and local that Fay and Reed examined Climate 200's first iteration. Delivered in March 2021, their review found that Climate 200 had 'definitely worked. People were interested in the idea, and donations were made to some candidates that won, so there was a nice little proof of concept there,' Fay says. 'But they spread their resources way too thin. The money they had was just way too widely dispersed and, because Simon had only come up with the idea eight weeks out, he was raising money six weeks out and spending money four or three weeks out. Even the last week, they were spending money.

'It was all just too late. I was very influenced by the US experience, which was a very long-term campaign,' he says. 'Even Trump was big on this. He got into trouble because he'd spent a lot of his money six months out. But they have an always-on philosophy, and I think we kind of took that.'

Time was also crucial because of the quite peculiar nature of the Australian 2022 independents variant. 'I very much had a view that, if you're going to do something like this, which is so non-traditional, and with these candidates who are going to need to build everything from scratch, you can't do it in six weeks,' Fay says. 'It was going to take at least three months, probably six months, and then you need to factor in fundraising time.'

While Steggall had not been among those funded by Climate 200 in 2019, her victory had established categorically that 'this can work in these inner-city seats, which was pretty unique because independents to that point had all been in rural, regional areas, except for Andrew Wilkie [in Hobart],' says Fay. Anthony Reed, as the man who had been on the ground with Steggall, 'had a lot of really useful insights that informed a lot of our recommendations. Because the question was "How do we replicate the models we have—Zali and Helen and Cathy—at scale?"'

In addition to going bigger and earlier, a further recommendation made by Fay and Reed in their March 2021 report was to employ the sort of data and analytics both men had seen at work in campaigns. 'We had to see a good, viable pathway to success through the analytics,' Fay says. 'Mostly it's polling, but also demographic change analysis. North coast New South

Wales is a perfect example. Lots of people moving into the area after Covid, which largely explains why [independent candidate] Caz Heise did so well in Cowper. It also explains why Eden-Monaro is now a safe Labor seat, because you've got all these retirees moving from Canberra to the south coast and it's becoming more progressive.'

A fourth recommendation by the two men related to strategic communications: 'Firstly, that was to get our message out there, to make sure that people were aware of what we were doing, so we could raise money,' Fay says. 'But we also had a philosophy that a rising tide would lift all boats when it came to the independents movement. So if we could talk up the notion of voting independent in the broad, it would help everybody.'

There's another entry in Byron Fay's CV that says a lot about the contemporary independents movement. Between Green Climate Fund and going to Oxford, he was climate-policy adviser to accidental South Australian independent Tim Storer, who had found himself a senator after the incumbent, Skye Kakoschke-Moore of Nick Xenophon Team, resigned as part of the parliamentary eligibility crisis in 2017.

It was a brief interlude, given Storer didn't contest the 2019 election. But for Fay, that eighteen months had been a revelation. 'We'd done a Senate inquiry into electric vehicles, we'd knocked back a big business tax cut, and we'd advocated for Murray–Darling Basin environmental reform,' he says. 'It was all pretty progressive stuff but we would get these calls from probably quite conservative rural voters who were very interested in what he was putting out there. It struck me that the conversations wouldn't have even happened had it had Labor or the Greens branding on it. The ability for an independent to cut through and have an honest discussion on the policy merits, without all that baggage, was quite clear to me.'

Fay also became close to Jim Middleton during this time. The former ABC chief political correspondent in Canberra was a senior adviser on Storer's team. 'I find it hard to remember this, but Jim always says to me, "You talked about this like four years ago, at least. When you were with Storer, you just wouldn't shut up about how you thought there could be this way of supporting independents at scale,"' Fay says.

Nor, bizarrely, was his work with Storer Fay's first brush with an independent candidate. Leah Ginnivan, the niece who had rung Cathy McGowan to suggest she run for parliament and make Indi marginal, setting in motion McGowan's 2013 tilt, had also been at ANU at the same time as Fay. Not that the latter exactly grasped the potential of the moment: 'I remember them saying, "We're going to go get my aunty elected to parliament in rural Victoria,"' he says. 'I said, "See you later. I'm going to go campaign for [Labor member 2007–13] Mike Kelly down in Eden-Monaro."'

A decade on, though, his time with Storer looked determinative: 'I'd had this big experience—"Wow, this independent model is too powerful"—and I was wrapping up because Tim wasn't going to recontest,' Fay recalls. 'I was up in Brisbane at the Al Gore Climate Reality leader training event [in June 2019], just after the 2019 election, which was when I met Simon. We just hit it off; we had this really intense hour talking about Climate 200.'

That experience highlights a major motivator at all levels of the 2022 community-backed movement: the inspiration taken from independent forebears. Kylea Tink typified the 2022 crop in being an incisive critic of the Morrison government's performance on the environment. But independence was an equally fundamental part of her campaign's DNA, right down to 'Tink pink', an exception to the so-called 'teal wave'.

As she wrote in a piece in the *Australian Financial Review* on 1 June 2022: 'North Sydney has been a Liberal seat for almost all of its 121 years since Federation, with the exception of six years under the independent Ted Mack.' By then, the man they call the father of the independents—the former mayor of North Sydney who went on to represent the area as an independent in state parliament and then federal parliament between the 1970s and 1990s—had been baked into the narrative.

This was reflected in the first Kaldor-funded survey, which North Sydney's Independent had found so reassuring. It showed that 'North Sydney had a very high approval rate of independents,' says Kristen Lock. 'It had a generally high resting rate [the percentage of respondents who would vote for an independent, before their identity was introduced], probably the highest in the country, around 16 per cent, as opposed to 10 per cent elsewhere, probably because of Ted Mack.'

Nor was the inspiration that an effective independent in action could provide primarily an urban phenomenon. The reverse, in fact. In Queensland's Groom in the Darling Downs, Suzie Holt first met the woman who would become her campaign manager, agricultural consultant Meredith King, in a quintessentially community-independent way: Twitter, followed by some expert shepherding from that ubiquitous Indi veteran Denis Ginnivan.

Both King and Holt had commented on a 2019 tweet from Helen Haines about a renewable energy project for Yackandandah in Indi. 'We both said something like "That looks wonderful. Imagine what could be achieved up here in Groom if we had an independent candidate," and then Denis said, "Have you two met? You need to have a coffee,"' King recalls. 'Denis then harassed us for a couple of months, until we finally caught up in early January 2020.'

By the time I spoke to the former consultant two years later, she had suspended her career and she and Holt were joined at the hip. A large part of her inspiration, says King, who grew up on a small cattle station north of Inverell, was the example of another independent, Tony Windsor. 'I've been interested in politics forever. We were one of those families that sat around and discussed politics from an early age. But, as a girl growing up on the land in northern New South Wales in the 70s and 80s, I just tottered along and voted National without thinking about it. Not because I firmly believed in them. It was just a generational thing.'

Windsor's 2001 run in New England, which he would hold until retiring in 2013, changed all that. 'My mum, who is a teacher, is very politically switched on and was becoming really disillusioned with the same old, same old,' King recalls. 'A good friend of ours in the media in Tamworth got to know Tony and she said, "You've got to come and hear this guy speak." So about twenty of us rolled down to the pub in Inverell one night to listen and that was it. We were sold.'

King's mother volunteered for Windsor. Her daughter began her own political odyssey. 'I travelled, and I lived in Sydney for about a decade and overseas, and I just started to open my eyes and broaden my political horizons.' More recently, her open eyes began to trouble her: 'I thought, "These guys have got their eyes closed and their heads stuck in the sand, and I don't think they're going to be right for the country." And I had probably begun thinking like that from about the time of Tony Windsor.'

~~~~~

Nor did the independent candidate have to be successful to inspire. In Wentworth, Allegra Spender's volunteer ranks expanded frantically in early 2022, as did her schedule of meet and greets, runs and swims, and politics-in-the-pub events. None of those supporters were more stalwart than retired teachers Annette Guerry and Evelyn Foltyn. The pair were omnipresent across events in their Spender-blue T-shirts.

Guerry's path to independence began when she and a group of what seems to be an endless supply of friends approached their then local member in the early 2000s. Former NSW state Liberal president Peter King had won Wentworth in 2001, having previously stood for preselection in Warringah in 1994 and been defeated by none other than Tony Abbott. 'There was an issue that a few women and I were concerned about and we went to see Peter, and he was very helpful and very available to the community,' Guerry says. 'That just opened my eyes; I'd never thought he would be so available and talk to the plebs. People usually use Wentworth as a stepping stone to where they want to be.'

When King lost preselection to Malcolm Turnbull, he ran as an independent for Wentworth in 2004. 'We supported Peter, my friends and I, everything from handing out leaflets to scrutineering,' Guerry recalls. 'He was resoundingly defeated, but it got me thinking about the power an independent can have in a real democracy and the role they can play. People kept telling me it didn't work when there was a majority government, but I thought, "I don't care if it works or not, I just want to find someone whose values align better with mine."'

Typically, involvement in one independent campaign bred deeper involvement. 'One of the girls went to [anti-racism group] Courage to Care, another got involved in the Sydney Alliance,' Guerry says. 'Another ran for council, unsuccessfully and then successfully. I learnt a lot through supporting her.'

Meanwhile, a friend from Evelyn Foltyn's book club, who lived in Fairlight near Manly—and, not coincidentally, also belonged to Manly's Bold and Beautiful swimming group—said, 'I'm fed up with Tony Abbott, we're going to get an independent to run.' Foltyn says, 'They didn't even know who when it started, but every book club he'd tell us what was happening and we'd just listen in awe at his passion and his drive. It got to the stage where I said I wanted to hear Zali speak and to volunteer. But he said, "No, we have enough supporters," and I just thought, "Wow, this is something."'

~~~~~

While Byron Fay and Anthony Reed had recommended that Climate 200 go bigger and earlier the second time around, no one could have imagined how much bigger it would get, or how much earlier. 'My theory was that Australians didn't engage until election season started,' Holmes à Court said in September 2021. 'So we would raise maybe a million this year, a million before the election was called, and then another million in the first two weeks of the campaign.'

Even that aspiration had been a major revision of the original target. Having been paid $50,000 for his services as a consultant early on, Fay set about proving the concept in April 2021 by raising the equivalent funds. Equipped with a rudimentary Canva slideshow, Fay pitched to Climate 200's original donors over Zoom during Covid lockdowns. 'I did it time and time again,' he says. 'When we'd passed that 50-grand threshold, Simon said, "All right, time to go public, we need to put it out there."'

A design agency donated a logo while Fay worked on a website, discovering the perils of back-end. 'There's a complicated series of things you need in order to accept payments from people through the internet . . . you need to bolt it onto your website and make sure the data flows to a spreadsheet.'

Initial expectations were modest: 'The advice we'd been given was that it was hard out there: "You're going to spend more than you'll raise on a crowdfunder for the first year, and then people build up a kind of affiliation with the organisation and eventually you'll see some return."'

But one of the first donors to the 2.0 iteration of Climate 200 was green-tech investor Simon Monk, who agreed to give $100,000 on condition that 100 people matched it at $1000 a pop. He said that he would issue his challenge on Twitter. 'We were not ready at all,' Fay recalls. 'The website had literally just gone live and Simon didn't give us a heads-up. It was a rainy Sunday afternoon and we just saw this tweet pop up, "Yeah, I'm raising money for Climate 200."'

Before they knew it, $30,000 had rolled in. The first matching challenge was complete in a couple of weeks. 'We were like, "Okay: a. people are keen; and b. Twitter's super powerful, because there's a really excited Simon Holmes à Court fan club out there prepared to give . . . This is good." We went hard on the matching challenges, rolling them out back to back for the first couple of months. The people who'd said we'd spend as much as we'd make were shocked. They said, "We have never seen anything like this. It's nuts."'

By the time Holmes à Court and I first spoke in September 2021, Climate 200 had already beaten the $3 million it had hoped for by the election, raising $3.3 million from 4200 donors in a few months. 'We joked at the start about calling it Climate 2000, but that's already happened,' he said.

~~~~~~

It is telling that when Climate 200's founder first neglected his law studies for student politics almost three decades ago, it was for the French-founded, non-aligned AIESEC.

Holmes à Court describes the organisation as 'a bit like a model UN'; it introduced students to 'fundraising, running events and plenaries and constitutions and stuff'. That he chose a non-aligned path through university politics reflected the very particular conditions of his childhood. 'As you can imagine, I had a fairly bizarre upbringing, with politicians of the day around the dinner table,' he said. 'My parents never saw themselves as partisan. I guess for most of my father's professional life Labor would have been in power, [and] some of the last days of the [Liberal] Fraser government, but his later years were very much internationally focused.'

His parents were unaligned in more essential ways, too. 'They weren't very social as a couple,' he says. 'They didn't really have friends, my dad particularly. He loved working, and he worked seven days a week. They both felt that, if something was wrong, you fixed it. And you don't complain, you just made it happen.'

A line in the *Australian Dictionary of Biography* entry on Robert Holmes à Court, whose takeover targets ranged from Ansett to BHP, catches the eye: 'He had a gift for seeing an opportunity and soon developed a legendary reputation for his daring company raids.' It's tempting to see something of the same eye in his son, albeit trained on very different opportunities.

'Simon wouldn't be onto this unless it was a winner,' Cathy McGowan tells me when we first speak in September 2021. 'And I say that with genuine respect. He can pick a winner. What makes him so special is that he gets how the high-level corporate world works—which very few community people do—through his father. But he's also the son of this most amazing woman, who is all about community, and he gets that, too.'

When I asked Janet Holmes à Court in 2021 what she had noticed about her second-youngest child, from that original toddler tilting at a power socket to now, she didn't hesitate: 'He was incredibly brave,' she said. 'He's courageous, he's forward-thinking and he's compassionate. And he's fortunate that in the role that he's choosing to play now, he can't be sacked. Because he doesn't work for anybody.'

For Holmes à Court, as for so many others involved in this latest chapter of the independents story, there was a sense of fate—finding the thing that made sense of all the twists and turns that had gone before—in his involvement in the movement. 'I'm just part of a much bigger team, right?' he said six months into Climate 200's second coming in 2021. 'Everyone has a superpower. I'm trying to find mine, and I think I have with this. I guess it's a convening power: kick-starting this and convening the people who can make Climate 200 work, and developing the strategy to help these campaigns.'

Those same qualities—his penchant for standing outside the system, alone if necessary or as part of a community as much founded as found—could also polarise. His family name, presumed inherited wealth and the slight awkwardness that clings to him would make him a lightning rod. Because, right from the start, Climate 200 had critics as well as fans. And they would be almost uniquely vitriolic in the lead-up to 2022.

It had started even before Climate 200, in fact. A long piece in the *Australian Financial Review* in October 2018 by Aaron Patrick reported that, according to allies of the then-new energy minister, Angus Taylor, Holmes à Court had an 'obsession' with Taylor, even driving to Taylor's home town in southern New South Wales to argue energy policy with him at a pub appearance. 'He doesn't accept the irony of a mining entrepreneur's son becoming an anti-coal evangelist,' Patrick wrote in the piece, which opined that Taylor, who was 'required to deliver fast results in a highly political and contested portfolio, [didn't] need any more critics. His job is complicated enough by adversaries' attempts to portray him as a climate change sceptic, a charge Taylor has denied many times. Even *The Economist* reported the claim as fact.'

The government would pursue a similar line, on and off the record, in the lead-up to the 2022 election, questioning Holmes à Court's stability and integrity. This time around, though, it focused more on Frydenberg, the subject of Senator Andrew Bragg's February 2022 Senate speech involving Holmes à Court. Meanwhile Dave Sharma accused Climate 200 of using a 'sickening' holocaust slur during the week leading up to the election.

The latter related to a 17 May 2022 tweet ahead of John Howard's arrival in Melbourne to campaign in the seat of Kooyong in which Holmes à Court summarised his view of the former prime minister's climate record and referred to him as the 'angel of death' in this context. Reports of Holmes à Court's tweet resulted in him sending a letter of concern to both the Sydney *Daily Telegraph* and the Australian edition of the *Daily Mail*, which published a story on 18 May headlined 'Multimillionaire puppet master of wealthy independents attempting to tear down the Liberal Party denies comparing popular ex-PM John Howard to Nazi doctor who tortured Jews'.

For his part, Frydenberg reportedly described his nemesis as 'gutless' for founding Climate 200. The treasurer was much more voluble in his not-for-attribution backgrounding of journalists, however, both before and after the election. Holmes à Court was a 'strange cat' who had an unhealthy fixation on him, Frydenberg rang to tell me when I checked the Climate 200 founder's Kooyong 200 story with him for an October 2021 *Good Weekend* profile. Not that he would be quoted, even off the record. 'Old mate' would know and come after him, his press secretary said at the time.

The fight would expand in the lead-up to the election. In an interview with Peta Credlin on Sky News in February 2022, superannuation minister Senator Jane Hume, with whom Holmes à Court would later clash, on both the hustings and TV, described Climate 200 donors as 'wealthy, trust fund babies', who constituted a 'new bunyip aristocracy . . . essentially providing themselves the equivalent of colonial titles with hereditary privileges in order to subvert democracy'.

On 10 April, the ex-chairman of the Coalition's Indigenous Advisory Council, Nyunggai Warren Mundine, tweeted that Holmes à Court was a 'filthy rich man' trying 'to influence the election via the All White . . . Climate 200 party' after Holmes à Court had described Mundine in a tweet as a 'grub' and a 'flog' for drawing attention on Twitter to a 6 April article in *The Australian* that accused Zoe Daniel of anti-Semitism. An editorial in that paper on 12 April said that Mundine had 'made an astute observation that Climate 200 party founder Simon Holmes à Court is a left-leaning equivalent of mining entrepreneur and political aspirant Clive Palmer'.

A few days earlier, on 9 April, in the same paper, Dave Sharma had called Climate 200 'the party of white privilege—just look at the candidates they are running, and their leader, Simon Holmes à Court', after the group turned down a funding application from Tibetan human rights activist Kyinzom Dhongdue, who was a candidate for the Drew Pavlou Democratic Alliance. Climate 200 was 'a movement which claims to be "grassroots"', Sharma said, that was 'run by elites and for elites'.

Through it all, Holmes à Court rarely resisted a bait, engaging in hand-to-hand comment on Twitter and in person. None of it was particularly edifying. But the breadth, stridency and persistence of the government's attack did seem to be a clear symptom of growing heat stress.

Nor was it only the Morrison government that found Holmes à Court and Climate 200 polarising. Within the independents movement itself, some viewed Climate 200's attempts to promote independence more broadly, in keeping with one of the recommendations by Fay and Reed, as a branding exercise that threatened to eclipse the broader movement. While no one questioned the benefits of Climate 200's involvement, which was seen as a game changer, there had been a degree of nervousness in the days leading up to Holmes à Court's scheduled appearance at the National Press Club in February 2022. Some within the movement questioned why he was doing it.

In the end his speech, which paid abundant homage to independents past and present, assuaged many of those doubts, but they never entirely disappeared. When the Press Club followed up by inviting Fay to speak in July 2022, post-election, some wondered why it hadn't asked McGowan or any one of the newly elected MPs instead.

As one community group leader who worked with Climate 200 to successfully get their candidate elected explains: 'They did an astounding thing and I don't want to take that away from them, but I did find it fascinating how much they became the story. I wondered how much that was external interest in making them the story and how much they wanted to be the story, for branding and other reasons.'

Margo Kingston is far less circumspect. Kingston started her No Fibs citizen-journalism website in 2012. From McGowan's Indi win on, it has chronicled and championed the 'Voices of' movement, continuing work Kingston started much earlier. While a senior political correspondent at the *Sydney Morning Herald*, she chronicled the rise of Pauline Hanson after her hometown of Maryborough in Queensland fell to One Nation in 1999, and subsequently wrote *Off the Rails: The Pauline Hanson Trip* that same year. In 2004 Kingston's *Not Happy, John!* was published.

The latter is cited by many as another eureka moment. Louise Hislop, for instance, dates her politicisation to a comment Kingston made at an appearance to promote *Not Happy, John!* at a bookshop at which Hislop worked: 'Look, it's okay for you white, privileged, North Shore types to come along here and listen to me speak about my book,' Hislop quotes Kingston as saying in a November 2021 No Fibs piece. 'But at some point you're going to have to get off your arses and actually do something.'

For Kingston, a self-described 'purist' of the movement, change has to be about capacity-building from within communities. 'I am extremely critical of Simon. I think he has made a number of fundamental mistakes,' she tells me in early May 2022. 'He was very, very wrong to make himself the face of the movement; to see that the chief donor of a lot of the independent campaigns was the person at the Press Club was devastating. The media needs a leader. They want a leader and he delivered for them.'

As a former *Australian Financial Review* journalist who sought out Simon Holmes à Court for a profile when news of Climate 200's comeback broke in mid-2021 as a way into the community-backed independents story, I can attest she has a point.

To Kingston, 'Climate 200 is not a problem in a city blue-ribbon seat, but it is a net negative in regional seats. It's a huge problem. I see the whole thing as an experiment now between, basically, the big end of town and the grassroots.'

Post-election, at least a couple of regional candidates that declined Climate 200 funding and didn't prevail will speculate that they should have taken it. 'This would not have happened without Simon Holmes à Court,' Jim Middleton said of the independents' election result in August 2022. 'It was Simon who worked out the building blocks to this. Those building blocks came from what he learnt from Robert and Janet; what he learnt from setting up a community wind farm up in Daylesford; what he had learnt by engaging with Twitter. Each one was an "aha" moment for him.'

To Cathy McGowan, speaking in 2021, being a lightning rod was a large part of Holmes à Court's role in 2021 and 2022. 'What I think he's done in being so public about his fundraising, and because he has such a high profile, is send a message directly to the Liberals and the Nats that they're in trouble,' she said.

While some saw him as changing the conversation, or sticking his blasted finger in the power socket of Scott Morrison's government, Holmes à Court distracted many in the Coalition ranks, just as Climate 200's funding of the campaigns in once blue-ribbon seats forced the government to spend huge sums and valuable time defending them.

Neither the Coalition nor media critics ever focused on Holmes à Court to the exclusion of the candidates or their campaign staff, who also copped considerable attention. But as 2022 wore on and the government's supporters became fixated on the brahmin with the billionaire father, Morrison continued to put off the inevitable election, allowing campaigns the time to find not only candidates but also their feet and then stride.

8

LET ONE HUNDRED
START-UPS BLOOM

Cathy McGowan had expected maybe 50 souls to attend her two-day 'Getting Elected' Zoom conference in February 2021. When 300 people turned up online from 81 electorates, even the woman dubbed the godmother of the movement was taken aback by the richness of the vein she'd tapped.

Seven months later, however, it was still unclear how deep or far that vein ran. When McGowan and I first spoke in September 2021, only Kylea Tink in North Sydney had announced her candidacy, spurred on by nervousness among her backers that the election would be called for later that year.

Media reports said Communications Minister Paul Fletcher might face a challenge in Bradfield, following a public 'Voices of' recruitment drive there. But while there were 'probably 80 electorates [with groups] that are interested, and I would say there are about ten to fifteen active groups that seriously want to run a candidate', McGowan said, there was 'still only one candidate'. Climate 200 had decided to go earlier and bigger second time around, but it was anything but clear that campaigns of any calibre would rise up in time. 'Give me two months to see the campaigns,' McGowan said at the time. 'Because if you don't have the right candidates and the campaigns, Simon's funding is going to make no difference at all.'

The comment underlined just how much still hung in the balance months out from what would become a May 21 election. As Simon Holmes à Court later quipped, Kooyong was still just 'a short bespectacled political scientist' even by October. Beneath the surface, feet paddled frantically, as they had at a similar point in the 2019 Warringah bid, as campaigns desperately tried to bag the big-game candidates they knew were critical if they were to succeed. Others were sorting through nominees from recruitment drives. Still others, unable to find a willing victim, were deciding to run themselves. And some were attempting all three at once.

But it was a live question in September whether any of it would amount to a hill of beans at an election that could still arrive before Santa Claus.

The reason McGowan was underlining the odds against, too, was that she knew them better than anyone. Fewer than 50 independents had been elected in the almost 120 years between Federation and Zali Steggall.

'I think about [95] people stood as independents at the last election, and only three of them got up,' McGowan said. 'People always run, but it's really hard to win, which is why I'm happy to share any of the strategies that I have learnt about community organising to help people. But I keep coming back to saying, "Look, I was really lucky in 2013 to win. I won by 439 votes."'

That reference to community organising is anything but casual. McGowan had learnt not only the odds against independents but also what it took to overcome those odds. And she had learnt the hard way. Her 2013 victory had been, she said, 'a bee's dick away from a real stuff-up'. By the second and third campaigns, however, 'we knew how to organise and how to get things done. What I've learnt is that it's really hard for a one-off independent who doesn't have a community base to get elected. Ted Mack did it, Peter Andren [the independent MP for the federal New South Wales seat of Calare for more than a decade] did it, but it's almost impossible.'

Which is why her mantra—heard repeatedly throughout the run-up to May 2022, as she delivered masterclasses, and geed up candidates and volunteers—was that a campaign comes down to three Cs: the backing of the Community, the right Candidate and a real Campaign. As she explained in September 2021: 'The campaign has got to be bigger than just your organising group. It has to speak to the whole community, and that's a real tricky ask. The ["Voices of"] group can do the first-level engagement with the community and find out what the issues are and whether there's a will in the community to organise. But then one of the technical questions is whether the community group can then transition to a campaign. A Voices group is usually democratic sort of stuff. The campaign is about winning: you need a bigger group, you need to fundraise and you need to get into the real competition.'

Which is precisely how Climate 200, too, saw the game. 'We're not the inventor or the product. We don't start the campaign and we don't choose the candidate,' Simon Holmes à Court told me in April 2022. 'They come to us. And if they have a great candidate, great campaign manager, 300 volunteers, and they say, "We've got a business plan, we've raised 80 grand,

and we have ten fundraisers planned for the next few months" then . . . that's our job: helping good campaigns scale. Ninety-five independents ran [for the House of Representatives] at the last federal election. Most of them got a few hundred votes, which is family, friends and donkey votes. Our job is to look at something that could get 8000 to 10,000 votes on its own, but with our help can get 20,000 to 30,000.'

As its founder saw it, Climate 200 was the political equivalent of a venture capital fund looking at start-ups. To its CEO, Byron Fay, the first of Cathy McGowan's Cs was particularly crucial in giving away what they never forgot was 'other people's money'. 'Community is just fundamental for us,' he said. 'We looked to factors that evidence that. How many volunteers have you got? How is that growing month on month? How much funding have you raised from the local community? What's that growing month on month? How many events have you held? How many people are you getting to them?

'For anyone who believes the theories that Climate 200 is pulling the strings or masterminding things: we couldn't. [Clive] Palmer tried quite overtly, and it was a miserable failure because there was no community movement. It was just money. We always knew that—without a strong community-movement campaign, this wasn't going to work.'

Which is why McGowan needed a couple of months to gauge the field when we first spoke. 'I've got to see the campaigns and the candidates,' she said. 'Because while there are communities that are organising, until they get a quality candidate, they can't win.'

The point was reinforced by the first round of polling Climate 200 undertook in July 2021, as soon as it had scraped a few dollars together. Three seats where Zali Steggall's brand was thought to be strong—Mackellar, Wentworth and North Sydney—were chosen to go first. Respondents were asked both whether they would vote for a generic independent, and whether they would vote for a Steggall-like candidate.

North Sydney's high resting rate of 16 per cent for a generic independent catapulted to 28 per cent—a potentially winning position with preferences—if the candidate was Zali-like. Results in other electorates were similar. That created its own conundrum, however, given that, as one sceptical donor told Byron Fay at the time, 'Zali Steggalls don't grow on trees, mate. She's a bloody barrister and a four-time Olympian!'

Wentworth was a less sports-obsessed demographic than Warringah. But 'rockstar candidate' was still near the top of the to-do list Wentworth Independents took from Warringah. That didn't necessarily mean celebrity. More what Lyndell Droga terms 'latent awareness': a familiarity from which a story could be fashioned that said 'smart, community-minded and driven; fiscally conservative, socially progressive'.

By late October 2021, about 30 names had accumulated on the spreadsheet that the Wentworth group, which called itself the 'Windies', kept on a shared drive. As the prime movers behind the group, Maria Atkinson, Blair Palese and Lyndell Droga approached potential candidates. At the time, word would filter back occasionally of the latest woman who had been approached, from newspaper editors and high-profile journalists to business-women. 'We were all being given names left, right and centre,' Droga confirmed in March. 'Some were a flat "no". Some were like being on Tinder—you'd look at the profile and think, "They'd be amazing!" Swipe! And they wouldn't even reply.'

Allegra Spender had been mentioned to Droga by Art Gallery of NSW philanthropy executive Jessica Block, a friend of both, who introduced them by email. By then, however, Sydney's eastern suburbs were back in lockdown. Even a coffee was impossible.

Instead, in June, Spender and Droga met for the first time like spies in Centennial Park, for a brisk, legal walk, during which Spender explained that while she might contemplate politics in a decade, the timing was all wrong. Crucially, though, just as Tim Flannery had done previously in Warringah, she said she was happy to be the Windies' Plan B but was sure they would find someone better.

You can see why Spender was reluctant. She had three children under ten and what she described as a 'very purposeful' job as CEO of the Australian Business and Community Network, which mentors kids from lower socioeconomic backgrounds. Nor was she a natural gladhander. 'I find it strange that everyone picks up on that,' she said when I ask her about the gentle, polite demeanour that was such a feature of her early appearances. 'No, I'm not a natural extrovert, but to be honest I like people. I like understanding what's important to them.'

What followed her initial refusal was a delicate dance. 'We kept in touch,' Droga said. 'I sent her updates on research findings. I wanted to keep her interested but without being pushy or disrespectful, because she is a woman of integrity. We had such a big fish potentially on the hook that we had to be careful.'

Droga promised Spender she would let her know if they found their Plan A candidate. 'I did ring her at one point and tell her we'd found someone promising. I said, "If it happens,

I'll let you off the hook." But it didn't, so she was back on the hook.'

Meanwhile, as in Warringah three years earlier, time was wasting. The Windies had a corporate campaign vehicle, a professional manager (Anthony Reed), an ad agency (Brains) and a market-research agency (Retail Oasis) already working on the brief. 'But we were tearing our hair out—we just couldn't find anyone,' Droga said. 'One of the donors said, "Lyndell, you're just focusing on the egg, you're not spending enough time on the nest," and I thought, "Actually, we've got a really good nest, I've even leased office space, we're just waiting for the best egg and it's not coming."'

Then, at the end of October, four months after they'd first met, Droga got the call. 'I've never said yes before,' Spender told her, 'but I'm saying yes now.' 'I nearly dropped the phone,' Droga says.

For the candidate, the clincher had been Scott Morrison's 26 October announcement of a zero-emissions-by-2050 target that relied partially on future technological breakthroughs. When the government's response 'was just so hopeless', Spender told me in February 2022, she decided she 'couldn't not stand'. 'I felt that if [Wentworth Independents] thought that, out of all the people they'd gone through, I was the best candidate for the job, then I should do it.'

She had also consulted widely, including speaking to John Daley on how independents could break the policy gridlock his report had anatomised, and testing 'the appetite in Wentworth for change'.

'There's been a huge appetite, across the board, from some of my mum's very good friends to a lot of people of my generation and people younger than me as well,' she said. 'That breadth has been what has really driven me.'

On 19 November, Spender's candidature hit the papers. A week later, she made the formal announcement at Paddington RSL. The venue had to be changed that morning from a local park, due to the storms lashing Sydney at the time. It was still standing room only, even in the spill-over venue, as one of those old friends of her mother's, Jillian Broadbent, introduced Spender, recalling Carla Zampatti's lament that her younger daughter didn't 'seem to care about clothes at all'.

Taking the public stage for the very first time, the newly hatched candidate then delivered a pitch-perfect launch speech. 'I'm not a radical; I am standing for the same values as my father and grandfather,' she said, between waves of applause. 'We cannot afford one more election cycle of spin, denial and inaction on climate change.' The die was cast.

In the bayside Melbourne electorate of Goldstein at much the same time, a very similar candidate play was unfolding. Voices of Goldstein had been launched in early 2021 after Denise Shrivell introduced Sue Barrett to Katarina Gaita via Twitter. A website had been knocked together, and purple T-shirts printed promising 'Our Independent's Day is coming' in Goldstein gold.

It was very much the sentiment Voices of Goldstein had been picking up as it ran kitchen-table conversations in early 2021 on what mattered to those in the electorate. 'It grew to about 1000 supporters quickly,' Barrett recalled. 'What was clear was that people were really pissed off and wanted change. We realised we had an opportunity. Call it guesswork if you like, but we thought, "Let's have a crack."'

As we spoke for the first time, on the morning of 22 September 2021, that crack became literal. Barrett and Gaita were still the spokespeople for Voices of Goldstein at the time; Project IndiGold was barely a glimmer in their eye. Halfway through our Zoom chat, however, the two rooms in lockdown Melbourne began to sway as their occupants scattered. The Mansfield earthquake, measuring 5.9 on the Richter scale, had just hit.

We joked about clumsy symbolism and quakes to come; but it would transpire that, even then, Barrett had a move up her sleeve that would prove every bit as seismic. Voices of Goldstein had consulted the community on what it wanted in a candidate and established a selection panel: three men and three women, aged 22 to 70, and a variety of political stripes. After Voices of Goldstein started promoting its quest for a candidate on social media in June 2021, fourteen people had nominated.

To one side of that process, Melbourne journalist Angela Pippos had also direct-messaged Barrett, who was chairing the panel. Barrett had been thrilled to think that Pippos was considering running, she told me in April 2022, but it turned out that Pippos was actually throwing her friend, Zoe Daniel, under the bus. 'She's not on board,' Pippos told Barrett. 'We'll have to talk to her.'

The three women caught up on Zoom in late July. 'Absolutely no chance in hell, I'm not doing that,' is how Zoe Daniel would later recall her response. 'I don't think so. But I'm not sure,' was Barrett's version: 'So I said, "If you like, I can stay in touch and just keep you abreast of what's going on."'

As with Spender in Wentworth, what secured Daniel was the stalled, divided Morrison government—particularly on climate—and a multipronged approach. Cathy McGowan had also sent Daniel 'a note saying perhaps I should consider being a representative', Daniel recalls. Pippos continued to argue the case, as did another old friend and colleague, Jim Middleton. As for Barrett: 'I did my very best key account management,' she says. 'I stayed in touch and kept her up to date without pressuring her, because there was no point.'

As a December election was still possible, Barrett contacted Daniel in October, a few weeks after our earthquake call. Voices of Goldstein 'had a candidate who'd been through the [application process] and done well', Barrett says. 'We were at the pointy end, no mucking around anymore, so I said I needed to know whether she was in or not. We'd love her to go, but we had a candidate, and she'd have to go through the same process if she was. No free passes.'

To Barrett's surprise, Daniel was in. Voices of Goldstein began work to launch its secret weapon at Sandringham Rotunda on Saturday, 27 November. 'We wanted to go a week earlier, but we couldn't do it that quickly,' Barrett recalls. 'Meanwhile, we were pulling this team together. While a couple of us had worked on Voices of Goldstein, none of us had worked together in a team, which is very different. My husband always says a community campaign like Voices of Goldstein is like a dot org. It's a social movement. Whereas a political campaign is a dotcom.'

The Thursday before the Saturday launch, however, the news leaked. Like so many subsequent potential setbacks for campaigns across the country, it proved a boon. The website may not have been ready when the news got out but, once it was, '$7000–8000 in donations rolled in in a couple of hours from around the country'. The 300 T-shirts that Barrett had ordered for the official launch three days later, fearing she'd overdone it, sold out in ten minutes.

In all, 600 people turned up. 'It was one of the most joyful days I've ever experienced,' Barrett said. 'People in the crowd were crying with relief that we had someone of such stature and candour and dignity to put our efforts behind.'

Around the same time, push was coming to shove in a different way in one of the electorates that borders Warringah in Sydney. Mackellar differs subtly from its neighbour. For starters, it is nothing like as homogeneous. Even on the coast side, it spreads from the well-heeled Liberal strongholds of Palm Beach and Whale Beach and the progressive lifestyle hub of Avalon. The major intersection that is Mona Vale leads down from the suburbs known collectively to locals as 'The Hills' (Frenchs Forest, Terrey Hills, Duffys Forest) to Warriewood, Narrabeen and the more raffish beach suburbs of Collaroy and Dee Why.

According to census data, Mackellarites have a similar median weekly household income to Warringah overall, are slightly more likely to be married (and legally married as opposed to de facto), but less likely to have a bachelor's, or higher, university degree (27.8 per cent versus 42.3 per cent in Warringah when last measured in 2016).

Nor was Mackellar experiencing the rich and varied currents of revolt that had characterised Warringah in 2019. The local

'Voices of' group had, nonetheless, picked up a definite desire for a Steggall-style independent (confirmed by subsequent Climate 200 polling), which led Dr Sophie Scamps and Anyo Geddes to form Mackellar Rising.

In doing so, they took advice from Warringah veterans, which had reinforced that there was 'a reason why there's not many independents in parliament and that's because it's a David and Goliath battle', Scamps told me in April 2022. 'You're a tiny person trying to come out of nowhere with no profile to fight against the party machine. It's a huge job.'

Which is why their initial advice was to find 'somebody with a high profile, because it is really difficult to build a profile from scratch to win an election', she said. 'We were talking to lots and lots of different people and we put it out via Mackellar Rising. We did have some wonderful people who considered it, but for whatever reason—family or work or whatever—they just couldn't commit.'

The more people they spoke to, the more people asked why Scamps herself wasn't running. 'Anyo had said she didn't want to do it, but I wasn't jumping up and down to do it either,' Scamps recalled. 'What drives you is the passion for what needs to be done, and that's what it came down to.'

Margo Kingston, who did a podcast for No Fibs with Scamps after she set up Mackellar Rising, was one of many trying to persuade her to run. 'She had absolutely no intention of standing,' she recalled of that moment. 'Sophie was desperately looking for other people and that to me is one of the crucial attractions of all of these candidates, that they were reluctant. They're not public figures. They either came from outside the Voices and had to be talked into it [like Spender and Daniel] or, in cases like Sophie and Suzie [Holt] in Groom, they loved community engagement and founded groups and tried everything to get a high-profile candidate.'

Just how reluctant became clear when Cathy McGowan introduced a slightly older and wiser Scamps at a Community Independents session watched by 250 people in early August 2022. 'So, Dr Sophie, tell us why you stood as a community independent and what it means for you,' McGowan said. 'Ah, Cathy, thank you,' Scamps replied, smiling. 'Cathy knows she played a very big role in my standing. I blame her entirely. All that talk about flexing your courage muscle, "If not you, then who?" and "There's no cavalry coming, there's only us!"'

No one was more convinced that Scamps should run, however, than Anthony Reed. From the Phelps campaign on, a medico was talismanic. 'The doctor element was really important,' he said in June. 'It's shorthand for someone being very intelligent across wide values.' In addition to being a GP and emergency doctor at Mona Vale, Scamps had completed Masters degrees in both public health and science, the latter at Oxford.

And that was just for starters. She'd also run for Australia in her teens, qualifying for the 1992 Olympics as a middle-distance runner and helping to set an Australian record that still stands for the 4 x 400 metre relay. She could even say, hand on heart, that she'd once beaten Cathy Freeman. For good measure her husband, Adam Magro, was a former Wallaby (rugby union international). Mackellar might not have been quite as sports-obsessed as Warringah, but after Climate 200 had polled the electorate and detected its desire for a Zali-style candidate, Scamps was about as close as you could get.

A week after Daniel's launch, and a fortnight after Spender's, Scamps was quietly announced in the 5 December Sunday papers as an independent candidate for Mackellar. The whole pitch became 'Dr Sophie', across every van, banner and corflute, with 'vote 1' and 'Scamps' in a far smaller font and a different colour. And the background was light blue, rather than teal, to appeal to a slightly more conservative electorate than Warringah.

What was less clear at the time, though, was whether any of it would work. When I spoke to Warringah's Mark Kelly in late February 2022, he was in no doubt: Mackellar was, he said, 'a very different electorate, not as rich, more family and more tradies, but they're a great team. I'd put my money on them.'

None of which was immediately evident at Scamps' inaugural 'Meet the candidate' event, held in a function room at the back of the vast new Forest Hotel deep in 'The Hills' of Mackellar. Three months into her run, the fledgling candidate had had to postpone our interview after catching Covid and then putting everything on hold to take a deep dive into policy.

The soft rain that had become Sydney's default had begun to fall as a handful of people scurried past a Dan Murphy's 'concept store' the size of an airport hangar and negotiated the maze of the spanking-new mega-pub. Inside, the 70-odd attendees weren't quite filling the function room. The crowd was mainly older and heavy on volunteers, judging by the T-shirts, with a few fit-looking younger folks, who might have been tradies but were too fast out the door afterwards for me to find out.

'Enjoy the fact that these independents aren't media trained,' Simon Holmes à Court urged journalists at his February 2022 National Press Club speech. Scamps was a case in point. Like Spender, she was clearly more a listener than a talker. And more dot org than dotcom. Tentative, almost diffident, she had to be cajoled by the MC, author Michael Robotham, into her runner–doctor–mother-of-three spiel. A great candidate on paper was yet to translate into a great candidate on stage.

But like the vibe in the room, that would soon change. Barely out of the gate, the dark horse of the urban independents field was about to break away. As Kingston later observed: 'The charm of the reluctance, the early nerves and the growing in confidence—it's so special.'

A lot has been written about the money spent or earmarked in the lead-up to the last election, from the $3 billion the Coalition promised to the lucky constituents living in just ten marginal seats, to Clive Palmer's reported $100 million advertising spree, or the $2.5 million Populares says it outlaid in key seats as part of its digital strategy.

The real currency of the independents' campaigns wasn't money, paid or promised, however. It was social capital. Strategic communications and advertising could only amplify what was already there. And as Byron Fay says, Palmer's wildly expensive, wildly ineffective UAP campaign—which managed just one senate seat and less than 4.2 per cent of the vote, translating to a spend upwards of $165 per vote—was the proof.

It's no accident that more 2022 candidates came from the health sector than any other, from Scamps and Dr Monique Ryan to Caz Heise in Cowper and Suzie Holt in Groom. Doctors remained the most trusted profession in Australia in 2021, according to an Ipsos poll. As Reed observed, the word alone was shorthand for smart enough to get into medicine, compassionate enough to practise it. And when you think about it, who better to diagnose and heal our ailing body politic than people who had dedicated their lives to healing?

'A lot of us do come from a health background,' Cowper independent Caz Heise said in July, also pointing to Helen Haines, a former nurse and midwife with a health-related PhD. 'All of us are fairly highly educated in the health sector and have a really good idea of what's impacting people, their health, the health of the natural environment, and how it's all interconnected. Plus, most people who dive into a career in health naturally have a level of empathy and willingness to give to the community. You don't go into health for the money; it's not that kind of job.'

In a 30-year career, Heise had gone from nurse to director of nursing and midwifery at Coffs Harbour Health Campus. Along the way, she had met a lot of Cowperites. 'Health, including aged care and NDIS, is by far our largest employer,' she said. 'The local health district has a footprint that's very similar to the footprint of Cowper. It encompasses Port Macquarie and Coffs Harbour and all of the smaller places in between, so I'm well known,' she says.

Voices for Cowper (aka V4C) had been established in 2019, inspired, as elsewhere, by Mary Crooks of the Victorian Women's Trust and Voices groups in Indi and Warringah. Between August 2020 and July 2021, it had held almost 50 kitchen-table conversations with 260 people between Port Macquarie and Coffs Harbour. Desire for a stronger connection with, and access to, its local member was the first finding. Heise was selected by a vote of 461 V4C members after an online V4C forum on Sunday, 23 January 2022.

It was late to launch a candidate. But Heise was surprised by 'how quickly we gained momentum', including more than 1000 volunteers and hundreds of thousands of dollars in donations between late January and the election. Those donations included accommodation for four regional hubs—in Port Macquarie, Nambucca Heads, Bellingen and Coffs—critical in an electorate of more than 7200 square kilometres. And one that is as diverse as it is large: from the migrant melting pot of Coffs itself—where the big blueberry long ago replaced the big banana, often grown on Indian, particularly Sikh, family farms—to Port Macquarie, where retirees predominate, via the farming community of Dorrigo, the more bohemian Bellingen and the holiday hub of Sawtell. As Heise says, 'It's a really tricky seat to actually get around, and to transition between the different cultures of the different towns.'

'The volunteer and in-kind support was next level,' Heise says. 'Some of them ran those hubs, some of them did mailbox drops, and doorknocking, and phone-calling.' Nor was it just volunteers. 'We had a meeting in the town hall in Dorrigo, a beautiful little farming community up on the plateau. I thought it might be interesting because there are a lot of traditional National Party voters up there. So I called this little meeting one night and 65 people turned up. It doesn't sound much, but it's huge. Some of those farmers are on struggle street, because of Covid and because of fires and floods. And they were saying, "The Nationals have let us down. They've turned their eye towards the big extraction industry, and they've taken their eye off the local people that are trying to keep communities alive and producing our food."'

Caz4Cowper not only took Climate 200 funding but was grateful for it. It 'was great, because you can do things like TV commercials and billboards', she said. 'But that stuff's never going to win you the seat, especially in regional areas where you need to win people's trust. It was the community's engagement that blew me away.'

In Groom, 500 kilometres north, the same considerations—who had the highest profile and broadest community reach—meant that it always had to be Suzie Holt rather than Meredith King who stood. As King volunteers: 'To be very pragmatic, Suzie had the social capital and existing networks that I lacked to start the ball rolling.'

The question arose because Voices of Groom, which King and Holt had set up after that initial Denis Ginnivan–brokered coffee, was another grassroots group that had been unable to find anyone willing to stand. Kitchen-table and other conversations had made it clear there 'was a mandate for an independent here', Holt says. A campaign vehicle was incorporated and they began beating the bushes. While 'a few people were kind of interested in running, none were interested enough', King says. 'In the end Suzie and I had a conversation and Suzie said, "Okay, well, if no one else is going to stand, then I will."'

'Part of the reason Miles [Holt's husband, Toowoomba anaesthetist Miles Brodie] and I started "Voices of" and agreed to run was that, even though we don't have a huge profile, we were both known because we're both in medical,' Holt says. 'We were using that social capital—it's a terrible way of looking at it, but we were using our medical contacts to get us over the line, including Miles being in theatre and being able to speak to nurses across four health services.'

Sandwiched between the federal seats of North Sydney, Warringah, Bennelong and Berowra, the electorate of Bradfield, on Sydney's upper north shore, is one of the country's most affluent, taking in Killara, Gordon, Pymble, Turramurra and Wahroonga. It is also another melting pot. Almost half its inhabitants were born overseas, including a significant Chinese Australian population, meaning that the pot had only become more molten as the Morrison government upped its anti-China rhetoric.

Towards the end of the second-last week of April 2022, I'm sitting in a Korean tea house in Westfield Chatswood with Sam Graham, founder of Voices of Bradfield, and the group's candidate, Nicolette Boele. As myna birds scream in the twilight outside, Boele is parsing the electorate she has lived in for 41 of her 51 years.

'So 46 per cent of the electorate's born overseas,' she says. 'Fifteen per cent were born in the Straits, Hong Kong or China, and another 15 per cent of Bradfield's Australian Chinese were born here to parents born in China. They stayed behind after Tiananmen, or more recently they've come as economic refugees, seeking a better life for their kids. Their motivations vary, of course, but they want to be able to go and visit their friends and family in China. They want to be able to trade with China. They feel the racism every day as citizens. You say "Dutton" and people shut up.'

Bradfield is also an electorate where people come to retire, Graham points out. 'We've got twenty residential care homes, which is almost twice the average you'd expect in an electorate. They're principally female, because they're outliving their partners, and traditionally conservative, but the lack of caring with this government's policies is too much for them.'

Boele and Graham first met at a European Union young leaders forum twenty years ago. They had been running into each other every five years since, before joining forces five months ago to try to oust their local member, federal communications minister Paul Fletcher. When we speak, they're about to head out—in wet-weather gear and 'Vote 1 Boele' T-shirts and wristbands—for another 6 to 10.30 p.m. stint, talking to commuters and late-night shoppers in the mall. 'He is Risen' banners punctuate the main drag outside Chatswood Chase. Graham and Boele aren't sure if their campaign is following suit, but they're certainly giving it a red-hot go.

The former executive manager of the Responsible Investment Association Australasia (RIAA), Boele is another accidental candidate. Like Jacqui Scruby, among others, she had previously worked at the intersection of policy and politics, including the Clean Energy Finance Corporation and the Climate Institute. But she'd given up on politics as a solution, she says, when Kevin Rudd announced in 2008 that his government's emissions target would be a 5–15 per cent reduction by 2020. 'I felt betrayed,' she said. 'We had had the apology [to the Stolen Generations] just a few months before. I thought, "This is it. We're breaking through."' When it didn't happen, 'I had what people now call climate change anxiety syndrome. It's like a number of people in the movement: we know the science; we're systems thinkers; we look at the interactions between what's happening and, if you're an empath, you can get sucked in and drown. That's why I went into capital markets and got out of public policy.'

Like Tink, she took a career break, in her case after six years at the RIAA, as 'part of the great resignation' that followed

Covid. 'It was time to move on,' she says. 'There are fantastically talented young people coming into impact investing, responsible investing. We'd set up the RIAA Human Rights working group. We had this cracking First Nations working group.'

One of Boele's last acts before leaving the RIAA had been 'congratulating the government on its 2050 target in the media, and suggesting it was not quite enough for business certainty and business planning'. Which made it seem like fate when she ran smack-bang into her federal representative after she had resigned.

'The universe put Paul Fletcher on Bobbin Head Road, where I'd just moved,' she said. 'There were a few people lined up to talk, and the man in front of me was very emotional. He was telling his grandkids not to have children because he was so fearful about the state of the planet, and I was thinking, "This is amazing. This is Turramurra—who is this guy?" When it was my turn, Fletcher looked at his watch. He was ready to go. But I said, "No, Mr Fletcher, please, I just have one question: I would like to know whether you, like Matt Kean, wish that you could have got a bill that offered a bit more certainty and targets that were closer, like 2030 and 2035."'

'"Don't underestimate how hard it was to get that 2050 target," was the reply,' says Boele, still incredulous. 'Of course it was hard! Barnaby didn't want it. But you also had a prime minister who had used a lump of coal as a prop in the Lower House. There had been no leadership. None.'

Boele had earlier been approached by Graham, who had founded Voices of Bradfield after a similarly dismaying meeting with Fletcher, and, sounding out Tina Jackson on what to do about it. 'But I'd just disconnected from politics,' says Boele. 'I'd worked in parliament. I'd had a lobby pass . . . it's too negative.'

Eyeballing her elected representative changed that, however, as it had for Scamps and Droga. 'I went straight back to my house and put in my expression of interest to Voices of Bradfield,' she says. 'I'm cranky at Fletcher because I didn't want to be a politician. He pushed me over the edge.'

Boele says she started with the aim of giving 'the people of Bradfield a choice'. But since announcing her candidature in late January, she's been 'staggered' by how she has been received: 'I've lived in an electorate most of my life where I haven't been able to talk about politics,' she says. 'Talking about those things wasn't something you did here.'

Three months into her run, she is 'breathless with the opportunity that now presents itself. When I hit the streets, people say, "This is a party that I voted for my entire life, but that I cannot in conscience vote for anymore." If I meet ten people, that's what seven of them tell me.'

The question, when we meet in late April, is how far she can get and how fast. A couple of weeks before, Morrison finally called the election, which will be held in a month's time. That day her volunteer ranks cracked 400. 'I'd like 600,' she says. 'Someone asked me if I could spend an extra $200,000 if I got it today and, yes, I've got a wish list. We'd get more dual-language people on the street. It all comes down to a 20–24 per cent swing. I'm not a former Olympic athlete or a football player. How do people know that I exist and that I'm a safe pair of hands? At the moment, it's about asking the people I meet. Six or seven out of ten go, "Thank goodness you're standing." It's that palpable. But they're the ones walking up to me.'

She and Graham start to get their stuff together for the evening ahead. A day that began with ABC Radio National at

6 a.m. will end around 11 p.m. Boele tried a catnap, but it didn't take. 'I was lying in bed and it hit me: "Fuck, this might actually happen,"' she smiles. 'It's my only point of agreement with our current prime minister: this is the most important election of our lifetime.'

~~~~~

Jo Dyer was crystal clear when we spoke a month before the May election: her chances of taking the South Australian seat of Boothby were remote compared to those of her comrades in east coast urban seats. But she was running in the state's most knife-edge electorate, held by the Liberals since 1949 nonetheless, because things had to change.

We were speaking the day after I talked to Boele and Graham, 22 April, a little over three months since Dyer, fresh from both her most recent gig as director of Adelaide Writers' Week and her very public advocacy in relation to the Christian Porter accusations, announced her candidature as a community-backed independent.

In that time, Dyer had cited as motivators everything from the 'existential threat of climate change' to her own experience campaigning for women's justice. But when we spoke, there was another factor she wanted to highlight: 'the level of just sheer frustration, if not rage, that exists in the Australian population at the moment; this really strong, fervently dismayed realisation of the extent to which we are being failed by our current political leadership. I think that is why there are so many ordinary people in so many seats who've said, "You know what? Fuck it. I'm going to put my hat in the ring, even if in some seats there's less chance of success."'

While Dyer does not say it explicitly, it's clear she is running, as she sees it, for the good of the game: backing change, and the groundswell that might finally bring it, above her own chances. She is certainly one of the most articulate commentators on the movement that started in Indi and blossomed after Steggall's 2019 victory; a movement without which, she says, she wouldn't have run. Before McGowan, 'running as an independent was a somewhat quixotic thing to do,' she says. 'We've all had that experience of driving past a lone corflute waving in the breeze.' But the McGowan 2013 and Steggall 2019 campaigns had both had 'another, mostly local, galvanising force' behind them, she says, the unpopularity of Tony Abbott in Warringah and Sophie Mirabella in Indi.

The 2022 campaigns were 'the first great attempt to take what have been really effective community grassroots campaigns, concerned with the idea of reviving democracy as much as particular local issues, and then extrapolate that out to the big national issues: climate and integrity in particular, and then a spotlight on some of the issues based around women and girls in relation to harassment, discrimination and violence.

'That's what I think both Cathy and Climate 200 have done so well: the sense that it's now or never, and "If not us, then who?", is real. I think that 2030 is literally two elections away after May and there's a sense that time is running out. People were losing hope that maybe we would get back on track. If there is a Coalition victory on 21 May, the chances of any kind of action on climate change in that closing window are zero. I think that level of frustration is a really powerful fuel behind a lot of this.'

In October 2021, as rubber was hitting the road in electorates around the country, Dyer had been approached by 'a couple of people', one of whom was Denis Ginnivan, to see if she'd consider running. Timing was everything, given she was committed to delivering her final Writers' Week in March 2022. 'If the election had been called for last year—and there was that moment when Morrison was contemplating not going to Glasgow, when everyone thought he was going to call a late November, early December election—I wouldn't have run. Only once it was clear that wasn't going to happen did I start thinking about it very seriously. I looked at the numbers and the idea that, within Boothby, there is a centre-left majority that just never seems to be able to translate into a progressive victory. Every election, Labor says, "This election will be the election that we win Boothby," and they never do. It was a combination of all of these things that made me take it seriously. Victory, winning the seat, would be a great victory, but I am very clear-eyed about my chances.

'If Labor wins the seat, then that, too, would be considered something of a victory for me, if preferences flow in the right way. Which is not in any way because I'm running as anyone's stooge or any of the other facile arguments the Coalition are attempting to mount because they're so terrified of the imminent loss of major blue-ribbon heartland Liberal seats. It's because in the end . . . the lesser of the two evils clearly for candidates running on climate and integrity is a Labor government. They actually believe in climate change and want to take action, have meaningful targets, are not quite as captured by the fossil fuel industry, and will establish a robust national integrity commission.'

In that context, Dyer said in April, an independent-heavy crossbench could enable faster action, given Labor 'would have the independents as a cover. There are a whole range of policies that would be much bolder . . . but which they have not been prepared to take to the election, because they're so terrified of the dark art of the wedge.'

9

TWO HORIZONS

The answer to Cathy McGowan's September 2021 question of how many community groups would mount their own campaign soon became apparent. Climate 200 ended up contributing to 23 campaigns in the May 2022 election.

And as 2021 turned into 2022, and those start-up campaigns began to proliferate, find their faces and gain momentum, two horizons opened up within the community-backed independents movement.

The immediate one was the looming election. The goal was to win the sort of leverage that would trigger action on various fronts, from integrity to gender equality, but most urgently on climate. The second horizon belonged to a deeper, longer and less visible game: encouraging and facilitating community participation in politics broadly.

The first horizon was the one Climate 200 was working towards. As Cathy McGowan said in January: 'Simon and his team are absolutely dedicated to doing something about action on climate change, and to do that, they need the balance of power. He's very specific, and he's very upfront about what he's doing.'

The second was open-ended, spanning not only electorates but elections at different levels of government: federal, state and local. This was where McGowan had decided to concentrate her efforts, she said in January 2022, with a particular focus on rural and regional Australia. 'I've picked six of them in the short term, which might come up to eight or nine, where I'm working closely with mostly the candidates to actually help them understand what you need to do to win. It's a journey that is longer than this election.'

'That's my passion,' McGowan said. 'How can I most influence long-term policy decisions in that area? It's gaining a huge amount of momentum ... the challenge is how to direct the momentum in a useful way, because it's a grassroots movement ... so encouraging people to be involved, and giving optimism.'

The second game embraced the first—what McGowan termed 'the pragmatic fact' that a federal election loomed—but continued beyond it. That made her long game not only about those who won seats but also about those who did the hard work and didn't. Or, as she put it: 'How do we give people the sense of the emotional return on their investment?' How did you ensure the long-term and short-term games worked together to complement, rather than undermine each other?

Right on cue, the tension between those imperatives began to manifest as campaigns geared up. McGowan's apparently simple comment in January 2022, that 'one of the technical questions is whether the community group can transition to a campaign', hid a multitude of risks. How, when and how cleanly a dot org morphed into a dotcom became a critical issue in 2022 campaigns. When that segue was seamless, things went smoothly. In Melbourne, for example, Goldstein's Project IndiGold became the vehicle for Zoe Daniel.

In Sydney, Wentworth Independents threw the keys of their corporate vehicle to Allegra Spender to drive. By March, Sue Barrett, the head of Voices of Goldstein's selection panel, was Daniel's campaign manager; while Lyndell Droga, who'd recruited Spender, found out during the week before we spoke in early March that she would be co-managing her candidate's campaign with Anthony Reed.

That had in no way been a given at the start, as Droga explained: 'We saw Wentworth Independents as a rocket launcher: the booster that gets it off the ground, then falls away. And that is what we've done—we've handed our company over; Wentworth Independents is now Allegra for Wentworth Pty Ltd, and the original Windies have become an advisory committee.'

North Sydney had a rockier transition, however. The incoming candidate established her own campaign vehicle, Kylea Tink Ltd, rather than subsuming North Sydney's Independent, which had originally selected and announced her. Along the way, tensions emerged between the Warringah-style dotcom campaign and its community, dot org origins.

One critical question was the balance the campaign should strike between focusing on getting the candidate elected versus assisting other campaigns, particularly as North Sydney was the first non-Senate campaign to be announced in 2021.

North Sydney was hardly alone in navigating the issue. Helen Haines had faced it after her election in 2016. 'Zali and I are quite different on this one,' she said when we spoke in June 2022 about the Steggall campaign's extensive outreach in the lead-up to the election. 'I didn't pay that much attention to trying to grow the independent movement. My focus during my first term [from 2016 on] was 100 per cent on Indi and being the best independent member for Indi that I could be. While I would happily take phone calls from people who were interested in running . . . and give whatever insights I could, I really did very little actively to encourage that.'

As to why: 'We're different people, with different goals and aspirations,' Haines said of herself and Steggall. 'And I won Indi on a tiny margin, 1.4 per cent; Zali [had] a much bigger margin up in Warringah, so maybe she had a little bit of wriggle room up there.'

For North Sydney, a related issue was the expense of, and potential return on, Reed's involvement. 'I have to say I didn't support Anthony's appointment initially,' Renata Kaldor says. 'He wanted this amount of money, and he was doing Warringah and he was doing Wentworth, which was a big one, and I thought, "This is ridiculous. How is he going to have time to do us?" My concern was we wouldn't be his main focus. But I have to say, in the end, Anthony was the right person. It was the right thing to do.'

You can see the attraction of a Warringah-style campaign organisation for a candidate such as Tink, a marketer by training who had been Australian managing director of global communications company Edelman before heading the McGrath Foundation and Camp Quality, and who was now putting all that on the line. As Kaldor said: 'We already had Kylea on board and Kylea wanted her own team around her.'

It highlighted an essential paradox of the 2022 community-backed independent campaigns: how could they fulfil the promise, particularly to volunteers and early adopters, of doing politics differently—democratically, consultatively and transparently—as they entered the realm of traditional politics: old-style, top-down, corporatised, tightly and centrally controlled?

By early 2022, Kristen Lock, North Sydney's Independent's founder, and Denise Shrivell, who had been handling communications, had decided to step back from the front line. 'Kylea's corporate separation from NSI mid-campaign came with risk; it could have been destructive, implosive even,' Lock says in August 2022. 'We'd expected she would either take over the NSI vehicle that had been prepared for the candidate or we would have a discussion much closer to, or even after, election day—not mid-campaign. But the gravity of the bigger goal, winning North Sydney, kept us aligned and moving forward.'

In the end, those involved agree that it worked out. The campaign achieved its dotcom goal on 21 May. And the dot org that is North Sydney's Independent was freed up to focus on the longer-term game, including the upcoming March 2023 NSW state election. 'Had we stayed tied tightly to Kylea's campaign, we would not have had this independent community machine ready to go for future elections at all levels of government,' Lock said.

Anna Josephson smiles when she talks about what became a key part of her involvement with the 2019 Steggall campaign. 'We spent a lot of time in Warringah, and I actually did personally, talking people out of running and into joining us,' she said. 'I drank a lot of coffee with people who were thinking about it.

Some of them were potentially great candidates, but we already had Zali.'

One of those potential candidates was former Turnbull adviser Alice Thompson, who would make a late run in 2019 as the only independent candidate in Mackellar that year. Jane Caro, too, considered running against Abbott but, after speaking to Louise Hislop and Kirsty Gold, 'mutually agreed that that was probably a risk they didn't want to take'. As she explained to me, 'I was happy with that, because I was in two minds. I'm fairly radical, particularly in the area of public versus private schools, and real-istically ... that's the deal-breaker for a lot of voters, because, tragically, they send their kids to private schools, and I'm fiercely of the view that this is a bad idea for the country.'

In terms of herding the cats running loose in Warringah in the lead-up to the 2019 election, many pay tribute to the stake-holder work of Julie Giannesini. The former Liberal Party member, who would go on to become Steggall's electorate officer, was critical in keeping all the various anti-Abbott groups and contenders informed and on track within the Zali tent. 'She was the one who got me into it,' Anna Josephson said. 'She became a conduit to make sure everyone was informed. Because it was a real people's movement. Groups could have chosen to support us in Warringah or not.'

The same kind of diplomacy was critical in Goldstein three years later, from forming that initial campaign team to keeping everyone on song as dot org turned dotcom. 'We really had to find our sea legs as a team, because everyone is very strong-willed,' Sue Barrett said in April. 'A lot of my work is stakeholder management, and people and culture. One of the challenges is that we have an embarrassment of talent here and everyone wants to have their say. Managing all of that is some-thing in itself. I'd say it takes up 50 per cent of my time. You have to keep people engaged, but also directed.'

~~~~~

That did not work out smoothly across all the campaigns, however. It's the end of March 2022 and I'm sitting on Station Street in Engadine in Sydney's Sutherland Shire, talking to the independent candidate for the Sydney seat of Hughes, Georgia Steele.

To a non-local, Hughes looks like a story that writes itself. Firstly, there's the candidate herself. A former commercial liti-gator, Steele is driven and articulate, saved by a ready sense of humour from the perfectionism evidenced in everything from her CV to her immaculate business attire—an orange suit, her campaign colour—and teal nails.

In 2018, after working as in-house litigator for a major bank during the banking royal commission, and with two kids under six, Steele took a career break. She started a Masters in litera-ture and, dismayed at the Morrison government's inaction on climate change, began volunteering for a couple of community groups, Hughes Deserves Better and We Are Hughes.

'I turned 40 and, when women turn 40, they grow their confidence,' she says as we sit outside her shopfront. 'I kept having visions of Scott Morrison at the lectern fondling a piece of coal, and thinking, "I could do better than that guy." All my female friends could do better. They're hopeless, these guys.'

One night, 'after a couple of glasses of wine', she floated the idea of running to her husband, who was at first incred-ulous, then supportive. 'I'd been working with [local] groups and reading everything I could get my hands on about political campaigns, including Ruth McGowan's *Get Elected*,' she says.

Steele also attended the first NSW Pathways to Politics for Women course, held at UNSW, which included Ruth McGowan and John Hewson. 'It was brilliant,' she says. 'It was selective— about 30 women—and you were taught how to be a political candidate: how to campaign, fundraise, everything you needed to know from campaigning experts, speech writers and CEOs of think tanks. Four women from the course got elected to local council in December.' Two more were running federally, Steele and Sally Sitou, who would win the Sydney seat of Reid from Liberal Fiona Martin.

When we meet in March, Steele and her family are all in on the campaign. The tall young volunteer inside, who is sorting signs and corflutes, turns out to be her husband, who's taken his own career break to support her. She also backed her 30 October 2021 candidacy announcement with her own money. 'An election was still possible in 2021 when I announced, and I have no profile,' she said of the decision to launch early. Since then, she has won the backing of Hughes Deserves Better and Climate 200, and has also raised significant funds. All up, the kitty will total $700,000, more than half of it from the community.

That broader fundraising has come from every seat around the country, driven by a second factor that makes the Hughes story seem to write itself: place. If every campaign is a reflection of its locale, few are as freighted with political significance as Hughes in 2022.

Craig Kelly has been the federal representative for more than a decade. The last couple of those years have been particularly tumultuous. Having been backed by Scott Morrison in the lead-up to the 2019 election, against a pre-selection threat from a Liberal moderate, Kelly denied any link between global warming and the bushfires ravaging Australia on UK TV in January 2020. A year later, he was spreading misinformation about Covid vaccinations, leading Morrison to defend him at a National Press Club address on 1 February 2021. 'He's not my doctor. And he's not yours. But he does a great job in Hughes!' the PM said. Three weeks later, Kelly quit the Liberal Party to sit on the crossbench. Six months later he joined Clive Palmer's United Australia Party as its parliamentary leader.

'I don't think Hughes would normally have come into play at this election, because of its demographics,' Sue McKinnon, founder of the unaligned local community group Hughes Deserves Better, told me in August 2022. 'It's outer suburban, the average income is good, but so is the median, with less stark wealth disparity than many other places in Sydney. And it's always tended to the status quo. Right now the social norm is to vote Liberal. It wasn't always. And it can change again in the future. What brought Hughes notionally into play was Craig Kelly.'

But it wasn't just Kelly. Hughes adjoins Cook, held by the PM himself. As McKinnon says: 'They might be two separate seats, but it's all the Sutherland Shire. People live, work, go to the beach, shop and identify with both electorates.' Home of the 2005 Cronulla race riots, the Shire is homogeneous, substantially white and has more churchgoers than average. Labor held Hughes after 1969 until it fell to the Liberals in their famous 1996 victory. And for the architect of that victory, John Howard, it always remained, as he said in 2001, 'special'—a mirror of his very particular version of middle Australia.

All of which made Hughes an epicentre in 2022. As we discuss why she decided to run, sitting on the park benches arranged outside her office like a fish trap for passers-by, Steele's eyes keep flicking across Station Street. Eventually I follow them to what it suddenly dawns on me must be Engadine McDonald's, where, as a plaque outside memorialises, on 'the evening of the 20th September 1997, Scott Morrison defecated in his pants after the Cronulla Sharks lost the Super League Grand Final'. A graffiti face of the PM—who denied the story, but only after letting it run long enough to bolster his everyman credentials—adorns the wall opposite, the words 'Engadine Maccas' scrawled across his forehead. Hallowed ground indeed.

But if Hughes looks too good to be true from an independent's point of view, it is. A couple of weeks after Steele's 30 October 2021 launch, the founder of We Are Hughes, Linda Seymour, announced she, too, would run as a community-backed independent.

Among other things, this is another dot org/dotcom collision. An architect and communications consultant, Seymour had been part of the March 4 Justice and the QT evening in Canberra at which so many of 2022's candidates and campaigns finally met. Through Tina Jackson she had also volunteered to coordinate the local chapter of Climate Action Now (CAN). And having arranged CAN T-shirts and pamphlets just in time for Covid to hit, Seymour was one of those whose activism was driven online. We Are Hughes became a 'Voices of' equivalent, holding kitchen-table and other conversations, on the advice of Denis Ginnivan who, with Kerryn Phelps, launched Seymour's campaign in November 2021.

'We Are Hughes was always going to run a candidate,' Seymour says when we speak in August. 'We had been working on selection for some time. The fact that another candidate announced was reflective of a vibrant democracy, but our process continued.' Steele, who had applied to We Are Hughes to be a candidate in May 2021, says she withdrew from that process due to delays and with an election potentially looming later in the year.

Regardless of how and why it happened, two community independents running was hardly ideal. A cautionary tale was unfolding in real time in early 2022 in what seemed from the outside a bellwether seat to rival Kooyong.

In retrospect, the ACT Senate race would seem perhaps the most strategically important independent campaign, generating not only a resounding win but also that all-important balance of power opportunity in the house of review. But if the upshot was as historic as it was emphatic, the path to victory was complicated, involving another contest between two independents and another dot org/dotcom dilemma.

Constitutional and citizenship law expert Professor Kim Rubenstein was the first of the two candidates out of the blocks. In fact, the distinguished ANU academic led the field nationally, given Rubenstein announced she would run in mid-August, a month before Tink.

Within a month of announcing, Rubenstein had the 1500 signatures necessary to form a party, Kim for Canberra, allowing her to appear above the line on the ballot paper, in a territory where almost 80 per cent of people had voted above the line at the previous election. By February she had raised close to $200,000, including $30,000 in seed funding from Climate 200, and gathered hundreds of volunteers. Her daughter and son had paused their own lives to organise volunteers and digital and social media, respectively. The latter included a snappy showreel of her appearances as a legal expert on ABC TV's *Q&A*.

She also had an impeccable foundation story. Rubenstein told me in September 2021 that she had become an academic precisely because of the independence it afforded her to be able to critique whichever party was in government. 'The last eighteen months have amplified the long-term problem in our political process,' she said, 'which is that the parties, no matter which party, have their own problems in managing internal party policy, and that has been a hurdle and a block to good policy being developed. I think we are at a moment where independents have not only the capacity to disrupt that in a positive way, in terms of forcing the parties to really deal with the pressing issues, but also . . . bring out the best in the parties.'

But another move was already afoot in the ACT. Clare Doube and her husband, Glenn Flanagan, had set up proACT, a 'Voices of' equivalent, after attending the February 2021 McGowan conference. A former accountant, Flanagan had analysed the results of the previous election across the ACT's 90 booths to get a picture of both the lower house and upper house voting patterns. Their goal was to 'identify where there might be a possibility', Doube says, their conclusion that 'the greatest chance for change in the ACT was in the Senate'.

The maths of the Senate, however, make it harder for an independent, requiring the successful candidate to gain more than one-third of the total votes in the whole territory. The ACT had returned one Labor and one Liberal senator at every election since 1975. This time around, however, Doube and Flanagan, like Rubenstein, saw potential in the polarising conservative Liberal incumbent, Zed Seselja.

In the country's most left-leaning jurisdiction—home to what the *Canberra Times* summarises as the country's 'most educated, vaccinated, politically literate and engaged voters'—Seselja had not only opposed same-sex marriage while representing a constituency that recorded the strongest Yes vote (74 per cent), and abstained from the final parliamentary vote, but also been Peter Dutton's numbers man in his 2018 bid to unseat Malcolm Turnbull.

Doube and Flanagan had spent early 2021 'testing the waters, asking people, "What do you think? Is there something in this?"' she recalls. 'The response was an overwhelming "Yes, there is potential for doing politics, not only differently, but better. Let's make this happen."'

The couple's Sunday afternoon kitchen-table conversations, initially consisting of ten to fifteen people, grew to about 400 people over the course of the year. One of the questions they asked was who people wanted representing them. In all, 26 names came up. But the most frequent—in a territory as sports-leaning as it is left-leaning—was former Wallabies captain, and climate and marriage-equality activist, David Pocock.

Bizarrely, given his sporting profile and political activism, Pocock said when we spoke in June that he had never been approached to run until proACT first contacted him in May 2021. 'Not personally,' he added: 'I've read that I was going to run for almost all the major parties.'

It makes more sense when you speak to him. Like many 2022 independent candidates, the self-described introvert seems more reticent and less inevitable in person than on paper. That wasn't his dilemma, though, when proACT approached him.

Pocock had joined top Japanese team the Panasonic Wild Knights after playing for the Wallabies at the Rugby World Cup in Japan in 2019. When Covid hit, the Japanese 2019–20 rugby season was cancelled and he returned to Canberra, devoting himself to what until then had been a conservation-and-agriculture side project. In February 2021, he and his brother left Australia for Zimbabwe to work on the project full-time, amid power outages and with intermittent internet.

'It's a great project that I think will make a tangible difference,' he said. 'When I was approached, we were cracking on with it, building on all the work that we'd already done, and it was going very well. I had to really weigh up what I wanted to put my time into. At the end of the day, it felt something that I would've regretted not having a crack at, given there are all these issues that are close to my heart and the ACT hasn't had the representation we deserve.'

He was, he said, 'approached by a number of people in the ACT' to think about nominating for proACT endorsement. 'Having thought about politics, I really have no desire to have to toe a party line that doesn't square with my values or with the community . . . The more I thought about it, the more it seemed like an opportunity to make the contribution I'd want to make.'

But proACT faced its own moment of decision. By August it was feeding its kitchen-table findings back to participants and finalising selection criteria. As Canberra went into lockdown from mid-August, it held online kitchen-table conversations and webinars, and finalised a six-person selection committee.

While there was pressure from some quarters to simply back Kim Rubinstein, the highly accomplished female candidate who had already declared her candidacy and cleared significant hurdles, proACT was committed to seeing its community-driven process through.

Online town halls, a feature of other campaigns such as Hume and Cowper, were held with each candidate in December 2021, viewed by 120 people each. Pocock and Rubenstein both presented and responded to questions. Viewers fed back to the selection panel, which then also interviewed both candidates. Pocock is understood to have been the clear favourite online, commanding support from three-quarters of those who provided feedback. The panel was unanimous. In mid-December he announced that he would be standing as a community-backed independent candidate.

Climate 200 funding followed. The organisation was 'very aware', Byron Fay said in July, 'that the community is broader than potentially just the kind of "Voices of" group', but proACT endorsement was 'obviously a good sign of community interest and support. The Senate's quite challenging. Kim had started early and was running a really solid community campaign. David's entry was obviously very high-profile and had a lot of potential, but he started later. We backed both campaigns, but it became pretty apparent to us that David was a real contender, and so that's where we put the lion's share of our support.'

Pocock says of Climate 200: 'We took funding from them initially to help set up and then, once it was clear that we were a real chance, they gave us more and more as we went along.

But we were very much running our own race. It was about the ACT, and all of our advice was coming from people who lived in the ACT, who worked in the ACT. [Climate 200] had no input on our strategy in terms of issues.'

As for running against another independent, 'I was aware that she was running,' he said of Rubenstein. 'I think it's great for democracy to have lots of good options for voters. Looking at the pathway, I didn't think that she'd be able to pull enough votes from where she would need to win.' Had he thought Rubenstein could do so, 'I potentially would've just . . .' Pocock trails off, before finishing with: 'It was pretty clear it potentially wasn't going to work that way.'

The challenge of Canberra was unique, says his wife, Emma Pocock, who was integral to both her husband's decision to run and the campaign: 'There is this perception that Canberra is affluent, it's where all the public servants live, but that hides huge variability in our population. It's the most expensive city in the country to rent and the second most expensive to buy, but we have real challenges with poverty and homelessness.

'The challenge to actually represent the electorate well looked quite different from some of the other successful independents' races, which tended to be in fairly affluent areas, which of course have differences across them, but not to the extent that a territory does. And no independent had ever represented the territory in the Senate. A lot of people told us it couldn't be done.

'You had to have exactly the right candidate, who could appeal broadly enough across the electorate that you could pick up votes from everywhere . . . Canberra's a very Labor town. You have to pull from [the Labor and Green] side of politics but also a significant chunk of the Liberal vote. And I think that was something that was exciting for us. We weren't running a politically partisan campaign. We were actually trying to build a platform that really represented the vast majority of Canberrans and had this political philosophy, which we've always had, that there's more that unites us than divides us.'

David Pocock adds: 'The media often lumped me in with the community-endorsed lower house candidates, but in reality I was running a very different campaign. The issues that seemed to really cut through and resonate in the ACT were around housing affordability, cost of living, territory rights, and climate and integrity. In a Senate race, you simply can't just run on climate and integrity. It's much more diverse.'

10

THE CRUELLEST MONTH

My interview with Dr Monique Ryan opens into laughter. Mine. As I hit the record button, Ryan said something, I don't recall what, you tend not to when someone sideswipes you with funny.

Of all the brilliant women who fronted independent campaigns in 2022, Ryan is perhaps the most accomplished. She is also the most amusing. Faced with the dual imperatives of authenticity and positivity that each candidate has to balance in 2022, she has clearly opted for authenticity.

Take her aside to Melissa Fyfe in a *Good Weekend* profile in July as she ponders what handover material Josh Frydenberg might leave in his old electoral office, which she is in the process of taking over: 'I'll be lucky to get more than a packet of prawns in the air-conditioning vent,' she says, glasses perched atop what one volunteer called Ryan's 'unelectable' hair.

Then again, why pussyfoot around when your old day job was life and death? 'It sounds grandiose, but a bad day for me is when I go to work and a child dies,' the former paediatric neurologist tells me. 'I know I can do this. I look at [my Liberal opponents] and this sounds arrogant, but I think a lot of them are not that bright.'

It's Monday, 11 April, the day after Scott Morrison finally called the election. That Sunday, 10 April, was also coincidentally the day a flurry of independent launches wound up. Ryan's was at the former Hawthorn Town Hall on the Sunday night, a few hours after Zoe Daniel's official launch in a park in Sandringham. Rob Priestly's rally at St Paul's African House in Shepparton had been the Friday night before; Allegra Spender's the day before that in a hotel ballroom in the harbourside Sydney suburb of Double Bay.

If that sounds coordinated, it wasn't. Kooyong wasn't even aware that the Goldstein event might clash when I rang to check times a week ahead. It was just that no one could afford to wait any longer.

'April is the cruellest month,' T.S. Eliot wrote of the northern spring a century ago, new growth pushing through dead ground in the wake of the war to end all wars. In Australia, of course, April is autumn. But *The Waste Land*'s opening line kept coming back to me, like a gag, watching the convulsions of mid-April 2022, as the election turned real, the independents launched into campaign mode and the government redoubled its defence. The question was to whom April would be cruel in the end: the incumbents, or their shiny-faced disruptors? Were we watching the former's autumn? The latter's spring?

The independents' makeshift headquarters didn't give many clues. When we meet, the day after her launch, Ryan and her team are camped out in yet another defunct bank—Westpac this time. Not a dollar had been wasted on repurposing. The candidate and her team are spread across former managers' offices and interview rooms like squatters. Or a nest of vampires, which is pretty much how the Liberal Party has come to view them.

Hawthorn is arguably the new ground zero for the community-backed independents, much as Manly was when the movement first emerged in 2019. This is Kooyong after all, a seat held by the Liberals and their predecessors since Federation. And, unlike Warringah, which was held by a former leader and conservative warrior, this one has been held for twelve years by a man considered by many to be not only a future leader but also the future of the party.

Kooyong isn't just home to Josh Frydenberg, though. A few minutes' drive along Glenferrie Road, Simon Holmes à Court lives in the Federation bungalow from which he first approached the treasurer as a constituent five years earlier. These days the Ryan corflutes in Holmes à Court's front yard are part of a pitched battle being waged—street by street, corner by corner—across the electorate. Ryan's corflutes predominate: small, guerrilla enough for apartment balconies and windows, they're the physical equivalent of the digital ads upon which her campaign has focused its resources on the advice of Ed Coper of Populares.

The big billboards at major intersections are Frydenberg's. All up, the treasurer will reportedly spend $2 million to $3 million, more than double the budget for his 2019 campaign, on advertising that includes billboards, cinema trailers and sandwich boards on paid workers. That spend keeps Ryan's face off prime sites at major intersections such as Camberwell and Kew junctions, 'where nine-metre-wide billboards featuring Mr Frydenberg's face dominate the suburban skyline', as the *Australian Financial Review*'s Patrick Durkin reported in

March. The approach of the Ryan campaign is, again, guerrilla: they rent the ground-floor shopfront of the same building
that carries Frydenberg's billboards above its second storey and
plaster it with Ryan's face.

The face-off underlines the fact that, as Simon Holmes
à Court later tells me, 'the Kooyong demographic is not your
grandfather's Kooyong anymore'. That shift plays out across the
opinion pages of *The Age* ten days after my visit. On 21 April,
former Victorian Liberal premier Ted Baillieu writes a piece
spruiking the Morrison government's credentials for meeting
'unprecedented challenges' post-Covid that Australia has 'not
seen since World War II'. In it, Baillieu contrasts that 'tested'
leadership with the independents' 'limited experience of political or civic engagement'.

'The energy around these independents is coming not from
the candidates but from the money spent on those campaigns,
and ugly trolling on social media,' he writes. 'Candidates are
hardly seen or heard. They have campaigns but no answers.'

A day later the former premier's 24-year-old son, Rob
Baillieu, a volunteer manager for the Ryan campaign, strikes
back. In an opinion piece titled 'My father was Liberal premier,
but I can't support his party', Baillieu, who is gay and an army
lieutenant, argues that the Liberals' commitment to small-l
liberal values had collapsed due to greed and infighting.

'In 2016, I was encouraged to work for a "moderate" Liberal
Party MP,' Rob Baillieu writes. 'The notional interview was one
of the most homophobic experiences of my life. The climate
scepticism, sexism, and disregard for basic scientific principles
didn't help. If these are the moderates, who on earth are the
conservatives? As the son of a Liberal premier, I could be in

the mix . . . running a Liberal MP's campaign. But I can't . . . I don't want to be rich, nor powerful, at the expense of others . . . I don't claim to be a good person. But I'm trying to be, and that's more than I can say for many modern Liberal Party MPs.'

In case the generational punchline is missed, the same paper reports on the same day that a record number of people had enrolled to vote, led by 80,000 eighteen- to 24-year-olds.

~~~~~

In truth, the blue ribbon that once held Kooyong safely in place had been coming adrift for a while. In 2019, barrister (and former Coalition voter) Julian Burnside had received the highest non-Liberal, two-party-preferred vote there in almost a century (44.3 per cent). At the same election, Frydenberg's first-preference vote fell below 50 per cent for the first time, despite the Liberals having reportedly doubled their campaign spend to $1 million in anticipation of the threat.

A redistribution two years later, in 2021, added parts of Surrey Hills and Glen Iris, cutting the Liberal two-party preferred margin from 6.7 per cent to 6.4 per cent. And while Frydenberg was a local son, his unrelenting criticism of Melbourne lockdowns had sounded by all accounts like attacks on his home town rather than its premier, from a man Ryan would label 'the treasurer for New South Wales' in their Sky News debate.

Climate 200 calculated that, in 2022, 20,000 people would vote in Kooyong who had never voted there before: one-third of them newly registered young people; one-third, people who had recently moved into the area; and the remaining third people newly redistributed to a seat that had already registered a strong progressive vote in 2019.

The night before I met Ryan, I got talking to two nurses in their fifties at her campaign launch in the sumptuous Second Empire hall of what's now the Hawthorn Arts Centre. One was a lifelong Liberal voter who fondly remembered both Fryden-berg senior and junior, and whose family had long been friends of John Howard's. She had been brought to her first Ryan event by her old friend, an equally rusted-on Labor voter. As they bickered companionably about past differences, they were now united as never before in their support of Ryan.

But when I see Ryan the next day, hope remains provisional despite the flux apparent everywhere. The TAB will shortly firm the treasurer's odds from $1.65 to $1.45, with Ryan's increasing from $2.15 to $2.65. The candidate has heard, too, that the Liberal Party still has something horrible up its sleeve for her and is waiting for it to drop. That aligns with the prevailing wisdom, as exemplified by a Tony Windsor tweet a few days earlier, which warned that the current independents should 'beware the last week because, if you are a threat, that's when they'll really pile it on. You'll be accused of being tied up with the Nazi party in Ukraine, or with Putin.' Windsor will repeat this warning when the last week dawns.

There had already been a couple of tasters. The first, in *The Australian* newspaper four months earlier, revealed that Ann Capling, 'director of the campaign to oust Josh Frydenberg', had been named in a WA Crime and Corruption Commission nepotism probe six years earlier. The investigation had actually been into the person who recruited her as provost of Murdoch University, rather than into Capling herself, and the watchdog had explicitly stated that its findings 'should not be read as adverse to Professor Capling's abilities or suitability for appointment'.

Cross currents: swimming groups like Manly's Bold and Beautiful were typical
of the community networks that fed into independent campaigns.
(Amanda Grant/Bold and Beautiful Swimming Squad)

Crossbench MPs Rebekha Sharkie, Julia Banks, Kerryn Phelps and Cathy McGowan
exit the chamber after the final question time for 2018. (Alex Ellinghausen/Nine)

Climate 200 founder Simon Holmes à Court addresses the National Press Club in Canberra on 16 February 2022. (Lukas Coch/AAP)

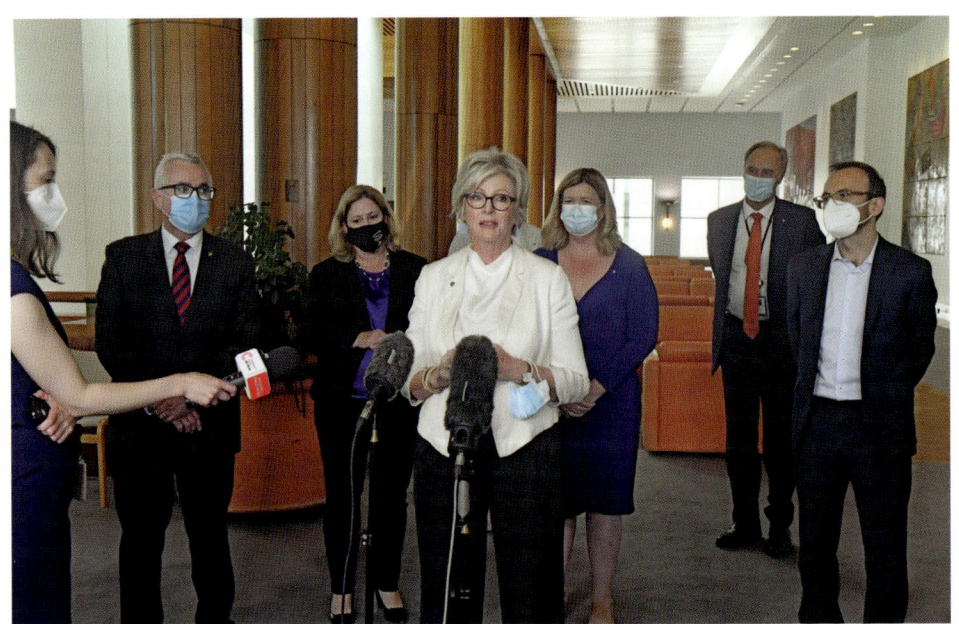

'The 46th Parliament is coming to a close, and this government has failed . . . the nation on integrity,' member for Indi Dr Helen Haines (pictured addressing the press) told the Parliament on 17 February 2022. 'I will never stop bringing this to the attention of this House, even in the dying days of this parliament.' (Mick Tsikas/AAP)

The godmother of the movement, former Indi MP Cathy McGowan, was everywhere in the lead up to the 2022 election, helping to get the proliferating community-backed independent campaigns she had inspired from good to winning. With Allegra Spender at the Truth + Trust event at the North Bondi SLSC on 4 April, the night McGowan realised how much trouble the Coalition was actually in. (Allegra Spender/Instagram)

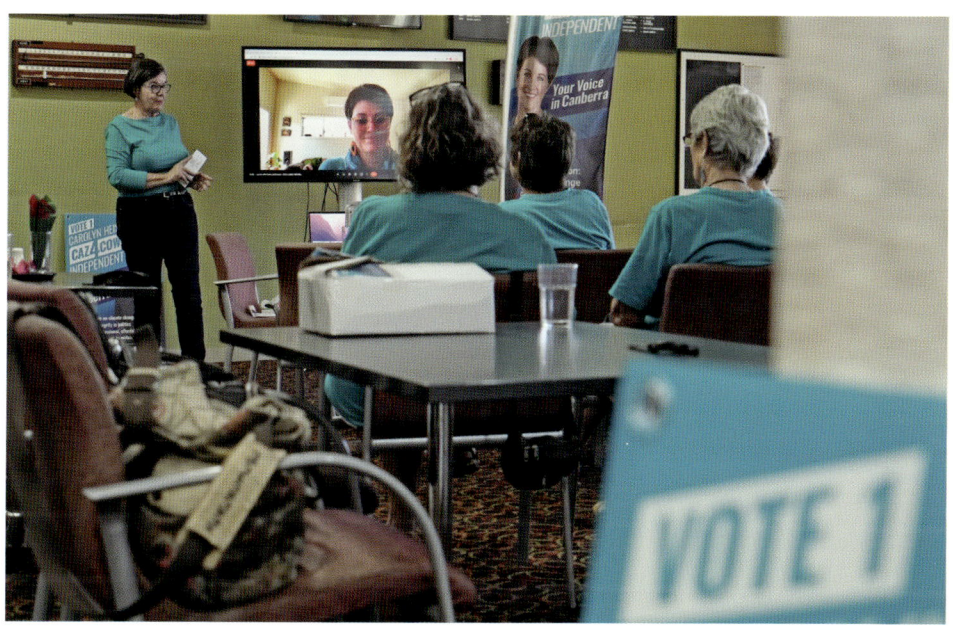

McGowan delivering a masterclass to Cowper independent Caz Heise (on screen) and her volunteers. (Erin Semmler/*Australian Story*)

Matt Murfitt addresses a Politics in the Park event in Hume in late March 2022. The Vote Angus Out campaign, founded by Alex Murphy and Murfitt, garnered support from around the country. (Matt Murfitt)

Independent ACT senate candidate David Pocock addressing locals and volunteers, who would eventually number 2200, at a Politics in the Park event in Watson, Canberra, 27 March 2022. Pocock had to decide how and where to concentrate his efforts before running to create history in 2022. (David Pocock Election Campaign)

Independent Groom candidate Suzie Holt's community outreach was surprisingly effective, from the early 'kitchen-table conversations' that inspired her campaign to the subsequent heated public rallies that won her respect across the political spectrum. Holt (right) at a 'Conversation and Coffee with your Candidate' session in early April 2022. (Suzie Holt/Instagram)

Stirring a mixing-pot electorate: local businessman and independent candidate for Nicholls, Rob Priestly, with his wife Sonia at his 8 April campaign launch at St Paul's African House in Shepparton, Victoria. (Daneka Hill/Country News)

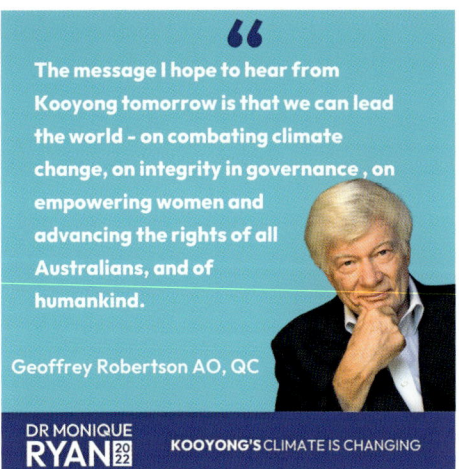

The message I hope to hear from Kooyong tomorrow is that we can lead the world - on combating climate change, on integrity in governance , on empowering women and advancing the rights of all Australians, and of humankind.

Geoffrey Robertson AO, QC

DR MONIQUE RYAN 2022

KOOYONG'S CLIMATE IS CHANGING

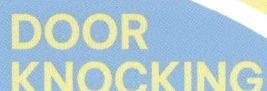

DOOR KNOCKING

DAVIDSON
Thursday 12 May meet at 4.00 to 6.30 Kambora Reserve, Cnr of Kambora Ave & Borgnis St Davidson

FORESTVILLE
Saturday 14 May meet at 2.00 to 4.30 Wombeyan St Reserve opposite 6 Wombeyan St, Forestville

BEACON HILL
Sunday 15 May meet at 2.00 to 4.30 Gilles Reserve, 28 Gilles Cres, Beacon Hill

INDEPENDENTS **MAKE LAWS** PERSUADE GOVERNMENTS **+ STAND UP** FOR THEIR COMMUNITIES

We need Affordable Childcare

DAI LE VOTE LOCAL

Daile.com.au

Borrowing from corporate marketing and cutting-edge US political campaigns, 2022 independent campaigns were digitally primed as never before, as Populares co-founder Ed Coper later trumpeted, upending old orthodoxies. Clockwise from top left: Instagram tiles from the 2022 campaigns of Dr Monique Ryan, Dr Sophie Scamps, Dai Le and Allegra Spender.

Caz Heise, independent candidate for Cowper, chats with her supporters and volunteers at a cafe. (Caz4Cowper/Facebook)

Waterworld: Independent candidates Allegra Spender (Wentworth), Kylea Tink (North Sydney), Zali Steggall (Warringah) and Dr Sophie Scamps (Mackellar) against the backdrop—environmental rather than Liberal blue—that featured in many campaigns. (Oscar Coleman/Nine)

In marked contrast to their political competitors, the independents moved it like it mattered at Mardi Gras 2022. Left to right: Spender, Steggall, Tink and Scamps. Equality was a key plank of independent campaigns that drew inspiration from the 2017 marriage equality debate and 2021's March 4 Justice. (Ash Berdebes)

Political differences replaced fence disputes in Goldstein, as neighbours declared their colours for independent Zoe Daniel (left) and Liberal incumbent Tim Wilson (right). Few knew what a corflute was before 2022. But Cathy McGowan's rallying cry that whoever had the most tended to win turned them into a major battle front. (Benjamin Crone/Alamy)

Walking the talk: Jo Dyer, independent candidate for Boothby in Adelaide, and her supporters made climate a kerbside call to action. Like doorknocking, mass sign-and-corflute waves helped convince voters in a way that surprised even the campaigns themselves. (Jo Dyer/Instagram)

Putting some faces to a name: On 11 April 2022, the candidates and volunteers in North Sydney (top) and Wentworth (bottom) lined the streets with corflutes. The show of human, real-time support proved much more persuasive than expensive traditional advertising. (Bianca De Marchi/AAP; Allegra Spender/Twitter)

Candidates for Kooyong, federal treasurer Josh Frydenberg (left, Liberal) and
Dr Monique Ryan (right, independent) debating on Sky News, 5 May 2022.
(Andrew Henshaw/AAP)

The fight between Ryan and Frydenberg, perhaps the bitterest of 2022's battles,
resulted in a silent vigil by Ryan volunteers when a campaign mural was painted
over a week before the election. The treasurer's huge paid ad on the building's
roof would prove no match for a thoroughly galvanised community movement.
(Chris Hopkins/Nine)

Independents' corflutes were defaced or replaced by groups that included conservative lobby group Advance Australia with stickers and fakes that suggested Labor and Green affiliations. While the AEC would eventually declare the signs breached the Electoral Act, the accusations proved less damaging than those making them may have hoped. (Top to bottom: Peter Kelly/Twitter; Dr Sophie Scamps/ Twitter; Elesa Kurtz/Canberra Times/ACM)

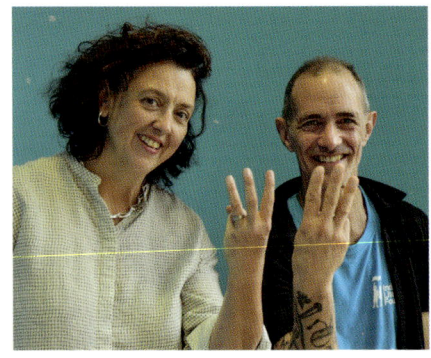

Celebrities and media personalities turned out big time for the independents, whatever the risk. Top left to bottom: Simon Baker braves the rain for Allegra Spender at a polling booth (Allegra Spender/Instagram); Dr Monique Ryan and Andy Griffiths support the It Takes 3 campaign in April 2022 (Dr Monique Ryan/Instagram); Lime Cordiale play Pied Piper at Dr Sophie Scamps' Election Beats concert in May 2022 (Dr Sophie Scamps/Instagram); Zali Steggall with Blak Douglas, winner of the Archibald Prize, in May 2022 (Ash Berdebes).

Dai Le talks to voters at a polling booth in Fowler, Western Sydney. Dai Le had the sort of grassroots community support that tended to carry the day in 2022, defeating star Labor candidate Kristina Keneally. (Dan Himbrechts/AAP)

'5 p.m. in the carpark of uncertainty'; independent candidate for Curtin, Kate Chaney, with Tony Fairweather and Sarah Silbert at the end of election day. (Tony Fairweather/No Fibs)

Dr Sophie Scamps (middle right) with her campaign manager, Jacqui Scruby (middle left), and volunteers at a polling booth in Mackellar. (News Ltd/Newspix)

A still-incredulous Zoe Daniel, independent candidate for Goldstein, delivers her victory speech on election night surrounded by family and supporters. (Joel Carrett/AAP)

Political scientist Dr Ann Capling (centre), campaign manager for Dr Monique Ryan (left), celebrating as the wave washes over Kooyong, carrying the treasurer away, on election night. (Louis Trerise)

Downstairs at the same venue, volunteers at Ryan's election night party rejoiced as Capling shouted out the booth results as they came into the improvised tally room upstairs. (Joe Armao/Nine)

Newly elected MPs arrive at Parliament House for their first day, on 14 July 2022.
Left to right: Dr Monique Ryan, Zoe Daniel, Kate Chaney, Kylea Tink, Dai Le,
Libby Watson-Brown (Greens member for Ryan, Queensland), Dr Sophie Scamps
and Allegra Spender. (James Brickwood/Nine)

Day one of Doing Politics Differently: independents (left to right) Daniel, Chaney,
Ryan, Spender and Steggall confer during their first session in the House of
Representatives, 27 July 2022. (Lukas Coch/AAP)

Then on 4 March, News Corp's other Melbourne publication, the *Herald Sun*, had given Ryan both barrels. Titled 'Ryan's Labor of Love', the front-page splash was subtitled 'Election "cleanskin" exposed/Independent candidate's hidden anti-Lib, pro-ALP past revealed'. Ryan had once been a member of the Labor Party, it disclosed, only quitting twelve years previously, in 2010, the year Frydenberg first won Kooyong.

Worse: 'The *Herald Sun* can now reveal Dr Ryan continued for years to support Labor's leaders in a string of effusive Facebook posts, while also sharing anti-Liberal Party memes, attacking Coalition minister Peter Dutton as "Toxic Potatohead", and blasting Malcolm Turnbull's asylum-seeker policies as a "national disgrace".'

What hurt, Ryan tells me, was that access must have been given to the paper by someone she knew, given that the posts were to friends only. In every other way the story was a godsend: 'In a week in which half of New South Wales and Queensland was under water and Russia had invaded Ukraine, they put an unknown independent on the front page of the country's highest-circulation paper,' she says, still incredulous. 'That was three pages of advertising I could never have afforded.'

When I visit, the piece has its own altar, pinned across the tea-room message board. 'It was a great way to raise Monique's profile at a time when our polling was showing that we still really needed to,' Capling later told me. 'It also gave permission to the progressive left of Kooyong to vote for Monique, that she was safe. And then the Liberals just kept hammering the message home with mailouts. It cost us $20,000 to send a flyer as unaddressed mail. And the Liberals put pictures of Monique in people's mailboxes a number of times. They did our campaign work for us.'

Dealing with what Capling calls 'The Hun piece' was where Populares was invaluable: 'What Ed [Coper] was crucial on was how to deal with shit that came at us,' she says. 'And his advice was that we couldn't buy advertising that good.'

The Kooyong campaign also purchased Populares' marketing data, allowing them—like Warringah and Wentworth—to understand block-by-block demographics. 'We knew we could also target our messaging, but we decided not to,' Capling says. 'For me, targeting was a bit cynical. It was more important that we knew our electorate read *The Age*, watched ABC and SBS, so that, when the Murdoch press turned dirty on us, we just stopped responding to their daily requests.'

From the moment the election date was announced, the momentum shifted, however. As Capling later explained, 'We told each other the gears would shift when the election was called. But we didn't know what we meant, because none of us had ever been involved in an election campaign at this level.'

That shift had pluses and minuses. 'The downside is we now understand how the Liberals are going to campaign,' Capling told me on 23 April, a few days after Guide Dogs Victoria CEO Karen Hayes featured in a Frydenberg video endorsement and letterbox drop that would lead to her being stood down. The upside, however, was seismic. 'Volunteers literally poured through the doors, saying, "Where can we sign up? What can we do?"' Capling said. 'They were literally signing up by the hundreds each week.' In the end, the Ryan campaign, which started with 600 legacy volunteers, thanks to Oliver Yates's 2019 campaign, would reach 2000, and doorknock every accessible property in Kooyong, plus part of the neighbouring electorate of Higgins by mistake.

Their inspiration became a mash-up of Cathy McGowan's campaign-trail refrain that her victory had come down to 500 votes, and the old Zen proverb 'Before enlightenment: chop wood, carry water. After enlightenment: chop wood, carry water.' 'We had these Weekends of Action, with wild targets like 5000 houses, and we always met and exceeded them,' the campaign manager recalled. 'And the way we campaigned didn't feel like politics. It genuinely felt like community. And you could feel that happening by the momentum.'

'The doorknocking crew really took that to heart,' Holmes à Court says of the campaign down the road from him. 'It's funny. Talking to strategists early, they'd said don't bother about doorknocking. They said it had a very, very low success rate.' Anthony Reed is upfront when we speak, admitting that he had been one of the naysayers initially. It would prove one of the great lessons of 2022: talking to people in the flesh, in real time, where they live, really matters.

Mantras keep the candidate focused, too. 'The only stress I have out of all of this, apart from physical fatigue, is the stress that it matters so much,' Ryan says in April. 'We just chop wood, carry water, 500 votes. Every day that's what we do. And my personal mantra is that I'm just swimming in my own lane.' Ryan has continued to attend squad training three or four times a week at the Hawthorn Aquatic Centre, handily located directly behind the Glenferrie Road HQ. 'I'm a swimmer; I'm happiest and most relaxed in the water. When they come at us and say, "She's a fake independent, she's a Labor stooge," what I see is that incrementally we're making progress.'

In that context, the ballot draw on 22 April, in an Australian Electoral Commission district office near Camberwell Junction, took on a special significance. 'It was the weirdest thing,' Capling recalls. 'Josh bounded in and did his hail-fellow-well-met thing and Mon, Julia [Ryan's diary manager] and I were sitting there barely able to breathe with anxiety. They blindfolded the AEC official and asked if anyone wanted to crank the machine. We nudged Mon, so she went up. She crossed herself I think, which is a reflex from her Catholic schoolgirl days. Anyway, she gave the handle a crank and she came out number one on the ballot. Mon said it was the first time in her life she'd ever understood what going weak at the knees meant.'

The Australian Electoral Commission representative then called out the other ten candidates ceremoniously, one by one. 'We were right behind Josh and I saw his hand clenching into a fist behind him as they went. He was drawn seventh. There was no more hail-fellow-well-met after that. He got the hell out of there.'

The three women followed. 'We got outside and checked nobody was watching and then screamed and jumped up and down like schoolgirls.' They 'grabbed two bottles of champagne, took them back to HQ and gathered everybody together for a scream and a toast and a laugh. It was the first moment of levity we'd had. It lasted half an hour and then we got back to work.'

~~~~~

That feeling of mounting community will, and corresponding Coalition desperation, would crystallise a week before the election at a literal crossroad. Five main roads meet outside the boarded-up Junktion Hotel in Kew. A new message had gone up a fortnight earlier on the vast double-sided digital billboard that crowned the corner building. 'Keep taxes low. Keep Josh,' it begged, reportedly at a cost of more than $10,000 a month.

'It's the vibe of the thing,' *Age* associate editor Tony Wright quoted Frydenberg as saying in an 8 May piece, by way of explaining how 'the Treasurer of Australia, deputy leader of the Liberal Party and member for Kooyong—an electorate famously held for 34 years by the founder of the Liberal Party and Australia's longest-serving prime minister, Robert Menzies'—could find himself in such political strife that he has to contemplate defeat.

'There is an air of disbelief to his musing,' Wright noted. 'It is the sort of affronted disbelief ricocheting around other wealthy Liberal-held electorates, among them Wentworth in Sydney's east, Curtin in Perth's oceanside west and Goldstein on Melbourne's bayside.' As Wright and the treasurer walked through Hawthorn's Fairview Park as the sun set, 'many of the walkers offer him best wishes', he noted, adding: 'No one needs to tell Frydenberg that winter is on its way.'

Which may explain some part of what happened next. 'We couldn't afford billboards, so we decided to do a mural,' Capling recalled in July. Damien Hodgkinson had secured verbal permission from Junktion's owner, Jon Adgemis, a friend. The muralists had got as far as a portrait of Ryan and the words 'Active Hope', against a backdrop of blue sky and clouds, when they were stopped after the owner insisted he'd not formally permitted the work.

The next morning, the Saturday a week before the election, Capling got a text. 'I ran down in my pyjamas and saw they were painting it over,' she said. Climate 200 had given some technology to the Kooyong campaign that enabled it to 'text all of our volunteers instantly, so I texted to come down to protest the removal of our mural'. In less than an hour, 250 people had gathered to stage a vigil across all five corners on a rainy Melbourne Saturday in Ryan T-shirts, under Ryan umbrellas, carrying those handily sized corflutes.

'I never cry, but I cried that day,' Capling said. 'I was amazed at how many people turned up: young, old, everybody in between. People were saying, "I've never done anything like this before," and so many cars honked their horns. It was such a formative, galvanising moment for both our volunteers and the broader community.'

11

SURFING THE WAVE

In early April, the attacks on the independents' integrity and credibility turned serious. Under the headline 'ABC "independent" candidate Zoe Daniel backs Palestinian agenda', *The Australian* 'revealed' on 6 April that Daniel had 'signed an open letter accusing the Israeli government of unleashing "a brutal war against the besieged population of Gaza"'. The day before, the same journalists reported in the same paper that one of Allegra Spender's backers, Blair Palese, had spoken on social media about Australia's 'shocking support of Israel in killing unarmed children and civilians', sharing articles and tweets advocating a Sydney Festival boycott over of a $20,000 grant from the Israeli Embassy.

The Daniel story went on to quote 'Liberal MP for Wentworth Dave Sharma, who is facing a challenge by Ms Spender', as saying 'there was a pattern on Israel emerging among the independent teams. "This seeming pattern of anti-Israel views amongst the Climate 200 so-called independents is concerning and demands an explanation," said Mr Sharma, who was formerly the Australian ambassador to Israel.'

It mattered because it mattered. Anti-Semitism is indefensible; the accusation of making an anti-Semitic slur itself a slur. It also mattered because just under 7 per cent of Goldstein's population identified as Jewish in the 2016 census. In Wentworth, the figure was 12.5 per cent. Either percentage could be the difference between victory and defeat if the Jewish population proved any more monolithic than the rest of the electorate. 'Security is the primary issue for the Jewish community,' says Spender volunteer Annette Guerry, who is Jewish, like her friend, Evelyn Foltyn, and Lyndell Droga's husband, Daniel, for that matter. 'It's in our DNA: where will we go if Australia chucks us out?'

Though not Jewish, Sharma was 'very conversant and comfortable with the issues; he doesn't have the whole of that 12 per cent, but he's probably got about 10 per cent', said Guerry, who was doing some community lobbying of her own with Foltyn in March. There was a lot of quiet outreach going on in both campaigns at the time, including via Goldstein's demographics and community activism expert, and founder of The Sensible Jew blog, Alex Fein.

And some not so quiet outreach, too, including Daniel's apology a few days after her election launch for both the open letter and a 2017 ABC article, in which she said that then US president Donald Trump had in part declared Jerusalem as Israel's capital as a way of 'satisfying his wealthy Jewish donors'. The 'mischaracterisation of Jewish people, including myths such as their enjoying outsize wealth or power, must be identified immediately as the starting point for much worse', Daniel wrote.

Palese replied to the claims against her in an opinion piece in *The Guardian* a few days later: 'This week I was shocked to discover myself on the front page of *The Australian* and other Murdoch-owned media, where I was accused of being anti-Israel,' she wrote. 'It was a shock because, while I've been targeted for years for my climate change work, I have never been the target of a politically motivated hit job designed to undermine the independent candidates I support.'

These successive Australian strikes came less than a month after Andrew Bragg's comments to me highlighting his 9 February speech on '"independents" and anti semitism' in the Senate. To Holmes à Court, the main target of that speech, 'weaponising false accusations of anti-Semitism is itself anti-Semitic'. And to Voices of Goldstein's Sue Barrett, such accusations had real and local consequences. 'I will never forgive the Liberal Part for putting my family, Zoe's family and other people at risk,' she says. 'We hadn't had anything up until then, the occasional anti-vaxxer, but nothing to worry about. The Liberals were absolutely hell-bent on taking us down. Zoe got a lot of terrible trolling, death threats. I got trolled on social media, but someone also found my business email address, which I wasn't using for the campaign, and sent [messages] saying, "We're watching you."'

Zoe Daniel's Goldstein election launch four days after *The Australian* publishes its story looks like a bust twenty minutes before its scheduled 11 a.m. start. In a ballsy move, it's being held outdoors, at Trey Bit Reserve, next to Sandringham Football Club. Ballsy not because of the weather, which is post-card-perfect. More because the team is worried, after the recent controversy, that only 800 people have signed up to attend. Trey

Bit is looking huge and empty far too close to kick-off, the water of Port Phillip glinting in the distance, a bluer shade of teal, on an unseasonably hot autumn day.

There's a smattering of carnival tents for merch and tech, and an empty stage. Its backdrop is the new Goldstein message being unveiled that day: 'Same Is Not Safe.' Shadowed into each of the huge purple letters is the independents' secret weapon, Scott Morrison's grinning mug.

Organisers have been nervous they won't be able to get plausible numbers. While people trickle in, it's hardly a stream as I get talking to a Brighton East local, Chris Kortge. The 64-year-old joined Voices of Goldstein last year and has been volunteering with the campaign a day a week since December, calling to thank donors. 'Four words,' he says when I ask what had motivated him: 'Morrison and Barnaby Joyce. Where is the federal ICAC? Where is the action on climate?'

Kortge is another independents supporter whose eyes were opened overseas, including a decade living and working in Germany and the UK. 'Australia is a beautiful country, but it's not "The Best Country in the World",' he says, referring to the PM's default slogan. 'We're backward in so many ways. What the Germans do is for the good of Germany in the future. What we do is for the next news cycle.'

A working-class boy by birth, the former financial services executive voted Labor before turning to the Liberals. More recently he's become a disillusioned donkey voter. 'People have been putting up with huge amounts of shit from their politicians, but they won't any longer,' he says. 'I'm one of them and I'm not willing to be quiet anymore. Even if this independent move fails at this election, it's not going away.'

By the time we look up again, ten minutes later, something magical has happened. Trey Bit is suddenly as full as a country fair. 'Friends, can you feel the change in the air today?' Angela Pippos asks, warming up a crowd that already risks heatstroke and includes Ian McPhee, a former Fraser minister and member for Goldstein, and former Hawke and Keating minister Barry Jones. 'Today we have the chance to make history . . . as a community we are saying we will not be taken for granted anymore.'

Daniel gives a fiery speech, backed by a choir of supporters notably younger than most of the audience. 'Thank you for finding your voices and for helping me to find mine,' she begins. 'Thank you for being part of history. Because make no mistake, we are on the brink of great and optimistic change.'

'It would be much easier for me not to do this,' Daniel continues. 'I didn't aspire to be a politician. Instead of fending off hit jobs in the press and grappling with the toxicity of politics, I could be running my own business, taking my kids to [sport], walking the dog and hanging out with my husband.'

Then comes some very local code. 'I feel so fortunate that this experience is affording me the opportunity to build so many strong and enduring friendships with so many different people from many different backgrounds . . . [including] our Jewish community who have contributed so much,' Daniel said. 'Hate speech has no place in Australia. Holocaust denial has no place in Australia. Nor does the co-opting of the trauma of the Jewish community for political gain.'

The crowd at the launch, estimated at 1500, almost double those registered and more than double her candidacy launch four months earlier, suggests the controversy has done little to slow Daniel's roll. 'Without getting caught in the bubble of my own positivity, I think I've got a pretty good radar for momen-tum,' she says when we meet the next day. 'The momentum is there. It's just a question of the length of the runway.'

By that she means the time she has left. 'As an independent, you're starting from zero and you have to get to a hundred in a very short space of time,' she says. 'We know about 27 per cent of people are politically disengaged and we know 10 per cent of people make their decision in the queue on the day. So how can you at least create some awareness among them? It's about being out and talking to as many people as possible; getting signs up and getting T-shirts out there. It's phone banking, street-meets, car stickers and social media and billboards. Because I'm up against a six-year incumbent in an electorate that's always been blue-ribbon Liberal.'

That Liberal, Tim Wilson, had done his bit to help. The Assistant Minister for Industry, Energy and Emissions Reduc-tions had written to local party members in February, urging them to dob in Daniel campaign signs that were allegedly unlawful before the election was called. Climate 200 launched a donation drive on the back of the controversy, raising 'a hundred grand overnight', Daniel says. Overall, the Daniel campaign would raise $1.5 million, $450,000 of it from Climate 200.

'One thing that is really interesting is that the engagement with my campaign is across the political spectrum: there are a lot of disillusioned Liberals, [but also] pragmatic Labor and Greens voters who know they can't win the seat and are voting or volunteering for me,' Daniel said. 'It's the disruptor thing. They're like, "Do we want to stick with what we've got here or change something?"'

How that disruption is being reported is another interesting phenomenon to someone who isn't just a former journalist but also a former US correspondent. 'I would never compare myself to Donald Trump, obviously, but I covered [his] election and administration, and I think that there are some parallels in how the media's grappling with this independent movement,' she says. 'Because it's a disruptor movement, they don't really know how to box it. Is it a thing? Or is it just a flash in the pan?

'The initial coverage was all the novelty, which was exactly like Trump descending the golden escalator [in Trump Towers to announce his White House run in June 2015]. Everyone said, "He's just a joke candidate, it's a side show." But the momentum that then swung in meant the media realised something was actually happening. They didn't catch up with it in time. They still thought Hillary Clinton was going to win even on the day. I didn't, because I was out talking to actual humans in inland America, so I was very confident Donald Trump would win in 2016.'

Simon Holmes à Court's home office is where trophies go to die. A rocket launcher stands on the mantel; on the desk is an elegant kinetic sculpture by Melbourne artist Arthur Ganson, *Machine with 22 Scraps of Paper*. Its base is a cat's cradle of pistons and wheels that keeps those scraps rising and falling in sequence, like a flock of undulating birds. Or the 22 campaigns Climate 200 is helping to stay aloft in early April 2022.

Also on the mantelpiece is a small bottle, which turns out to contain an air sample from Hawaii's Mauna Loa Observatory.

The carbon dioxide in that tropical air was 397 parts per million back when it was captured. 'Before industrialisation, we were at 280. It passed from 300 through to 400 about five years ago, now it's 417,' he explains. 'One of the first things Angus Taylor said to me was, "You know, we're going to zoom straight through 500." I thought, "Not if I can help it, we're not."'

Each piece in his Wunderkammer marks a moment. Like the early Macintosh on a table by the window. 'I invested in Apple in 1992,' says Holmes à Court, who was nineteen or twenty. 'It seemed a silly thing to do at the time, but it worked out all right.' Not all are hits. What looks like a Hot Wheels car turns out to be a memento mori of a punt on the electric car company Better Place. Launched in 2007, in response to World Economic Forum founder Klaus Schwab's question 'How do you make the world a better place by 2020?', Better Place filed for bankruptcy six years later.

The Tesla charging peacefully in the yard outside his window is a reminder of how brutally a good idea can fail to translate. But Holmes à Court has no such worries about his latest venture, Climate 200. 'We're supporting 22 candidates,' he says. 'Someone put it to us about two months ago that coming second in 22 campaigns would not feel that good the day after the election; we really had to focus. That kicked something off in me, so now 70 per cent of our focus is on the top seven seats. That's not at all saying all seven will get in, but we want all seven to be in a position where we've done everything we can do to help them win. Obviously, most of it's up to them. So we do effectively have two tiers of support, and it's probably graduated in the second tier.'

Climate 200 polled those top seven electorates—Wentworth, North Sydney, Mackellar, Curtin, Kooyong, Goldstein and

Canberra—every three to four weeks in the lead-up to the election. When we speak on 11 April, that month's poll, which will show a critical uptick in support after the election is called, is still in the field. But it's already clear that the 'top seven to a dozen [campaigns] are on a track to be able to get over the line,' Holmes à Court says, adding that 'whether they do or don't on the night is somewhat out of anyone's control'.

He knows there will be a correction. 'The spread always narrows in the final weeks, people become more likely to go back to what they know. Undecideds become decided, and you see the gap close. We're not going to see 56 to 44 national TPP [two-party preferred] for Labor on election day,' he says, referring to a recent poll. 'And Josh [Frydenberg] dropped below 40 per cent in our polling in March; in fact, every poll since we started. He is not going to finish under 40. The question is, will he go above 44 or 45?'

He is nevertheless sufficiently sanguine to have made a significant decision. 'We decided recently that we're not putting Climate 200 to sleep after the election, like we did last time,' he says. 'It lived for just six weeks then, from the time we registered it on 6 April. We probably only started fundraising a week later. It was a tiny, tiny experiment.'

With state polls looming in New South Wales and Victoria, the political action committee he, Byron Fay and others built was eyeing other opportunities to level the playing field and support candidates whose policy platforms align. The move had been inspired by the way the independents had already influenced political debate. In early February 2022, the federal government had restored ABC funding to 2018 levels. That restoration had been a major platform for the new independents, as it had for their predecessors, from Rebekha Sharkie and Helen Haines to Zali Steggall. Later in the same week, five moderate Liberals, including Trent Zimmerman and Dave Sharma, had crossed the floor to strengthen protections for gay and transgender students under the federal government's contentious suite of religious discrimination bills.

And both of those developments had followed what Holmes à Court cited as a clear win for the independents in general, and for Mackellar's Dr Sophie Scamps in particular: Morrison's December 2021 announcement that he was ending the Petroleum Exploration Permit 11 (PEP 11) that allowed offshore oil and gas exploration along Sydney's northern beaches. That decision—which would turn out to have been made by Morrison as Resources Minister rather than as PM—was largely due to pressure from Mackellar MP Jason Falinski, who was joined for the announcement by Trent Zimmerman and Dave Sharma. 'To a certain extent, we've already won,' Holmes à Court said, echoing another refrain heard across campaigns in April.

The decision not to mothball Climate 200 after the election marked a real moment. The two horizons that Cathy McGowan had identified when we spoke a few months earlier, in January—Holmes à Court's immediate ambition of achieving climate action at the 2022 election, and her own longer-term project of involving people more broadly in their democracy— had now become one. It may not have been a dead cert that the revolution would happen in 2022, but if it did, Climate 200 was going to do its level best to make it perpetual.

Not that the election that had been called the day before Holmes à Court and I spoke was not still vital. As he observed, 'A few people have said, "Look, this movement doesn't finish on election night; you will have got so far that people have got a taste for it." But it'll be hard to do it again if we don't have any success.'

~~~~~

The Lyndell Droga I meet in late April isn't the Lyndell Droga of seven weeks earlier. It's three weeks after the campaign's election launch, and 'Allegra for Wentworth Pty Ltd', as Wentworth Independents has been renamed to reflect the shift of gear (and ownership), hasn't just turned the corner, it might be on the home straight.

It's 27 April, the day Spender overtakes Sharma for the first time on Sportsbet, firming to $1.80 from $1.95 overnight, while the incumbent falls back to $1.90. It won't last. Sharma will inch back to $1.85 to Spender's $1.87 on the eve of the election, as part of the ceremonial narrowing of margins that is widely expected.

Getting to this point, though, has not been without its casualties. That day, Droga forgot to check if her son made it back to school for the second term of Year 12. Her husband, Daniel, had to interrupt one of her meetings to check he had the date right. 'It's fair to say I've neglected my family,' she says sheepishly.

But for the moment Droga has allowed herself a single indulgence, a teal pedicure, on her way to our chat. She's out and proud in sandals on a still-cool evening. 'It's the first week I've felt really excited, that this could happen,' she says.

Nor is it just the chicken entrails of Sportsbet. In the campaign's view, Spender had held her ground against the incumbent in a 21 April Sky News debate. And while she'd only come fifth at the ballot draw the next day, that was two spots higher than the incumbent, who came last.

The ballot draw seemed a milestone, though not as big as the one that came the next day. On Friday, 22 April, Spender, Droga, Daniel and the campaign's media wrangler, Max Koslowski, also Jewish, attended a combined Passover and ANZAC service at the pluralist Temple Emanuel on Ocean Street, Woollahra, near Sydney's Centennial Park. Sharma entered the event to find his challenger not only officially invited but also ensconced at the front. And while Senior Rabbi Jeffrey Kamins had mentioned the sitting member first, he also acknowledged the 'elephant in the room': 'I want to also obviously acknowledge that Allegra Spender is here,' Kamins said. 'I think everybody has seen her face along with Dave's face around this electorate, so I know you would recognise her and so I want to welcome each and every one of you.'

It doesn't sound like a big deal, but it was. The 'conservative' Australian Jewish Association president, David Adler, had told the *Sydney Morning Herald* a fortnight earlier that Jewish voters in Wentworth were as divided on who to support at the coming election as the wider electorate. But a 'surprising' proportion of Jewish voters were backing Spender, said Adler, who gave the independent candidate his tick of approval.

The acknowledgement was enough of a boost for the candidate and team to celebrate it with their first glass of wine together at the nearby Hotel Centennial afterwards. 'There was a father by the door, tying up his little daughter's shoelace,' Droga recalls. 'As we entered, I heard him whisper, "Look, that's Allegra Spender."' As they'd walked through, a table of dining women jumped up, came over to tell Spender they were hosting corflutes and volunteering. 'It was just magical,' Droga says.

The mood continued with the campaign election launch on 7 April. MC Emma Alberici introduced special guest David

Haslingden, who had run Fox global television businesses, including 'all of Rupert Murdoch's TV channels', as Alberici told the audience, drawing catcalls from the crowd collected in the Ritz-Carlton ballroom.

Haslingden and his wife, Alexa, had, in fact, been drafted into Wentworth Independents in June 2021 by the Drogas, who are old friends. The catcalls ended as the man Alberici described as 'one of Allegra's strongest supporters' started laying into her competitor's 'modern Liberal' credentials: 'Mr Sharma's bid for re-election rests on a piece of logic that even *Catch-22*'s Milo Minderbinder would be proud of,' declared Haslingden, the embodiment of old-school media power in an impeccable black suit. 'On the one hand he argues he can't achieve his goals unless he's in power, and on the other hand he argues that to stay in power he must set aside his goals. Well, that's just not good enough.'

'That's right!' someone in the audience shouted, as Haslingden continued. 'There is a second string to Mr Sharma's argument. He says that a vote for Allegra or for any independent is a lost vote because, the way politics works in Australia, change can only be delivered by the major parties. But it is absolutely not the case. The Grattan Institute and others who have taken the time to go back and do a comprehensive assessment of policy initiatives in Australia over the last decade will tell you that exactly opposite is true. The best opportunity for policy change arises when independents are on the floor of parliament, and they have the leverage to pursue those policies.'

The candidate herself then took the stage. 'We are here for one reason . . . to win Wentworth,' Spender said, launching into her least polite performance yet. 'These are uniquely challenging times, I agree with the prime minister on that,' she said, citing issues ranging from security and inflation to climate change. 'Our response to these . . . must be leadership that is driven from the community because Wentworth is telling me that we need a leader who consults with the experts not with donors. We need to govern for the community not the party . . . the current member, he might be a nice guy, but he says he's not willing to stand up for this community. He needs to get out of our way.'

~~~~~

That week-long bubble would be burst, however, by a YouGov poll in *The Australian* on 10 May. The PM had by then segued seamlessly into campaign mode, his natural element. Opposition leader Anthony Albanese, on the other hand, had been unable to recall the Reserve Bank of Australia's cash rate and the unemployment figures. A combination of the looming election and Albanese's fumbles had shortened the TAB's odds on a Coalition victory from $3 a month earlier to $2.35.

The real shock of the YouGov poll, however, was for the independents. Based on a survey sample of almost 19,000 voters across all 151 lower house seats, it was billed as 'the most comprehensive poll ever conducted in Australia'. And while Ryan and Daniel would prevail 'if an election was held today', political editor Simon Benson declared on *The Australian*'s front page, 'over-hyped predictions of a "teal" sweep of moderate Liberal-held seats by an army of left-wing independents aligned under Simon Holmes à Court's Climate 200 banner would fall well short of expectations, with the Coalition retaining the three inner-city Sydney seats of Wentworth, North Sydney and Mackellar, which were also considered to be under threat'.

The four 'sitting independents, Zali Steggall, Helen Haines, Andrew Wilkie and Rebekha Sharkie, all elected under previous platforms but now laying claim to Climate 200 sponsorship, would be re-elected', Benson wrote. But 'only two of the 15 new candidates listed under the Climate 200 banner . . . are likely to be elected based on current voting intention'.

Independents' campaigns had become inured to prediction, not least from News Corp. But Anthony Reed's advice was to take the poll seriously, particularly as it wasn't the only one casting shade at the time. A survey for The Conversation suggested on 23 March that Sharma led 51–49 on a two-candidate basis with a primary vote of 42 per cent. A 9 April piece by the *Sydney Morning Herald*'s Michael Koziol cited that finding and reported that 'a Liberal source familiar with the party's internal polling' had said 'they were confident Mr Sharma's primary vote was "holding up well"'.

For Spender, balm of sorts came via another survey by The Conversation's Wentworth Project a few days later. The third and final instalment of focus-group research on 'soft' voters in the electorate (eight of the fifteen surveyed had not yet decided their vote) found that almost all agreed on one thing: Spender had run a better campaign than Sharma. That was significantly more than in the second round at the end of April. While focus groups are an attitudinal, rather than predictive, guide, Spender had 'gained momentum and there was a mood for change', Michelle Grattan wrote.

Interestingly, some people in other campaigns had questioned Spender's commitment when she had gone quiet after her November 2021 launch. It later turned out that she had taken a break with her family, as had been arranged with the campaign when she agreed to run. And from the minute she hit the trail, the intelligence and work ethic she brought to the campaign surprised even those managing it. As for the fledgling candidate, 'I've begun to really enjoy it,' she assured me on the couple of occasions I ran into her with that trademark slightly sad smile. Turned out she really did like people.

Her schedule was gruelling, though, as it was for all candidates. In addition to a constant stream of punter events and fundraisers, Spender seized every community opportunity. She swam in the North Bondi Oceana Classic. She ran—an activity she describes as her 'happy place'—around Bronte with 250 people from the 440 Run Club at 5 a.m. on Saturdays. And while Steggall, Tink and Scamps all entered fully into the spirit of the March Mardi Gras parade, only Spender truly danced like nobody was watching in her rainbow skirt.

As her later election launch would confirm, she had even found some vestige of an inner mongrel. The ABC was recording when the mic cut out at a March 'Politics in the Pub' event at the Charing Cross Hotel in the Sydney suburb of Waverley, the hour late and the room heaving with well-lubricated supporters and Allegra tourists. As the audience waited expectantly, Spender tried her version of shouting, but the punters just hollered for more volume. Frustrated, she raised her voice further, reaching the point at which she stopped being polite and became commanding, just as the sound kicked back in. 'I'm fighting a really hard election,' she said when what had become the question of the moment for independents—why they wouldn't declare all donations in real time—was put to her. 'I know that I need a lot of money to do that. Donors have come up to me and said, "Look, I can support you, but I can't do this publicly because I have a contract with the government, I'm on a government board, and I know that if I stand up and do this publicly, that will come under threat.'"

Droga later admitted that, hearing the waiting crowd, she wasn't above psyching the candidate into the zone with some version of 'Listen to that—it's you they want, go get 'em!' But as the campaign progressed, an increasingly palpable momentum carried them all. And as a pre-poll opened on 9 May, the machine swung into action. 'The last fortnight was joyous,' Droga recalls. One supporter gave up her office space in Bondi Junction, which became a warehouse for merch and corflutes and tape. A triage team ran a truck delivering emergency campaign supplies.

On the Thursday before the election, the campaign held the last of its 'banner waves', the displays of gyrating corflutes that had become a signature of the urban independents' campaigns. As Spender arrived at Edgecliff Station, the volunteers broke into 'Allegra', sung to the tune of 'Cecilia'. Cars honked. Droga cried. The candidate looked overwhelmed.

The emotion was an exotic mix, led by relief, Droga recalls. 'We had delivered: Allegra had done all she could, the volunteers had done all they could, we had all delivered for Allegra. We went into two weeks of pre-poll and the volunteers went into overdrive at every single polling booth, covering them in material, packing it away at night and doing it all again the next day. It was addictive. You'd go into the office and you'd say, "I'm just going out to the booth," and then you just wouldn't leave. Allegra was there all the time, as was Dave Sharma and his chief of staff.'

~~~~~

223

Collaroy Beach had a surf club even before it had a name. Built before World War I, to protect the growing hordes of sea bathers and surfers, the old clapboard shed has been replaced over the decades by a conglomeration of sun-bitten concrete boxes. Late on a Saturday afternoon at the start of April, the upstairs hall is buzzing as Mackellar holds its latest Meet the Candidate event.

This time around, Dr Sophie Scamps is being interviewed by SBS journalist and fellow sports parent Felicity Davey. The pair sit on a stage, with their backs to floor-to-ceiling glass onto the beach. It's only ten days since her first public outing, but Scamps is already at ease as she speeds through her origin story—running, records, Cathy Freeman, the fact that the most googled thing about her is her Wallabies husband—before getting to the meat: 'This election is going to be the most crucial of our lifetimes,' she tells an all-ages crowd of young parents with little kids, older teenagers, older adults. 'In Mackellar we have voted loyally for a government that wasn't representing our values for twenty years,' she says. 'I'm a mother. A lot of us have enjoyed a world that was safe and secure. I'm worried about the future we are leaving our children.'

Behind her, surfers zigzag back and forth on the heaving brown swell as if it's a piece of interpretative dance. Run-off from the northern NSW floods has turned the sea a light shade of sewage. As for the surf, it's the result of the third east coast low in a row, says TV chef Ed Halmagyi, who is again moonlighting as volunteer MC and tech guy. 'There's never been two east coast lows in a fortnight,' he says.

The next day, the *Sun-Herald* reports Scamps' call for a parliamentary inquiry into the health impacts of climate change, citing the postponement of a lifesaving championship due to a gastro outbreak resulting from the flooding. The accompanying picture of Scamps with a Mackellar local, veteran surf champion Tom Carroll, emerging from the water with boards under their arms, had been taken at one of the regular 'Surfing with Sophie' events. Scamps surfed with friends anyway on Fridays, says Jacqui Scruby, adding: 'We were looking at ways of not disrupting her exercise routine but still giving people access to her.'

For the Mackellar campaign, the major challenge was always going to be to raise Scamps' profile to a level where she was competitive with a less polarising incumbent than Tony Abbott in a seat that was close to, rather than exactly like, Warringah. Jason Falinski was a comparative newbie, having taken over from Bronwyn Bishop in 2016, but he held the seat on a comfortable 13.2 per cent margin. As Anthony Reed said in June: 'The community engagement work that Anyo and Sophie did with Mackellar Rising was really fantastic and important. But the campaign had to be perfect. We really had to promote her heavily. By the end, we were number two across the country in digital advertising. We invested heavily in Mackellar.'

The broader campaign, too, pulled out all the stops. 'If you'd told me what we would end up doing beforehand, I wouldn't have believed it,' Jacqui Scruby said. 'At the beginning volunteers were hesitant to wear a T-shirt. By the end, they were competing with me, and I wore Sophie's T-shirt every day, much to my family's horror, from December the 5th. Even my nails were blue and yellow.'

All up, Mackellar managed to attract more than 1200 volunteers, of whom about a third were 'very active, consistently turning up', Scruby says. 'I was also astounded at the way, when it was required, people self-organised and completely ran particular aspects of the campaign, like doorknocking or letter-box drops. It was incredible.'

As in Kooyong, the power of doorknocking—the ultimate, labour-intensive, hand-tooled form of engagement—proved a revelation. Even to Louise Hislop, who had done it in Warringah. 'We had decided early on that we weren't going to spend a lot of time on doorknocking,' she said post-election. 'It's a lot of work to speak to not too many people; advertising is a lot more effective. But it literally sprang out of the campaign itself. Someone else had experience and ran a training session. The volunteers were so enthusiastic and committed that the group just grew and grew, to the point where we had doorknocked a really high percentage of the electorate by the election day.'

In Wentworth, too, there would be a late doorknocking push in the final weeks. Again, initial advice had been that the effort outweighed the benefit. The campaign also lacked training and capacity. But with some quick tutelage from Climate 200, the campaign managed to roll out almost 100 volunteers, who doorknocked 15,000 houses, mainly in the central-west of the electorate, from Paddington to Surry Hills, in less than three weeks. 'I'd start with that next time,' Droga says.

More broadly, the way the multiheaded beasts that were community campaigns no sooner learnt something than they mastered it would become a major lesson from 2022—and potentially for those who might face such campaigns in the future. 'Banner waves' became another staple of urban campaigns. Mackellar's first go in Beacon Hill in April had been 'a huge logistical exercise', Scruby recalls. She only found out how effective it had been, however, at pre-poll, when 'people kept coming up and saying, "Oh, I'm voting for Sophie. If that many people can stand on the side of the road and wave a banner, she must be good."'

Scruby rang the campaign's volunteer leader and said, 'Look, I know you're all overworked, but do you think we could do another banner wave just before the election?' They were able to do it instantly because they'd done it before.

That final banner wave, at 7 a.m. on 20 May, stretched 3 kilometres. 'It was raining that morning and I thought, "This is going to be terrible,"' Scruby recalls. 'It was just pissing down as I started driving the van, but there were all these people, happy as Larry, waving banners. They weren't miserable or begrudging. They were dancing in the rain on the side of the road.'

It was less than the campaign had originally hoped for. Its homepage plea had been for 200 volunteers to cover 7 kilometres. But it did the job. The same went for what would become the centrepiece of the campaign, the Election Beats concert ('Dr Sophie Scamps speaks truth to youth in Mackellar') on 1 May, featuring Angus and Julia Stone, Lime Cordiale and Sons of the East. They were 'bands that sell out concerts within minutes all around the world', as Scruby says, but time and council limits on crowds meant they couldn't push things too far.

'Lime Cordiale came to us and said, "We want change, we've never really been politically active, but we're willing to do anything we can." The first idea was that they'd jam in a local park and people could come and listen. But then they involved Angus and Julia Stone, and a couple of other bands. We pulled together a whole huge event, council approvals the lot, in two weeks. To have those people supporting Sophie and what she was standing for, and being able to reach young people in a way that spoke to them, that was definitely the highlight of the whole campaign.'

∿∿∿∿

There are a couple of striking things about the Mackellar campaign as it hits its stride in April and May. The first is how low-profile it remains, compared to more celebrated urban campaigns such as Wentworth or Kooyong. 'We were very much under the radar the entire time,' Hislop recalls post-election. 'I had Covid on election day and I was flicking between ABC and Sky News all day, and they were talking about the seats to watch, and Mackellar was not mentioned once.'

The second is that, on the ground, it gives off an unmistakable whiff of impending victory even in early April that is all the more striking for its underwhelming start. Scamps hangs around at the Collaroy Surf Club event until she has spoken to every lingering punter, even me. She looks exhausted, but she leaves no constituent unturned.

Which means that by early evening she is already running late for the fundraiser in her honour 25 minutes' drive up the highway in the hills of Clareville. Money is reportedly an issue on both sides of the battle for Mackellar at the time. An item in *The Australian*'s Margin Call column a couple of weeks earlier reported Scamps telling a late-March fundraiser—at the Newport home of Harris Farm Markets founder David Harris—that she had received $1 million in donations but needed as much again to remain competitive.

'Liberal polling currently puts Falinski ahead in Mackellar but not by an enviable distance, according to campaign sources,' the piece continued. 'Perhaps this is what motivated a hastily convened fundraiser on Tuesday night with Treasurer Josh Frydenberg, a donor-magnet who happened to be in town and agreed to partake in a spot of gladhanding on very short notice. Falinski's minimally circulated invitation sounded promising: a 'private and limited dinner' with Frydenberg at an 'exclusive event' that would offer guests 'unparalleled access' to the treasurer.

The Scamps team denied the $1 million campaign hole. Still, the sold-out Clareville 'Soirée with Sophie' on 2 April is hoping to wedge about $20,000 into whatever gap remains. Again, the weather gods are smiling as it begins. After weeks of rain, it's a blindingly golden sunset as I run into the host, Richard Proctor, assembling banners outside his and his wife Eva's house, hidden from the road.

The 61-year-old retired fund manager turns out to be the man who led Mackellar's doorknocking campaign. It's something he had done in Warringah with GetUp! in 2019 to try to dislodge Tony Abbott, for whom he had once voted. Eva, who had been involved in Mackellar Rising's kitchen-table conversations, then got him involved in Mackellar.

The couple spent every weekend for months with up to 90 volunteers, doorknocking a total of 18,000 houses. 'Recruiting volunteers to get political for the first time in their lives was surprisingly easy because of the frustration they felt,' he said. 'And the people we spoke to really appreciated it, because it had never happened before in Mackellar. They'd never been approached by any political party before. The LNP hadn't bothered because they hadn't needed to.'

Even in early April, the reaction is already 70 per cent positive. 'It's definitely building,' Proctor says, before being called away to greet the arriving guests. 'We're sensing a real mood for change. Women especially are saying they want to see the back of Scott Morrison and the LNP.'

After he goes, I stick my head into what is already beginning to look suspiciously like a victory party. Newcomers literally dance through the open door as a band plays and the sun flames out on the huge deck suspended above Pittwater.

It's already apparent that there is, as Proctor later recalls, 'a real buzz in the air'. Silent-auction bids prove bullish, Scamps is on fire as she promises the audience a future where people and their environment are the priority. The night ends with Eva Proctor on the ukulele, singing her own version of Dragon's 'April Sun in Cuba'. The uke is in tribute to Scott Morrison's tone-deaf evisceration of the boomer classic a month or so earlier on *60 Minutes*. But Proctor's version has a new title, and refrain. 'Sophie's going to Canberra,' the chatelaine sings.

12

HARD YARDS

Of all the melting-pot electorates, none seems quite as molten as Nicholls in Victoria in the first week of April. Formerly called Murray, for the river that traces its northern border with New South Wales, Nicholls is something of a paradox.

Classed as rural, it's the second-safest National Party seat in the country, held on a margin of 20 per cent by well-liked former AFL footballer and coach Damian Drum. But it centres on one of Victoria's largest provincial cities, Shepparton, a regional-services hub.

So while it's tempting to project a tale of rural decline, walking into the office of local independent candidate Rob Priestly, in the shell of an abandoned bank, it isn't true. Diagonally opposite Priestly's office on Shepparton's main drag is the spectacular new $73 million Architectus-designed Shepparton Law Courts. Five minutes down the highway is the even newer and equally spectacular $50 million Denton Corker Marshall–designed Shepparton Art Museum. The rusted iron that clads both is a purely architectural element.

The hoarding around the Maude Street Mall, too, means renovation rather than neglect. As does the fencing around an empty block on the next corner, crawling with Bobcats and wreathed in dust. Every second shop has a 'help wanted' sign in the window, a skills shortage that extends to GPs and aged care. 'There are farmers here that are having extraordinary years, profits beyond their wildest dreams at the moment,' Priestly says. 'A good friend, who's a grain grower, had his best year two years ago. And this year will be double that.'

For all its energy, in early 2022 a lot still hangs in the balance for a seat situated on the floodplain of the Goulburn River, however. Murray–Darling Basin Plan water-saving deadlines loom in two years. 'The short version is that this region has lost half a billion dollars a year in economic activity through the Basin Plan,' Priestly says. 'And it's not over. If the plan is enacted to the most damaging set of circumstances, another half a billion dollars in economic activity is at risk.'

More broadly, a town that was a crossing point from the goldfields of Ballarat and Bendigo in the nineteenth century heading east, and a hub during the railway boom that followed, is again at a crossroads. Once soldier-settler territory, the area has been home to waves of European immigration, particularly Italian and Greek. More recently, they have been joined by newer waves from India, Afghanistan and Africa. Situated on Yorta Yorta land, it is also home to a significant First Nations population.

Those early waves are evidenced by everything from the Italian Ossario at Murchison to the larger-than-life statue that stands in the front garden of a wedding-cake mansion behind wrought-iron gates on Shepparton's main road ('Alexander the

Great, hero of Macedonia' reads the brass plaque). Four mosques, a Sikh temple and St Paul's African House cater to later arrivals.

As for the original owners, after it was redistributed in 2018 the seat was renamed for Yorta Yorta man Sir Douglas Nicholls, the first Indigenous man to be knighted and the only one to become a vice-regal representative. He and his wife, Gladys, were jointly powerful advocates for the 1967 referendum.

Nicholls' evolving identity has already begun to change the politics of a seat that has consistently recorded a conservative vote 20 to 30 per cent stronger than the rest of Victoria. In November 2014, the National Party lost the overlapping state seat of Shepparton District, which it had held since 1945, to an independent, Suzanna Sheed. Ten months earlier, Tony Abbott had rejected a lifeline request by SPC Ardmona. The company had asked for a $25 million co-investment so as to modernise and retool its business. Abbott's decision had put up to 3000 Goulburn Valley jobs at risk.

Sheed not only won the seat, after what she described as 'a short but successful grassroots campaign' in 2014, the year after Cathy McGowan won Indi next door, but, like her neighbour, also held it at the next election, in 2018.

Those victories had been 'transformative from a state relationship point of view', Priestly says. '[Shepparton] spent decades as a safe National Party seat. We had some elections where we'd seen the Bendigos, the Ballarats, the Geelongs get really substantial, positive investment. In the preceding election, I distinctly remember the paper running on the front page a column with the promises for each. For the city of Shepparton, I think the net promise was 50 grand.'

Right on cue, a Voices for Nicholls group was founded in April 2021 by a group described on its site as 'students, retirees, Aboriginal leaders, business owners, farmers, long-term and newly arrived residents of Nicholls' frustrated 'with the representation the major parties offer'. A month after my visit, as the election fight gets bitter, Priestly will reveal he had originally been approached to run by the Nationals, but didn't want to represent them. While the Nationals will deny doing so, something clearly got him thinking. 'My hope was that [Voices for Nicholls] would coalesce around a candidate and that would deliver someone from the community,' he told me in April. But while the group held kitchen-table conversations, it decided not to seek a candidate.

'Someone had to step forward,' Priestly continued. 'And to be successful, they were going to need financial resources, enough community profile, the right values for the issues that were important,' he says. 'If we were going to provide competition, we couldn't afford to wait. I had some people in mind I thought would be good, but they didn't think the same thing.'

Priestly announced his run on 15 October 2021, relatively early because an election was still possible later in the year. COP26, too, loomed at the end of October. 'I thought, well, if there's one thing I can do, it's help influence [the Nationals] to commit to net zero by coming out [just before], so they know they're going to have competition in this seat they'd be counting on, and net zero is going to be part of the conversation.' His original aim was, he says, to make Nicholls marginal to stem federal neglect, as McGowan had done in Indi almost a decade earlier.

A well-known local businessman and deputy mayor standing in a safe Nationals seat adjoining Indi ensured a flurry of publicity. But what really caught the national imagination was when Damian Drum announced in December he was retiring. Under the Coalition agreement, this allowed both parties to run candidates. A key Coalition seat—held for two decades by Liberal MP Sharman Stone until it was won by Drum in 2016—turned into a three-way race at what was already shaping into a crucial moment, not just for Nicholls but also Australia.

That contest was between Priestly; Drum's would-be Nationals successor, agronomist Sam Birrell; and local pomegranate farmer and teacher Stephen Brooks, the son of Southern Riverina Irrigators chairman Chris Brooks, who is leading a class action against the Murray–Darling Basin Authority.

The life-or-death issue of water policy was front and centre. But it was also a fight for whose version of, or vision for, Nicholls would prevail, as underlined by Priestly's 'TIME FOR CHANGE' banner. 'I come from a farming and business background, and that informs some of my values,' he told me in April. 'But I'm quite progressive on social issues. And I'm interested in good environmental policy.'

~~~~~

By mid-March, Liberal, National and Labor-linked polls all showed Priestly was competitive, *The Age* reported. With the Nationals vote 'smashed' by Drum's departure and Liberal competition, the local deputy mayor was 'capturing between 16 and almost 20 per cent of first preferences'.

By 5 April, the *Australian Financial Review* was reporting that the Nationals were concerned about Priestly's 'name recognition and positive polling', in an electorate where he'd received 'significant attention' in local papers belonging to regional media baron Ross McPherson, and where Nationals leader Barnaby Joyce was an electoral drag: 'Water is a real breach of faith from the Nationals, and they're looking for a way to express that,' Priestly said of local voters. 'Nobody will know until the day comes, and it depends what happens with the preferences, but we're way ahead of where I expected to be at this stage. It feels like we've got a lot of momentum.'

'It's possible, but it's a Herculean task,' he says when we meet on the afternoon before his 8 April campaign launch. 'On a normal day, we have ten to twelve people working in this building. You could have a hundred and still not be sure you were going to get there. It'll come down to all of our best endeavours and the vagaries of the electorate's mood.'

He is polling in the high teens at the time, with a name awareness of 50 per cent. That is 10 per cent lower than the campaign had hoped, but it also underlines what is possible if they can raise his profile. 'If we hit 25 per cent, with preference flows, we're probably in the box seat,' a campaign strategist tells me.

As his chances have improved, Priestly has raised his sights from mere marginality. 'The people who are funding the campaign are people that have known me for 25 years or so through business,' he says. 'They're the ones that see the value because they've seen the state member and gone, "Geez, that was good. We want one of them."'

Six months after announcing his candidacy, he's all in. His brother, Phil, is running Gouge Linen, their commercial laundry business. The candidate has also thrown in a fair whack of his own cash. Then there's the intangible investment. Outside the office in which we speak, Cathy McGowan is giving a tutorial on preferences to volunteers, including Phil Priestly, and Rob's wife, Sonia, a speech pathologist. 'My brother, his wife, and my wife are out there. They've all taken huge chunks of time. They've been [helping] on this for six months,' Priestly says.

A few hours ahead of his official campaign launch, he's clearly feeling the weight. 'The pressure to deliver is extraordinary,' he says. 'Everyone I know has put their hand in their pocket, taken time off work. For my kids [the couple have three sons] and my nieces and nephews, it's their family name. This has to be worthwhile. It has to be about using this opportunity to deliver all the values stuff. Because there's just zero interest in it if you can't do that.'

Those values align with those of the other community-backed independent campaigns. 'Integrity, anti-corruption measures, donations [reform], standards of behaviour in politics, treatment of women, refugee policy,' Priestly enumerates. 'I think middle Australia wants all of those issues dealt with. And a very elegant example of the failure of our system is gambling advertising in sport.' Those values have an extra immediacy in a city as visibly and vibrantly diverse as Shepparton. It's no accident Priestly's launch this evening will be at African House.

But the parallels with Indi are just as striking. The primary campaign colour is the orange pioneered by Nicholls' neighbour almost a decade ago. And Priestly said no to Climate 200 money. In part that's because he doesn't need it: the campaign will raise $700,000, including significant donations from local business-people and farmers. In part it's because Nicholls remains a conservative rural seat. 'People—not everyone but broadly—believe in climate change,' he says of locals. 'They think there should be action. However, there's got to be a pathway that actually is going to achieve that outcome.'

There are other parallels, too. Like McGowan, Priestly grew up in a Catholic family on a dairy farm. Indeed, the number of what might be called 'cultural Catholics' in the community-backed independents movement is striking, from Priestly to McGowan to Louise Hislop in Warringah and then Mackellar, Kristen Lock in North Sydney and Dr Monique Ryan in Kooyong. As McGowan's tales of growing up in her autobiography underline, the outsider status of Catholics historically in Australia, and their profound sense of community, seem tailor-made for the movement. Particularly at a time when religious and other traditional community affiliations had declined to an all-time low, an atomisation that was, like so much else, further dramatised by Covid.

It's symptomatic that Priestly speaks of that upbringing as a vanished world. 'My parents raised five kids and put them through university on a hundred acres,' Priestly says. 'We lived modestly, but you could afford to do that. When I grew up, there would've been a couple of hundred dairy farms in our community, all highly productive. Today there's two or three dairy farms left. The farms are being amalgamated and its dryland agriculture.'

But Priestly isn't McGowan. A few hours later he will introduce that self-described 'clever, sophisticated country woman' to the African House crowd as 'maybe Australia's most connected person'. While Priestly is just as clever, and his community connections just as deep, he's a businessman. And a policy wonk. His interest is more in ensuring someone seizes the opportunity he can see so clearly than in necessarily being that person.

That becomes clear near the end of our conversation. He has just outlined a flawless case for an independent candidate in Nicholls in 2022. But why him, I ask. 'That's still not clear to me,' he says, only half joking.

~~~~~

Cathy McGowan is a pale shade of white when I run into her a couple of hours later in Shepparton. She's been on the road for a fortnight, dropping into seven or eight campaigns, her visits strategically timed to help 'get campaigns from good to winning', she says. '"You've got three or four weeks [until pre-poll]. How are you lined up? Are you ready to grow?"'

Two hours later she is magically resurrected as she follows the candidate and an African choir onto the stage of Priestly's early-evening launch for another revival-style pep talk. 'You have a candidate who is one of the most outstanding candidates I've seen in Australia,' McGowan tells them. 'Imagine an Australia where two of the major electorates bordering the Murray have independents. Imagine what we could do with water policy. The opportunity is there, but the work still has to be done [of finding] 25,000 people in Nicholls who will put Rob number one and another 20,000 who will put him second.'

A little over a month later, signs are that that may have happened. National Party polling is rumoured to have Priestly leading 55–45 two-party preferred a fortnight before the election. A week out, ABC election analyst Antony Green tells *The Age* that he, too, thinks the seat of Nicholls is 'one of the most likely to be won by an independent', adding: 'It's a stronger chance than some of the urban seats.' It is certainly the rural seat that makes headlines most often alongside the urban contenders in the eastern capitals.

The scale of the threat is reflected not only by the number of non-Joyce Nationals who visit, including Bridget McKenzie, who announces $25 million for a sports and events centre, but also by a spooky robocall. 'You've heard a lot about Rob Priestly, but have you heard where he stands on really important issues?' it begins, segueing into ten seconds of air before the obligatory authorisation message reveals a National Party ad.

By 13 May, it's being investigated by a busy Australian Electoral Commission. Days later, Priestly also lodges a complaint about texts advising constituents they have been 'selected to participate in a survey . . . about Rob Priestly's endorsement by [Victorian premier] Daniel Andrews' Labor Party'.

~~~~~

Five hours' drive north-east, and a couple of weeks earlier, the path to victory is already clear in Matt Murfitt's mind in the heart-shaped NSW electorate of Hume. If preferences are kind and he can double his candidate's name recognition over the next month to six weeks, they might just manage an upset to rival Kooyong.

A campaign-commissioned poll had underscored the scale of the opportunity two months earlier, showing that support for Angus Taylor, who has held the seat since 2013 and increased his margin to 13 per cent in 2019, had plunged from 53.3 per cent to 31.6 per cent. Better still, the January poll also showed that almost half of those surveyed didn't think the Minister for Energy and Emissions Reduction had put the interests of the community above his own personal or business interests.

Taylor was how Murfitt first came to this fight. 'He is basically that prototype that everyone loves to hate about the Liberal Party,' he said when we first spoke in September 2021. 'He's renowned for not listening to his constituents. He doesn't want to meet with people. He's anti-renewables. He's interconnected with big money, and never deviates from that.'

So much so that Murfitt, a 40-year-old digital marketer who lives in Bowral with his wife and three kids, including ten-month-old twin girls, has spent the better part of three years working to oust Taylor, despite living 5 kilometres outside Hume in the ALP-held seat of Whitlam. 'My local member is Stephen Jones,' he says, 'but I was much more motivated to start change with Angus and move him on.

'I've always been concerned about environmental degradation,' he continues. The couple had just had their first child when Donald Trump took office in 2017. 'When Trump was elected, I decided it was time to pull my finger out and start applying my skills to change. You see an article about the Great Barrier Reef being on its way to 95 per cent death and you look at your kids and you think, "What explanation can I give them when I'm 80 years old and they're living in a radically different world?" I'm at the age now where you think, "People are actually listening to me now. I'm not just a follower anymore. It's my responsibility to do something."'

Murfitt initially founded Voices of Hume with 30-year-old local pilot Alex Murphy. Voices of Hume conducted kitchen-table conversations with 250 people and released a report in April 2021. In November 2021, it announced semi-retired teacher Penny Ackery as its candidate at a launch in Goulburn's Belmore Park by Julia Zemiro and Cathy McGowan.

It's a textbook independent campaign trajectory. But the January poll had a sting in its tail. In addition to showing Taylor's support falling, it also suggested that, two months after she was announced, Ackery was running last, behind Labor, One Nation and the UAP.

~~~~~

Things have improved slightly when Murfitt and I meet in late March 2022. A recent unpublished campaign poll indicates that just under a third of those surveyed are now aware of Ackery, and about a third of that third would put her first on the ballot. 'That's pretty much 10 per cent,' Murfitt says. 'So we just need to double her awareness and we double her primary vote. And that's all we effectively need to do. It's awareness, awareness, awareness. All I say to people now is, "Have you got a corflute? Have you got a sticker? Put it on your car, take your sign."'

But doubling awareness is easier said than done in a 17,250 square kilometre seat that the Australian Electoral Commission classifies as 'provincial' and that takes in some of Sydney's outer south-western suburbs, much of the Southern Highlands and major centres such as Goulburn and Camden. While the Voices of Hume social and digital marketing is predictably strong, there is no substitute for 'getting Penny in front of people and shaking their hands', as Murfitt says. Doorknocking, street-meets and democracy walks become fiendishly difficult in a sparsely populated area that sometimes seems to combine rural respect for the local community with big-town impersonality.

I visit on the day the campaign is hitting the ground: the opening of its brand-new office, rented for peak visibility on a roundabout leading into Goulburn proper. It's a significant milestone given that, between Covid, recent local floods and the constant of distance, the campaign's managers and the volunteers haven't been able to be in the same room together physically.

Murfitt, dressed in T-shirt, cap and shorts, is rousing the troops as I arrive. Outside, Murphy is trying to sizzle sausages as the skies open once more. The 30 or so mostly older volunteers are enthusiastic, if not quite a throng. Some are from outside the electorate, motivated, like Murfitt, by their desire to see the back of Taylor. It's clear the campaign remains underweight on supporters and key personnel. By election day it will manage between 200 and 300 volunteers, partly because it lacks someone to generate and organise volunteers. It also lacks people to do critical but mundane tasks, such as responding to the sheer volume of emails the campaign receives.

Instead, Murfitt is shouldering most of those burdens himself. Both he and Murphy stopped work three months earlier to devote themselves to the campaign around the clock. As we speak, Murfitt is slumped on a sofa, having slept three hours the night before, 'mainly because we had a ten-month-old squirming around all night, but I also couldn't stop thinking about how important the how-to-vote card issue is going to be and what we're going to do about it', he says.

He's driven an hour to be here, but that's 'a luxury', he says. 'My wife and I fight over who goes to the supermarket ... Looking after those tots is hard work. They're 10 kilos each. I'm walking around the house with one in each arm.'

As David and Goliath battles go, it's hard to better the one between the kid with the mobile and the Rhodes-scholar minister once touted as the man to watch. Murfitt has taken it on because he is, it's fair to say, one of the independents movement's true believers. Inspired by Steggall's 2019 win, he and

Murphy have since read the book, seen the movie and bought the T-shirt. He was also one of the original people who attended those early exploratory meetings at Kirsty Gold's house of individuals and groups looking to find candidates.

Denis Ginnivan advised the campaign on the kitchen-table conversations Voices of Hume conducted with ten facilitators, and on the online forums via which Ackery was subsequently selected during Covid. And Murfitt and Murphy modelled the other group they set up, Vote Angus Out, directly on Vote Tony Out, with Mark Kelly advising, not least on the importance of T-shirts as an engagement tool. Murphy had planned to attend Cathy McGowan's 'Getting Elected' conference in February 2021 but forgot. But he did buy her sister Ruth's *Get Elected*.

'We [he and Murphy] did Voices of Hume first as a community engagement project, where we asked everyone what mattered to them, and released the report,' Murfitt says in March. 'We also launched Vote Angus Out, which is largely social media. Basically: "Here's a website. Come and donate, or buy a T-shirt." We both agreed that we needed something that was more attack-driven than the kind of fluffy Voices of Hume brand. We realised that wasn't going to get us a long way, because too many people didn't know what it was.'

When we speak, the two arms of the campaign are raising about $7000 to $8000 a week in donations from a combined database of 2000. 'A lot of them are from outside of the electorate, but that doesn't mean that we can't hit them up for cash donations,' Murfitt says. In the end, the campaign will raise about $700,000. Predictably, most of Vote Angus Out's support comes from outside the electorate; most of Ackery's from within it.

Its war chest is healthy enough, given the campaign has been in two minds about Climate 200 money. It initially received a $50,000 grant—and had sought substantially more, according to Climate 200—but then returned the money. 'You just can't win campaigning on climate alone in this seat,' Murfitt says.

He points to previous Hume independent candidate Huw Kingston, who garnered less than 6 per cent of first preferences in 2019. 'I think he campaigned too heavily on climate,' Murfitt says. 'You can't just push that. I've looked at the numbers pretty closely and I'd estimate about 15 per cent of people here vote on climate.'

Indeed, the campaign will run ads disassociating themselves from Climate 200 due, he later explains, to the pushback they were getting from 'Liberal-leaning voters who were keen to vote for Penny. One of their main objections was, "Oh, I don't know about this guy [Simon Holmes à Court]. I don't know if we like him." And that was mainly because of what they're reading in the Murdoch press, with their incessant attacks against them. We decided, "Well, look, we've probably got enough money here."'

When we meet, they are at the pointy end of things, even though the election date hasn't yet been announced. 'We've been working on this for two and a half years,' he says wearily. 'It's been a labour of love for that long, but to be honest I'm quite looking forward to the fact that it's now reaching its climax. As much as I sometimes feel a little bit . . . not over it, just tired . . . now we know we've got no more than two months to push through to the end of this thing. And most of it's been done.'

I keep waiting to meet the candidate, whose face is plastered all over the corflutes that line the walls of the new office space and the fence outside. Turns out she is already there, indistinguishable from the other volunteers. She is pitching in, part of the team, as she has been since she helped to facilitate the kitchen-table conversations and even the Zoom forums that chose her.

Even before the forums, she was Murfitt's preferred candidate. As for her motivation for taking on the job, Ackery tells me she has reached the stage where she had the luxury of choice, working when she wanted, rather than needed. 'Why did I do it?' she says. 'Because Matt asked me and I thought, oh yeah. Why not? Just give it a crack.'

Conducting those kitchen-table conversations had also been a clincher, she adds. 'I'd never met most of those people and I was listening to them talking about integrity and climate change, and the fact that their representatives didn't ask them anything anymore, or even answer their emails. I realised I wasn't the only one thinking like that. That it was okay to talk about those things, because there was a whole network of people out there.'

And then, a fortnight after my visit, tragedy strikes. In mid-April, six weeks from the election, Ackery's husband, John Steel, dies unexpectedly after a short illness. The candidate drops out of the contest for a fortnight before resuming, as her husband had wished. By then posters had begun to appear, depicting community-backed independent candidates—including David Pocock, Dr Sophie Scamps and Zali Steggall—as Greens.

By mid-May, the Australian Electoral Commission has overruled its preliminary finding that the posters, authorised by the conservative lobby group Advance Australia, had not breached political advertising laws. As Tony Windsor says, it's a classic sign of how much of a threat the independent campaigns have become, as is the fact that locals report Ackery corflutes disappearing overnight, while Taylor's remain, some even post-election. By mid-May, various fake posters suggesting Greens or Labor endorsement of, or alignment with, independent candidates have popped up from Hughes to Kooyong. Hume gets a version, too. One, touting 'Penny Ackery & The Greens 2022', is attached to the fence of the graveyard where Ackery buried her husband a fortnight earlier.

13

BOOK OF REVELATIONS

By election day, Climate 200 calculates that close to 20,000 volunteers had worked on the community-independent campaigns it helped fund, not including the likes of Nicholls, Hume and Groom. On the day, in Wentworth alone, 800 people put in 4000 hours. Two hundred people joined the campaign in the last week.

The election came at the end of a particularly wet autumn in Sydney. Memories of the last election were fresh for Manly resident Ranya Alkadamani, who worked on 2019 and 2022 campaigns. And the atmospherics didn't help. 'It rained all week,' she says of the lead-up. 'There was just this feeling of doom and gloom. I really didn't really believe people were going to change or vote differently. It had been so clear the Morrison government had to go in 2019 but it hadn't happened.'

In Melbourne, the day was blue and brilliant, though cold, and close enough to Covid to curtail the sausage sizzles and cake stalls that usually lent a festive air. The theatre of the day was mounted with military precision. In Goldstein, 36 booths had been triaged into three tiers. By the night before, 24 were decked in full Zoe Daniel livery, with incoming Liberal teams complaining the best spots were gone. Volunteers guarded their real estate until midnight when security took over. By 6 a.m. on the day, the central operations team were drowning in texts and pictures from captains. All booths were locked and loaded.

In Kooyong, an underground car park behind the campaign office had been turned into a cross between Santa's workshop and a Vietcong bunker. Over six weeks, volunteers had constructed giant corflute frames on the sly to match Josh Frydenberg's maximalism on the cheap. Materials had been stockpiled, from the 12 kilometres of bunting that would be used across the 38 booths, to signs in Chinese, emergency supplies and rain gear.

Those giant banks of Ryan signs formed solid backdrops outside booths as the candidate and her campaign manager spent the day driving around, thanking volunteers, talking to voters, guided to the highest-traffic sites by an advance team. About 1300 had registered to work on the day. An extra 100 just turned up. Together they put in a total of 7000 hours.

The volunteer mood was 'gloriously, happily, politely feral', Ann Capling recalls, with people singing 'Vote 1 Mon and number all the boxes'. From the moment the election had been called, 'we felt like we had caught the wave', she says, adding: 'my concern was that we not hit the beach too soon or have the wave crash over us. That was the biggest challenge of that last six weeks, staying on top of it.'

As they left the last booth, however, Capling decided to take the scenic route as she drove Ryan and her thirteen-year-old son, Patrick, home, past streets full of corflutes and signs. 'This is the last time we'll get to take this crazy little journey,' she told the candidate. 'Look at your face in 200 front yards.'

'I shouldn't have done it,' Capling says. 'By the time I dropped her off at about 5.30 we had both decided we weren't going to win. We had a little cry in the car. I said, "This is the best thing I've ever done!" And she said, "Me too!"'

They were so swept up in the moment that they had forgotten they weren't alone. Until a voice piped up from the back seat. 'What are you talking about?' Patrick demanded, indignant. 'You've spent so much time on this, what do you mean you're going to lose?!'

~~~~~

In Curtin in Western Australia, a similarly concerted push was underway, if in a slightly lower key. In the final two weeks, the campaign had resolved to doorknock the more populous, less affluent areas in the north of the electorate, including Scarborough, Doubleview and Glendalough. Recognition of Kate Chaney wasn't as high outside the golden triangle of well-to-do suburbs such as Cottesloe, Tony Fairweather says. And some were newly redistributed into Curtin.

All up, the campaign would knock on more than 7000 doors in that final fortnight, almost 70 per cent of them in the last week, with residents reporting they had never been doorknocked, let alone listened to, before.

Even on this last push, the sense of a historic—even dynastic—changing of the guard was clear. Retired pharmacist John Guilfoyle doorknocked tirelessly on Kate Chaney's behalf. Yet another ocean swimmer swept into the movement, Guilfoyle, now in his late seventies, had doorknocked for both Sir Fred Chaney in the 1960s and his friend Fred junior in the 1990s. Fred Chaney himself also volunteered, together with his wife, Angela.

The week before the election, the former Fraser minister also wrote an opinion piece for *The Saturday Paper*. In the article, titled 'Independents are the shock the major parties need', Chaney cited many of the factors that Ted Baillieu had raised weeks before as reasons to stick with the experienced Coalition, but reached the opposite conclusion.

Australia faced 'wicked problems', including 'the ongoing gap between government income and expenditure', stagnant wages, inflation, tax reform and the need for climate action, Chaney wrote. 'But neither major party has the moral authority or the gumption to deal with these issues,' he said; for all these reasons voters had lost faith in them.

'The Liberals need the Nationals to have any hope of a majority and hence the hope of governing. Both need the support of the worst of their members or former members— people like Craig Kelly and George Christensen. In the same way, Labor needs Greens preferences to get elected and is unable to escape the tyranny of the faction system. All parties manipulate preselections in a way that undermines democratic choices and destroys party integrity.'

It was 'in this sorry context of an election campaign designed as a smokescreen for the failure to address long-term issues that the "teal" and other independents are so important', he wrote. To reform, the parties required 'an external shock and that is what independents represent', with 'the near hysterical attacks on these independents' reflecting 'how great a challenge this poses to a broken system'.

On the day of the election, 600 Kate Chaney volunteers converged on 38 booths. It was an impressive show of strength given the campaign's short life, and they outnumbered other teams. But while pre-poll had had a feeling of momentum, the mood on election day was less clear. 'It was hard to get a read on the result from most booths,' Fairweather wrote in a subsequent No Fibs piece. 'Many took only Liberal HTVs [how-to-votes], some took some or all HTVs from Labor, Green and Kate, and plenty took no HTVs.'

The final shot illustrating that piece was a selfie taken by Chaney with Fairweather and Sarah Silbert. Smiling but exhausted, they look into the camera as the sun sets over Doubleview. 'It was 5 p.m. in the carpark park of uncertainty,' Fairweather recalls. 'It was "We don't know what the fuck is going to happen."'

Ann Capling missed the TV coverage on election night. She missed the party, too, or at least its start. The Ryan campaign had searched long and hard for a venue big enough to accommodate the expected crowd. By 6 p.m., 1200 people were packed into the downstairs areas of the Auburn Hotel in East Hawthorn— the venue from which Holmes à Court says Frydenberg had had him removed at a 2019 fundraiser.

Upstairs, in an improvised war room, the number crunchers bent over laptops, including Capling and amateur psephologist Steve Adlard. A psychiatrist by day, Adlard had designed his own algorithm and predictive software, into which the incoming booth counts were fed. 'Steve only does scrutineering, that's all he does in an election. He said, "I'll be there on the night," and he was. He was so good,' Capling says.

Not so good, though, that they didn't both question the accuracy of his technology as the first two booths came in. Barely an hour after Capling had dropped Ryan off, they were showing big swings. More remarkably still, they were followed by booths in more conservative areas of the electorate, with a high proportion of voters from Chinese backgrounds. Black holes for Oliver Yates in his tilt at Kooyong three years earlier, they now showed even bigger swings.

'We were convinced it was going to be much, much closer,' Capling recalls. 'I looked at Steve and said, "Are you sure your software isn't wrong?" He said, "I know, I know I'm checking." But we kept seeing swings of 6 or 7 per cent being replicated broadly, which was more than we needed to win. I kept running downstairs as each booth came in and screaming out the name and the swing. Twelve hundred people would go wild because they were all so smart and informed, having door-knocked those areas, that they understood the significance of the swing at a particular booth. By about 8 p.m. I'd lost my voice. Someone who lived nearby said they could hear the roars two blocks away.'

A similar scene was playing out across town in Goldstein. The campaign's number crunchers, gathered at Brighton Bowling Club, had received their first taste of pre-polls just after 6 p.m., as Cameron Stewart and Carly Douglas reported the next day in *The Australian*. While Zoe Daniel needed a substantial 7.8 per cent swing to defeat Tim Wilson, the early votes were showing 12 per cent. 'Really? Can that be right?' one of the number crunchers reportedly muttered, staring at his screen.

That swing, like the others emerging around the country, would prove no mirage. By 7 p.m., hours before the pundits, Adler had called Kooyong for Ryan. After all, the algorithm didn't lie.

~~~~~~

The volunteer number crunchers' incredulity was mirrored by that of the professionals in more public forums on the night, as even seasoned commentators struggled to comprehend, and articulate, the scale of what was taking place. By the time it was over, the Coalition would lose eighteen seats, ten of them to Labor, six to independents, and two to Greens. In the House of Representatives, the crossbench more than doubled in size, from seven to sixteen, thanks to independents and Greens.

Climate 200's 11,200 donors, one-third of whom were from regional and rural areas, had helped elect six new independents in the House of Representatives and one senator. They also contributed to the re-election of Helen Haines, Andrew Wilkie, Rebekha Sharkie and Zali Steggall, who had accepted small donations from the organisation.

It would be more than a week before the Melbourne seat of Macnamara was called for the ALP, securing the party its 76th seat and majority government (Labor won it with 77 seats in total). The question that had dogged the independents throughout the campaign—which of the two parties they would support in a hung parliament—became moot. As many saw it, that was a lucky break.

Climate 200 may have set out with the balance of power in its sights to engineer urgent environmental action, but at least two members of its advisory council, former MPs Tony

Windsor and Rob Oakeshott, knew only too well the political cost of supporting a minority government, as they had done with Julia Gillard's in 2010. This way, the fledgling independents would have a chance to find their wings before they had to fly.

While how exactly government would be formed remained unclear on the night, the answer to the broader question—which reality would prevail, the status quo or the disruptors'—was crystal clear. For the combined LNP, the result was the worst since 1949. For the Liberal Party, the threat had proved existential, with talk of the potential dissolution of the Coalition, given the National Party had held seats and its vote.

On 26 May, the Liberal Party announced a wide-ranging review to probe the loss to independents in heartland seats, to be conducted by former federal director Brian Loughnane and Senator Jane Hume. On the same day, writer Richard Flanagan underlined the historic dimensions of the catastrophe. In an opinion piece in *The Age* and *Sydney Morning Herald*, Flanagan traced the 2022 loss back to the 'transformative' leadership of John Howard a quarter-century earlier, which had ushered in climate scepticism and the culture wars, and reversed progress on everything from the republic to reconciliation.

Widely credited 'as the architect of this annihilation', Scott Morrison was perhaps 'no more than the sinister final act of a larger story that began decades earlier', Flanagan suggested, with 'Howardism . . . taken up with a new aggression and misogyny by his self-declared love child, Tony Abbott' and 'continued, despite his postpartum revisions, by Malcolm Turnbull' until it reached 'its final decadent phase: the Morrison government, a rabble characterised by sleaze, scandal and self-interest'.

Morrison's defeat had 'put an end to not only the Morrison government but also the Howard ascendancy and with it, the two-party system,' Flanagan concluded.

Not coincidentally, that was the arc Margo Kingston had described in recent decades, shifting from mainstream to citizen journalism to do so. When her home town of Maryborough in Queensland had fallen to One Nation in 1998, she'd gone on the road to cover Pauline Hanson for the *Sydney Morning Herald*, which resulted in her 1999 book, *Off the Rails: The Pauline Hanson Trip*. She subsequently became editor of the *Sydney Morning Herald*'s first blog, Webdiary, because, she says, she wanted to explore what was happening politically in a way that went beyond the press gallery and two-party politics, welcoming what she called 'civilised voices from the left and the right'.

Tracing Howard's subsequent lurch right to counter Hansonism, or migrate under its cover, resulted in her second book, *Not Happy, John! Defending our Democracy*, cited by Louise Hislop and others as influencing their involvement in the independents' movement. Webdiary would in turn morph into Kingston's No Fibs citizen journalism site, which chronicled the rise of the new community-backed independents from Indi on.

Nor was the existential threat underlined by the 2022 election limited to the Liberal Party. All up, almost a third of the nation didn't vote for major parties, a new record. The Coalition's primary vote slumped to 35.7 per cent, Labor's to 33 per cent. 'We haven't seen a party win government with a primary of less than 40 per cent ever,' Liberal senator Simon Birmingham declared on the night.

Alongside the independents, the Greens were a major beneficiary, particularly in urban Queensland seats such as Brisbane and Griffith, where some commentators saw them playing a similar role to the independents in the absence of independent candidates. The 2019 blue wave in Queensland that had helped work Scott Morrison's miracle win had been washed away, as the ABC noted. Again, though, it wasn't only Coalition seats. In Fowler in Sydney's west, former Liberal Party member and local councillor Dai Le unseated Kristina Keneally, who had been parachuted into the safe Labor seat ahead of the election. More broadly, successful community-backed independents often took from the Labor and Green vote.

If there is a pattern to what was generally agreed to have been a very messy national picture, as ABC commentator Annabel Crabb said on the night, it was a 'real feeling of people not liking to be taken for granted'. As she would reflect a few days later, the old orthodoxy that Australians were politically disengaged had been resoundingly disproved. And the drivers of that change had been women, climate change and what she described as 'a vast and nebulous rage against the perfidy and shallowness of modern politicking, in which major parties take their voters for granted and stubbornly fail to do their one job, which is sorting out solutions to difficult problems'.

It was abundantly clear even on the night that Ryan had defeated Frydenberg. The man who would have been Scott Morrison's natural successor as head of the Liberal Party after a historic rout did not, however, concede until Monday. As he said, it was still mathematically possible he might win. But as *The Age*'s Tony Wright noted, the treasurer couched the speech that followed about his career entirely in the past tense.

As the evening wore on, the face of Ryan's son, Patrick, became a mood ring. 'He had been given a lot of grief at school about me standing and he was worried that he would be given even more if I lost, so it really mattered to him that I not do so,' Ryan explains. 'But the main thing was he couldn't believe that I'd been telling everyone we were going to win while not actually believing it. The poor darling was completely thrown; that look of terror was because he no longer believed anything anyone said about anyone winning anything. And who could blame him.'

In Wentworth, Spender defied Sportsbet, which had had her trailing Sharma again the day before the election, though the odds had narrowed from $1.87 to $1.85. At 35.8 per cent, her first preference vote was just 3.4 per cent higher than Kerryn Phelps's in 2019, but that 3.4 per cent had made the difference. Sharma's primary vote slumped from 47.4 per cent to 40.5 per cent, compared with the 62–63 per cent Malcolm Turnbull had recorded in the seat in 2013 and 2016, as the Poll Bludger website noted. The two-candidate preferred result was 54.2 per cent to 45.8 per cent, giving Spender a 4.2 per cent margin.

The second most heavily 'teal' voting booth in the country turned out to be in Wentworth, at St Sophia's Church Hall in the inner-city Sydney suburb of Surry Hills, where Spender got almost 75.5 per cent of the two-candidate preferred vote.

The most 'teal' was St Paul's Catholic College, near the former St Patrick's seminary overlooking Manly, where Steggall recorded a two-candidate preferred vote of more than 76 per cent. Overall, Steggall managed a swing of more than 3.7 per cent in her second election, recording a two-candidate preferred result of close to 61 per cent. She had indeed proved the model.

In Indi, Helen Haines evolved that model further. By winning in 2019, she had shown that one independent could succeed another; that it was a template rather than a personality cult. Back then, however, she had done it by the skin of her teeth, on a margin of just 1.4 per cent. This time around, she was returned with a swing of more than 8.3 per cent, securing almost 41 per cent of the primary vote, a good 10 per cent ahead of her nearest rival, Liberal candidate Ross Lyman. Two-candidate preferred, Haines now holds the seat on a safe margin of 9 per cent, with 59 per cent of the vote.

'There were swings to me in every single booth and in booths that we'd never won in Indi as independents, in Cathy's two terms or when I won in 2019,' she said after the election. That result reflected a number of factors, including the national prominence to which both she and Zali Steggall had risen through their integrity-commission and climate bills over the last year. 'Some of it [would also] be incumbency and satisfaction with performance. And some of it was the national mood,' Haines said.

In Indi, the private member's bill and the electorate's satisfaction with its representation were, in fact, the same thing: the electorate had demanded action on integrity and Haines had delivered the bill that had helped make the issue central to the election. In 2013, when they set out to make Indi marginal and ended up winning, 'we really hadn't envisaged barnstorming the parliament', she said. 'But that's what's happened ten years on.'

Indi had lived up to its name. Haines was up before dawn on election day, then drove around the polling booths talking to volunteers, some of whom had camped overnight after setting up. 'It was an incredible moment,' she says. 'Just the excitement, the happiness, the diversity of people who were out there participating in democracy, having fun, trying to get their independent re-elected.

'We now have more than 1800 volunteers; we've kept the ones we had and got more,' she says. 'People feel good about this. They feel good about being involved. They feel good about values underpinning everything that gets done. It was unbelievable on election night to be in a packed hall in Wangaratta, and just watch all of these independents coming in [on TV]. We knew here that the story was now way, way bigger than us.'

While the campaigns achieved the sort of numbers they would hardly have dared dream of even days before, voting patterns were, not surprisingly, neither simple nor monolithic. Not only was each electorate its own individual microclimate, but each was also composed of very distinct mini-microclimates. Spender, for instance, struggled to get above 32–33 per cent two-candidate preferred in a traditionally Liberal booth such as Dover Heights, which also happened to have a significant Jewish population. The fight narrowed in Double Bay and Edgecliff, hit almost 58 per cent for Spender in Woollahra, rose to 70 per cent in Potts Point and almost 75 in Darlinghurst, before hitting its Surry Hills high.

As Kos Samaras of polling outfit RedBridge Group noted in the *Australian Financial Review*, 'teal' candidates generally did better in the less affluent part of otherwise wealthy electorates. 'Their voters in general were younger, and the rental class skewed heavily toward the teals,' he said. Even in one of Australia's most homogeneous electorates, the picture was a patchwork. Not coincidentally perhaps, Spender polled best in the electorates on which the campaign had concentrated its late doorknocking push.

The candidate turned up at the Drogas' house at 7.30 on the night, after dinner at her older sister's house. As the Drogas watched the coverage with their kids and the Haslingdens, Spender knocked together speech notes in another room. All were pacing themselves for what they thought would be a long evening. By 7.45, however, they received a call summoning them to Bondi Bowling Club. 'Antony Green had just said Wentworth was looking good for Allegra,' Droga recalls. Spender joined them watching TV, then returned to her speech.

As they entered the party an hour later, volunteers broke into the Black Eyed Peas' 'I Gotta Feeling'. It took forever for the candidate to complete a lap of a room that had turned into a moshpit. From the start, Reed had told his co-campaign manager she must always be at her candidate's side in public, never leave her unprotected. At the bowlo, he gave Droga a last push. 'You have to go with her,' he said, old advice that now meant she should be up there, too. It was, she reminded a hooting crowd as she introduced Spender, little more than a year since they had formed Wentworth Independents, 'inspired by strong, real community representatives, especially Cathy McGowan'.

In the contiguous electorates of Sydney's northern shore and beaches, St Paul's near North Head, which recorded a Steggall vote of more than 76 per cent after preferences, proved the epicentre of a broader earthquake. The Zali effect was evident everywhere.

In North Sydney, Kylea Tink beat Trent Zimmerman almost 53 per cent to 47 per cent two-candidate preferred.

The fact that after Tink announced her candidacy the Labor Party had decided to run a strong female candidate in the seat, Western Sydney University law professor Catherine Renshaw, was seen as a sign of the competition she had brought to a safe Liberal seat held on a margin of 9.3 per cent. Not to mention the perils of announcing early. Tink's primary vote of 25.2 per cent compared to 21.45 per cent for Renshaw and 38 for Zimmerman. That Labor primary was actually 3.6 per cent down, Zimmerman's a whopping 14 per cent.

In neighbouring Bradfield, Nicolette Boele became the face of the largest primary swing against a sitting Liberal in the country. While Paul Fletcher retained the seat 54.23 two-candidate preferred to Boele's 45.77 per cent, a swing of nearly 15.3 per cent took his primary vote to slightly over 45 per cent, with Boele running second on almost 21 per cent. A seat classed as very safe Liberal, held on a margin of 16.6 per cent, was suddenly, stunningly marginal—vulnerable to a better-funded and better-resourced tilt next time.

In Mackellar, in a less crowded field than North Sydney, the dark horse romped home. Dr Sophie Scamps beat Jason Falinski 52.5 per cent to 47.5 per cent, managing a first-preference vote of more than 38 per cent to the incumbent's 41.4 per cent. The seat went from very safe Liberal on a margin of 13.2 per cent to independent on a margin of 2.5 per cent. Of all the independent campaigns, Antony Green said later, Mackellar had been the one he had thought 'least likely. But, in fact, it was one of the earliest to be called.'

The *Sydney Morning Herald* described the forlorn figure the incumbent had cut the week before the election, 'standing in a darkening suburban car park handing out fliers to every last straggler turning up at the local pre-poll station before it closes at 8pm'. Of the 127 hours of pre-poll voting in his electorate, Falinski said, he had been there for 124½ of them, every bit of it 'trench warfare'.

It was one of the things Capling was proud of in another trench-warfare electorate: the way their campaign had tethered the treasurer to his seat. 'We tied him to Kooyong and that was part of our plan to help the broader effort across the board,' she says. 'He was clearly pretty miserable there, because he should have been flying around the country, going from electorate to electorate, gladhanding, helping the cause. That's his role as treasurer.'

That broader cost of the independents was underlined on the ABC on election night by former deputy state director of the Victorian Liberal Party, Tony Barry. Having to fight so hard in heartland Liberal seats had 'eaten up millions of dollars and manpower which has been taken away from marginal seats', he said.

From Kooyong to Wentworth, concessions would take time, as candidates hung on to the forlorn hope that the centre might miraculously hold, as it had done three years earlier. Dave Sharma disappeared from Twitter after his concession, re-emerging some days later with an updated bio that read 'Ex-somebody'.

In Goldstein, Tim Wilson, the first Liberal to lose the seat, conceded on the night, however belligerently. An 'unholy alliance' of GetUp, Extinction Rebellion and the Greens 'all going under one banner to back so-called independents' had been put together for the sole purpose of displacing him and removing Goldstein from government hands, he said.

Daniel had managed a healthy 34.5 per cent of the primary vote to Wilson's 40.4 per cent, to prevail 53 per cent to 47 per cent two-candidate preferred. Meanwhile in the ACT, David Pocock became the first independent senator in the territory's history. Since the ACT and Northern Territory had first elected senators in 1975, every election had produced the same pairing, one Labor senator and one Liberal senator in each jurisdiction. It was just one more way the tectonic plates had shifted.

~~~~~

It wasn't long after that moment in Doubleview's 'carpark of uncertainty' that things began to look up for Kate Chaney. By 10 p.m. the fledgling candidate looked like she'd crack more than 50 per cent of the two-candidate preferred vote. An hour later Nine News's seat predictor called Curtin for her. 'Kate was looking likely to win by election night,' Fairweather recalls. 'We had a quick celebration and then went back to waiting.'

They did so because Charlie Caruso was adamant that the campaign could only really celebrate when they had definitively won. Postal and pre-poll votes were still to be counted. And she had been getting calls from her team of volunteers and scrutineers all night.

Covid had finally hit Western Australia in the weeks before the election. Volunteers constantly had to be subbed and replaced as infections rose. And not just campaign volunteers: those manning booths in an official capacity, too. 'The AEC did an extraordinary job in the circumstances, but because of Covid there were a lot of people who had never been a vote counter, or in charge of vote counting,' Caruso says. 'I'd received calls from our people and I knew there were certain booths where we should be sceptical of the numbers.'

That count and verification process would go on for days, with up to 50 Chaney volunteers competitively scrutineering the results ('savage' would be the word one observer from another team used on Reddit to describe their approach). They included a disproportionate number of senior lawyers and QCs, even a CFO whose lightning-fast mental arithmetic challenged at least one official's calculator. The team knew which boxes contained what votes. Early postal votes, tending to elderly voters, were expected to favour Celia Hammond; pre-poll to favour Chaney.

Caruso had told the team they would know whether or not Chaney had prevailed by box five. But that box came and went without turning the tide. 'Everyone was gutted,' Caruso said. The next box, six, proved the charm, however. 'We were counting pre-poll votes and we started to claw back,' she says. A frequent and easy error by tired polling booth workers proved to be simply inverting the Chaney/Hammond preference count (putting each in the other's column). As it was corrected, chunks of votes began to flow to Chaney.

Through those four days, Caruso didn't miss a shift. On the fifth, though, she had a medical appointment she couldn't reschedule. Hammond finally conceded, and the Chaney team finally celebrated. 'I missed the whole thing,' Caruso says. But while she missed the party, she did exit the experience with renewed respect for the very human and theatrical ritual of scrutineering. 'I would defend that process to the death,' she says. 'People talk about automating it, but having seen it in action, that can't happen.'

The experience of finally throwing herself into a campaign for which she had scanned the horizon for years also renewed her faith in our federal voting system. 'The ability of an independent to win is directly attributable to preferential voting,' she says. 'That singular innovation should be our greatest source of pride and is the strongest line of defence to ensure we don't end up like the US, in the stranglehold of the two parties.'

As for what had made the difference, both in Curtin and more broadly, one demographic stood out, says Caruso, who had watched her volunteers closely. Women 35–50 had carried Curtin, she says. 'I said throughout that if you didn't inspire those women and that demographic you lost and it was those women who got Kate elected. It was clear from the gender split of our volunteers. It was them reaching down to convince the younger generation and up to their parents to convince them. They had conversations with their husbands when they were dragging their feet. They convinced their neighbours, had dinner parties, literally turned streets around, house by house. In electorates where there wasn't an independent, women voted the way they usually voted. What was different in the seats that changed was that women were inspired.'

But that had all taken time, a luxury of which the Curtin campaign had little, having announced late and when the election date was still live, the length of the runway unknown. It had become a shake-and-bake campaign, shortcutting its way to election day on everything from advice from North Sydney's Independent founder Kristen Lock to the X factor everyone cites as determinative in the equation: the sheer star power of its candidate. Curtin also received the most substantial funding in the country from Climate 200, which contributed $450,000 of the $975,000 total the campaign raised, with the remainder raised from 650 donors.

Money wasn't what made the difference, Caruso says. Without the four scant months the campaign had to build, reach and persuade, cash and effort alone might have been for nothing. 'If we had been even a fortnight later announcing, or the election had been a fortnight earlier, it wouldn't have been viable,' Caruso says. 'Timing was crucial.'

14

THE ROAD LESS TRAVELLED

Outside the city electorates, the picture was less triumphant but no less telling. In Nicholls, Rob Priestly managed a healthy primary vote of 25.5 per cent, cracking the 25 per cent his campaign hoped for in April, but with 'no cigar', as the candidate quipped. Priestly lost to Sam Birrell 46 per cent to 54 per cent two-candidate preferred, despite a more than 25 per cent swing against the Nationals.

As might have been expected, Priestly's vote yoyoed across the electorate. In central Shepparton, it hit 61 per cent to Birrell's 39 per cent. In the Murray town of Cobram, on Nicholls' northern border, the vote was just over the reverse in Birrell's favour.

The Nationals were helped by drawing second position (especially behind Liberal Democrat Tim Laird, who managed just 3.5 per cent of first preferences), together with 'a few things we didn't expect', Priestly explains. Firstly, 'more Labor voters voted for me, so Labor's primary fell by more than we expected'. The ALP suffered an almost 8 per cent swing.

'The second thing is that we were told Labor voters usually follow the [ALP] card about 90 per cent. But they didn't, they followed it 70 per cent, and all the UAP and One Nation [prefer-ences] ended up in National Party land.' Priestly had, however, achieved his original aim. At 54 per cent, the very safe Coalition seat was now marginal.

Those election entrails would be construed, and spun, accord-ing to need. 'As the Liberal Party started its self-examination,' *The Guardian*'s Gabrielle Chan wrote a few days later, 'Barnaby Joyce was busy putting lipstick on a pig, talking up the National Party's stellar result on the weekend. He said that while it was disappointing the Coalition had lost the election, the Nationals held all of their seats . . . Clearly, it was the Liberals' fault.'

In fact, Rob Priestly's primary vote of 24,287 was less than 600 votes behind Sam Birrell's after 'millions of dollars of Coalition promises'. And Liberal candidate Stephen Brooks's 18 per cent primary vote had also sent a portion of preferences back to the Nationals. Now that their Coalition partner had held the seat, the Liberals wouldn't be able to run a candidate and help the Nationals with preferences next time. 'If Priestly decides to run again, Nicholls will be a very close contest,' Chan concluded.

'There's definitely an appetite,' says Priestly, who is 'leaving the possibility open' of running again, though you wonder if he wouldn't prefer to cheer another independent candidate to victory given his previous comments on the cost to family and friends.

In Cowper, on the New South Wales mid-north coast, Nationals MP Pat Conaghan claimed victory on 24 May with a two-candidate preferred vote of 52 per cent to 48 per cent for independent Caz Heise. But only after days in which Cowper was the only Nationals seat too close to call and 'a wait for the Australian Electoral Commission to provide "fresh scrutiny" over the count', as the ABC reported.

Heise's primary vote of 26.2 per cent took Conaghan's under 40 per cent, a swing of just under 8 per cent. A previously safe Nationals seat wasn't just marginal, it was the most marginal National Party seat in the country, down from 12 per cent to 2.3 per cent.

Claiming victory, a 'humbled' Pat Conaghan acknowledged that Heise had run 'a very strong campaign' and that change was 'in the wind', but he attributed the swing against him to 'an equally strong campaign by the One Nation candidate Faye Aspiotis', which he said had taken votes from him 'from the right. I think the most damage was actually done by them rather than the independent at the end of the day.'

'It's the same smoke-and-mirrors denial game that the Nationals play about everything, including the state of the climate,' Heise scoffed when we spoke in July. 'It's just outdated politics. They just don't want to own that they're a party in decline.'

The pattern continued into the Liberal stronghold of Wannon, another Indi lookalike, as campaign volunteer Dr Deb Campbell wrote on No Fibs. Victoria's second-largest electorate after Mallee, covering 33,600 square kilometres in south-west Victoria, Wannon had been home to centre-right Liberal Dan Tehan since 2010. In 2019, Alex Dyson, a Warrnambool-born former Triple J radio presenter, had taken on the Morrison government's trade minister in the safe Liberal seat, saying he would be 'happy if his tilt encourages more young Australians to pay closer attention to the political process'.

Campaigning as 'a different kind of politician', Dyson delivered his May 2019 policy pitch in a suit and tie 'via the medium of interpretive dance' on Warrnambool breakwater. In a video of just under 60 seconds, Dyson caught the groove of captioned policies ranging from 'Forward-thinking environmental policies' to 'Independent from the Canberra bubble', before taking the 'political plunge' into the cold grey waters of the harbour. The video had gone viral, as it was designed to, helping the 30-year-old to third position in 2019 on a primary vote of 10.4 per cent, behind Labor's Maurice Billi on 26 per cent and Tehan on 51 per cent.

In 2022, Dyson didn't need to dance. The youngest of the community-independent candidates almost doubled his primary vote to 19.3 per cent on a swing of almost 10 per cent, edging out the ALP candidate (down 6.8 per cent to 19.1 per cent) for second position. While Tehan retained the seat with a two-party preferred vote of 54 per cent to Dyson's 46 per cent, the trade minister's primary vote fell 6.6 per cent to 44.5 per cent. Another safe Liberal seat turned marginal.

Meanwhile, in Calare in central western New South Wales, 48-year-old Orange environmental entrepreneur and mother of four Kate Hook received 20.4 per cent of the primary vote, ahead of Labor's Sarah Elliott at 15 per cent. Again, that vote took from the ALP, which suffered a swing of 7 per cent.

At a distance, Calare, which extends from Mudgee to Bathurst and Orange to Lithgow, looked like a story that might write itself, having been held comfortably by independent Peter Andren from 1996 until his death in 2007. In fact, the vote for the veterans' affairs minister, Andrew Gee, rose 3 per cent, despite Hook drawing the top ballot spot (and Gee second last). But Gee had made sure there was no light between himself and Hook on climate and a federal ICAC, as Gabrielle Chan noted in *The Guardian*. He had also threatened to resign over veterans' affairs funding in late March.

Closer to town, Matt Murfitt had realised the teal wave probably wasn't going to break over Hume when he saw the campaign's early-May polling results. It showed Ackery at 13 per cent, 'at a point when she really needed to be up around 17 per cent, because people were starting to vote', he said in August. 'I knew it wasn't going to be enough and we were starting to get into the realm of maybe. I was hopeful until the end, but I knew deep down it was an outside chance.'

Ackery ended up running third in Hume, with 15.3 per cent of the primary vote, behind Labor's Greg Baines at 20 per cent. The ALP primary was down 6.65 per cent, Angus Taylor's more than 10 per cent. But Taylor still retained the seat 58 per cent to 42 per cent two-candidate preferred. Having worked as hard as anyone, Murfitt didn't even get the satisfaction of turning the seat marginal.

The illness and death of Ackery's partner had unavoidably taken her out of the campaign at a critical juncture. But there were still lessons, Murfitt says, including doorknocking and proper volunteer engagement and organisation. Interestingly, he has also reconsidered the campaign's Climate 200 position, having discussed the issue with Kate Hook, who told him that Climate 200 funding had not hurt her campaign. 'We really got bogged down in that,' he says. 'I think, in retrospect, we should've just accepted the association and moved on.'

~~~~~

Perhaps the most intriguing of the 2022 results came in the Darling Downs electorate of Groom in Queensland. Suzie Holt's plucky little campaign ran fourth on first preferences, garnering just over 8.2 per cent of the vote, behind the LNP's Garth Hamilton with 44 per cent, the ALP at 19 per cent and One Nation at 9.5 per cent. Another independent—nurse and mother of five Kirstie Smolenski—almost equalled Holt at 7 per cent.

Which made it all the more remarkable that Queensland's lone 'Voices of' candidate shot to second position after preferences, coming in at 43 per cent to Hamilton's 57 per cent. To Antony Green, that indicated just how 'well on the nose' the LNP was, with voters going to the trouble to ensure 'they voted for somebody else before LNP'.

Like Nicholls, Groom is another paradox. Classed as 'provincial' by the AEC, it centres on Toowoomba, Australia's second most populous inland city after Canberra. But it isn't just located on the rich, rural Darling Downs, it's also a bastion of conservative Christian politics, one that had voted against marriage equality, albeit narrowly.

The preselection in 2020 of mining engineer Hamilton, from the right of the LNP, to succeed retiring moderate John McVeigh, raised concerns within the LNP about a growing fundamentalist right-wing Christian faction within the Toowoomba branch. That fear had been Holt's motivation for entering the 2022 fight. And she was not alone in what *The Guardian* called a highly contested 'frontline in the battle for the soul of the Coalition'.

The interesting thing is how Holt catapulted to second in that field of eight. To Green, it was down to the unpopularity of the LNP and its candidate; someone had to come second, and six candidates had primary votes of less than 10 per cent. But as the candidate and her campaign manager tell it when we speak in July, the preference flow was the result of strategy and hustle. Holt says she got 75 per cent of all preferences where the vote was not for the LNP. And she did so because of the effort they put into the battle for the hearts and minds of those aligned with her competitors.

'We were a very small but mighty team,' she says. 'We didn't have the resources or volunteer base that a lot of the other independents had. But we did have real diversity, both within the [Voices of Groom] and our campaign. We had everything from the very hard right of the LNP, the UAP and One Nation to the Greens, and everything in between, coming together as our volunteer base.'

With a total budget of just $75,000, she and her campaign manager, Meredith King, used human and financial resources wisely. 'When we scattered people around pre-polling and polling booths, we were very strategic about the conversations we needed to have,' Holt says. 'People were slow to see what we could do, so we had to be strategic in our placement. We had one of our farmers who had stood for One Nation [previously] standing out in Jondaryan, which is a really small farming community, with an umbrella greeting everyone coming through.'

By pre-poll, the campaign had 43 volunteers for the four booths, all in Toowoomba. By election day, they had 130 volunteers for all 51 booths. But much of the work had already been done by then. Both Voices of Groom and the campaign used local business groups as a community network, including the Toowoomba Chamber of Commerce and the well-established local networking organisation the Toowoomba and Surat Basin Enterprise.

'We were able to tap into that network and then work closely with the Toowoomba Chamber to align ourselves on a number of issues,' says Holt. 'They began to see us as an asset, so we then started attending a number of their events, which gave us a huge networking base.'

Within a couple of weeks of the election being called, one of the local business groups started to hold candidate forums. A mid-May forum at the Toowoomba Bowls Club, before a crowd predominantly supporting Clive Palmer's UAP, became so heated that Garth Hamilton walked out. 'It was really more like a rally,' Holt says. 'The issue around [Covid] mandates was huge in our region. I had to grab the microphone off one candidate because he really was rallying. And because they knew that I had been supportive of the mandates, they flew at me. It actually got very loud. People yelled. I was called a sociopath because I was calm.'

Meredith King: 'I was sitting in the back going, "Suzie, just step back."'

Suzie Holt: 'And I said, "No, we're going to listen to every single person in this audience." Miles and I stayed till 10.30 at night and we spoke to as many of those people as possible, and we listened to them. We were exhausted, but we built a relationship with the UAP and One Nation supporters. And we got a lot of their votes coming through.'

King: 'It was a seminal moment for the campaign, because people started to respect Suzie for turning up with all of these other people.'

While Hamilton's 56.89 per cent two-party preferred vote doesn't technically make Groom marginal, Holt and King consider the difference academic. At 6.9 per cent, Hamilton's margin is a third of the 20.5 per cent that McVeigh managed in 2019. It's odds on, too, that Holt will run again. A candidate who started out tentative, and remains disarmingly easy to underestimate, has found her voice, and vocation.

'Someone had to smash it to start with,' she says. 'It's been worth it, because we've shifted the dial in a very conservative seat, which is a great outcome for our region. The feedback that we've had since is that the conversation has changed and the conversation is ongoing.'

Meredith King says one sign of that change is 'the number of people that have started to ring since May 21. We were like, "Do you realise the election's over?" Suzie hasn't said anything about what she's going to do but they're ringing and talking to her about all these different issues and things that they want to see happen.'

'One local journalist said it's like we are the opposition,' Holt adds. 'The minute we got that result, even though we were fourth initially, people came on board. We campaigned as if we were the member for Groom and I suppose that has just continued.'

15

UNLEASHED

The community-backed independents' 2022 triumph wasn't just a mutiny that hid in plain sight. To misquote the great Gil Scott-Heron, election night was a revolution that was entirely televised. As the results rolled in, two realities—one within the independents movement and one without—collided publicly and in real time.

The incredulity of the campaigns' amateur number crunchers early in the evening was mirrored by that of the professionals as the night wore on. This was partly due to the unprecedented scale of the challenge the independents had mounted. Their sheer numbers made the task of calling the election 'technically more difficult', the ABC's Antony Green told *The Guardian* on election day, without 'historical preference counts as a comparison'.

Even forewarned, however, the most celebrated psephologist in the country seemed discombobulated at times, manually overriding his algorithm at one point in the night because, if he didn't, seats such as Mackellar, Goldstein and Wentworth would 'tip over' into independent hands and he needed to be sure before declaring them.

It took some time to call North Sydney, 'because it was unclear for a while whether Labor or the independent was going to finish second', Green explained when we spoke after the election. Similarly, it was 'sensible to wait on Wentworth because of the pre-poll and postal vote being so heavily biased towards the Liberal Party', he said. 'Kooyong and Goldstein had a little bit of that as well, but in both of those you just make absolutely sure on some of these concepts, particularly with postals. There was an increase in postals [and] there was an increase in pre-poll votes . . . there was a high likelihood that the Liberal Party would do better with those votes.'

And for Green, not getting carried away by the kind of emotion that fuelled the community independents movement mattered. 'I refuse to be romantic,' he said. 'People always want everyone to be romantic about it, "Oh, they're standing up to the parties" . . . That's fine, but they have a limited number of seats. They're not government . . . It's easy for Clover Moore to campaign for her hospital. The difficulty for a government is to allocate resources across all hospitals. So independents have always got an easy task in that sense.'

A lot of media coverage of the community-backed independents was permeated by a suspicion that some kind of trick, if only of light and emotion, was being perpetrated. 'The media never really got it,' says Climate 200 adviser and press gallery veteran Jim Middleton. 'They never got this distributed model of democracy; they didn't get the Climate 200 phenomenon, and they didn't realise the reality of the independent challenge. Climate 200 was one arm of a pincer, providing expertise and offering money, money that was really necessary. I mean,

Frydenberg spent 3 million bucks. And the other arm was Cathy, the community project.

'They also didn't understand the extent to which the major parties were in secular decline, despite the evidence being right in front of them,' Middleton continues. 'You had people giggling on TV on the night, saying how much harder it was than they had expected. They found it hard to acknowledge the impact on the political agenda of the existing independents. All of them—Helen Haines, Zali, Rebekha Sharkie—were being viewed very favourably by the electorate, who saw what they were doing and thought, "Why can't we have one of them?"'

Middleton had, in fact, rung around television channels ahead of the election to offer expert commentators from the Climate 200 advisory council, which includes Kerryn Phelps, Tony Windsor and Rob Oakeshott. None of those approached took them up on the offer. Instead, the usual in-house commentators and party apparatchiks presided.

'They haven't plugged the independents into their psyches,' Tony Windsor said in early April of the press gallery. 'They have in the Senate, because it occurs in the Senate all the time, so they've adapted. But in the House, they can't come to grips with it. It's too hard for some of the journalists to deal with, both intellectually, I think, but also [because] their owners now are having a much greater say than they did even a decade ago.'

The television coverage just dramatised the sense that something strange and new was happening before viewers' eyes. 'They were in shock because things were not happening as their previous experience had taught them to expect,' former Wentworth independent member Kerryn Phelps said of the election-night offerings. 'They knew the number of independent campaigns out there, but they hadn't been listening to independent commentators. In the weeks leading up to the election, I had written that there was a big thing going on out there that could usher in a new era of democracy.'

The term 'the teals' was a misdescription that arrived quite late in the piece but immediately took hold. Teal was the colour that Dof Dickinson had originally chosen for Warringah. Choice had been limited. Brand colours have to hit hard. Red, blue and green already belonged to parties.

Variations on Warringah's blue–green spectrum did indeed proliferate in many of the 2022 urban campaigns. But Tink, a quintessential 'teal', remained resolutely pink. Zoe Daniel combined teal with yellow and purple. And beyond the urban campaigns was a riot of orange, purple, pink, teal and white; even—in the case of Hume—most of the above.

At its most benign, 'teals' was an attempt to group the independents for ease of reference. To pin a label on a phenomenon. But ease of reference, in a system schooled in party politics, was itself problematic. And often the misconstruction was purposeful, insistent, not least the claim that 'the teals' were a unified Palmer-style operation in disguise.

As Byron Fay said in July, 'Climate 200 is one cog in a very big wheel that powered the outcome that we saw. The idea that it could be controlled by one or a few people is absurd. The candidates themselves are independents first and foremost. If you think you can tell them what to do, you have another think coming.'

There is little question, however, that from the outside—and particularly from the other side—media coverage of the independents looked very different in the lead-up to the election.

The Australian's Simon Benson was hardly alone in calling the independents 'over-hyped'. And there were reams of copy to point to: Climate 200 alone counted more than 135,000 media mentions of its organisation or the independents during the campaign, far wider coverage than independents in the past had achieved.

The Guardian covered the movement in detail, from Steggall's 2019 bid on. Crikey and *The Saturday Paper*, too, covered the 2022 phenomenon extensively. The *Sydney Morning Herald* had dived into Warringah in 2019 and, no matter how much it and its sister paper, *The Age*, initially grappled with how extensively to cover the new crop of candidates, both papers increasingly did so as the energy and traction of the grassroots movement became obvious.

But media coverage was another Rorschach test: one man's over-hyped 'so-called Teal independents' became another woman's failure to come to terms with the depth, variety, momentum and integrity of the campaigns by the media.

The issue of Zoe Daniel and the ABC is emblematic. In his election-night concession speech, Tim Wilson accused the broadcaster of giving his opponent a dream run. When I spoke to Sue Barrett in early April, however, she said the opposite. Polling showed the candidate was in 'with a really good chance', she said, but the media was 'doing everything but helping', including the ABC, which was 'very afraid because she was an ex-ABC person'.

As to why professionals, politicians and commentators alike might have found contemporary independents hard to get their heads around, Ann Capling, a political scientist embedded in the movement, makes a stunningly simple point: 'It was a social movement, not a political movement,' she says. 'People were sick to death of politics the way they were done in Australia. A lot of good, thoughtful people, who would've been involved in politics in earlier eras, had just checked out. They came to us because we weren't a political party and the way we campaigned didn't feel like politics. It genuinely felt like community.'

That gave the Kooyong campaign a momentum of its own, she says. 'We didn't have to drive it. It was like a snowball going down a slope. It just kept getting bigger and bigger. People came to us saying, "I've never done anything like this in my life, but my friend said I should come." They came because they felt optimism; they felt joy.'

~~~~~

As for what's next, the way Groom has fixed its gaze on the 2025 horizon is one broad hint. As is Hume, where Matt Murfitt is already thinking of how he can improve his game, including through work experience at the looming March 2023 NSW state election. 'I'm going to tag along as an adviser for a couple of the New South Wales campaigns and take those lessons in and see if we can effectively test and refine various strategies,' he says.

For some, the 2022 results were so tantalising as to amount almost to a provocation. In June, Voices of Bradfield endorsed Nicolette Boele's candidacy for the 2025 election—or any intervening by-election. Boele has since hired her 2022 campaign manager of volunteers, Carey Francis, as chief of staff, and her campaign manager, Rob Mills, as strategist, kick-starting what is titled the 'Office of Nicolette Boele, Shadow Representative for Bradfield'.

Even Hughes in southern Sydney, where Georgia Steele

won just 14.3 per cent of the primary vote, behind Liberal Jenny Ware (43.5 per cent) and Labor's Riley Campbell (22.5 per cent), has taken on a whole new significance, given the speculation about a possible by-election in Cook, its Shire neighbour and some say twin, whenever Scott Morrison steps down.

It's worth remembering how often previous tilts helped crack the seal on seats that got a result in 2022. Before Allegra Spender there was Kerryn Phelps; before Kylea Tink, Ted Mack; before Dr Monique Ryan, Oliver Yates. Even Steggall's 2019 campaign had a precursor, TV presenter James Mathison's 2016 tilt at Warringah, a campaign managed by Louise Hislop.

Within days of the May 2022 election, Climate 200 was reported to be eyeing the November 2022 Victorian and March 2023 NSW elections, despite donation caps and optional preferential voting adding extra barriers in New South Wales. 'Reported' was the operative word, though. Simon Holmes à Court's actual quoted words were: 'There is no reason we wouldn't support value-aligned community campaigns at the state level, but we haven't yet settled on a plan. With differing electoral laws, our support model will need to be tailored state by state.'

That reflected the reality in the election's immediate aftermath. As Byron Fay said in July: 'We saw a wave coming. It was a very specific wave and we built a very specific surfboard tailored to that wave. And it did the job well. We surfed the wave in. But next time it's going to be a very different wave. Can we build a surfboard that rides the wave? We'll see.

'There are definitely things that give us a sense that we can make some sort of contribution,' he said. 'Is it going to be the same sort of contribution? Who knows? There's a saying in politics, "You're never as good as your most recent victory, and you're never as bad as your most recent loss.'"

By late August, Annika Smethurst reported in *The Age* that 'a wave of professional women' had been inspired to enter the Victorian election race by the federal result. They included hospital doctor Kate Lardner in the Liberal-held state seat of Mornington, and small business owner Sarah Fenton, who had founded an ocean-swimming group during Covid-19, in the Labor seat of Bellarine. A doctor and a swimmer sounded strangely familiar.

The article went on to mention former McGowan staffer Jacqui Hawkins in the Liberal seat of Benambra, and former Labor Party member and lawyer Nomi Kaltmann, who is taking on deputy Liberal leader David Southwick in Caulfield, held on a margin of just 0.1 per cent.

By early September, Climate 200 had a new 2022 election landing page: '11,200+ of you began to fix the broken party system. Help us continue pushing for greater action on climate, integrity and gender equality,' it said. The revolution would continue.

Federally, one of the possibilities under active discussion was how an effective surfboard might be fashioned to ride the wave in rural and regional seats. The successful new campaigns in 2022 had, after all, exclusively been in affluent, urban seats. The appetite beyond those seats was, however, underlined by the fact that one-third of Climate 200's donors had come from rural and regional areas.

'Since the election, one of the things that I've been really keen to pursue, and this is probably how we move forward, is something like a regional alliance to progress regional candidates to get over the line,' says Suzie Holt. 'We all had a similar outcome at the election. We got there in the end, but we definitely need a hand to make it happen, and I've certainly put that to Cathy and others.'

Caz Heise, who says she, too, will consider running in 2025, has been part of those conversations: 'Forming some kind of alliance is something that a few people like Suzie and myself have discussed. I don't know if that would work. The question is whether it takes away from the notion of being independent for your region. I'm not sure that what we're seeing in the parliament now is going to resonate with a lot of people in rural and regional areas. [Those independents] are very citified. I think we need to explore it more. I've had a chat to Climate 200 about it, and said, "We need to be thinking about the regions." Certainly people like Cathy and Ruth McGowan are a good resource.'

Having wondered if No Fibs had done its job post-election, a decade after it tracked Indi, Margo Kingston has also since decided to focus on the rural and regional areas that first inspired her. The moment is broadly reminiscent of September and October 2021, when Kylea Tink and Climate 200 had both announced their intentions, rumours abounded, but so much still seemed to hang in the balance. Now, as then, much of the action is offstage.

In August 2022, the Community Independents Project—formed after McGowan's inaugural Zoom conference, 'Getting Elected', in February 2021—held its first national convention, 'Empowered Communities: Next Steps'. The two titles marked the progression that had taken place over just eighteen months, as did the fact that the 300 people from 81 electorates who attended the first had grown to 460-plus from 100 electorates this time around. As Andrew Wilkie, who participated in a panel, says: 'If that doesn't send a shiver down the spine of the old parties, then they're not paying attention.'

The attendees' top three areas of interest should engender more shivers. 'For those who want to get going, they were keen to network. They wanted to know how this all worked, what's the magic,' Cathy McGowan said afterwards. 'For the ones who got elected, it was how they were going to put community at the centre; they ran as community independents and people are really keen to continue to be engaged. So that's obviously a work in progress.' The other area was how to continue to progress 'their issues politically outside their MP', whether or not they had a community-independent member.

None of which suggests that the very independent genie unleashed in 2022 is going back into a two-party bottle any time soon. The 2022 election politicised ordinary citizens in a way never seen before. Tens of thousands of Australians gave their time and money to the experiment, engaging with and learning about the political process as they did so. Cathy McGowan said that in 2013 she brought to parliament the 500 people involved in her campaign and in Voices for Indi. Since then, a few hundred in one electorate has become many thousands across many. The new candidates carry the hopes and expectations of those constituents with them to Canberra.

Meanwhile, a whole new cadre of community campaign managers has been minted, many of them formidable enough to beat experienced practitioners and the party machine in hard-fought seats. It's easy to see why the Liberal Party needed the contemporary community-backed independents movement to be the creatures of one man and one organisation in the lead-up to the 2022 election. That way, there was only one head to lop off. In reality, the movement was always a hydra.

Nor is it only political parties in Australia that are watching how community-backed independents fare. Within days of the May election result, the UK *Guardian* rang the alarm at Downing Street, warning of the result's implications for then UK prime minister Boris Johnson, another 'conservative leader so heavily disliked they can't even be featured in campaign literature; seen as lacking integrity; unclear about strategy in the face of a cost of living crisis; and unpopular with women and liberal graduates for his culture war posturing'.

The election had been 'uncannily familiar to followers of UK politics', Sam Freedman wrote. That was in part due to the two countries' shared politics and past. But more recently those parallels had been 'magnified due to the influence of conservative Australian strategists Lynton Crosby and Mark Textor, and their proteges', the masterminds of 'all the Australian Liberal Party's campaigns since 1996'.

Both the UK and US have very different electoral systems, of course. But in the latter, Elon Musk, fresh from his quixotic tilt at a Twitter takeover, tweeted that he was 'thinking of creating a Super Moderate Super PAC [political action committee]' to support candidates with centrist views from all parties as the mid-term primaries got underway in June 2022. 'hey @elonmusk, we kinda just did that in Australia with @climate200', Holmes à Court tweeted back. 'it was a huge success. happy to chat. #auspol.'

In August, Democrat Mary Peltola pulled off a major upset in a special election to succeed an Alaskan representative in Congress who had died. Alaska had introduced ranked (preferential) voting in 2020. In a field that included the quintessentially polarising Sarah Palin, Peltola 'won by appealing to Alaskan interests and the electorate's independent streak', the *New York Times* reported, adding: 'But Alaska's new voting system played a big role, too.' Again, it all sounded familiar.

Peltola became the first Native Alaskan member of Congress, as well as the first woman to represent Alaska in the House. Some commentators said it was more to do with Palin than Peltola, much as they said Warringah in 2019 was about Abbott not Steggall. But the scale of the threat was immediately apparent from the way Republicans mobilised to make sure the ranked-voting model, which some labelled a 'scam', didn't catch on more broadly.

'There's a seismic change happening, what they talk about as a post-democratic era and the failure of the two-party system, and we in Australia are behind the rest of the world,' Dof Dickinson said in July, pointing to English journalist Ian Dunt's 2020 book, *How to be a Liberal*, which sees the 2008 financial crisis, Brexit and populism as an existential threat to an illustrious tradition.

Pulling Australia into the currents of global progressivism, and shame at its backwardness, were major motivations for many involved in community-backed independents campaigns in 2019 and 2022. But 35-year-old political tragic and convenor of Australia's preferential-voting fan club, Charlie Caruso, for one, wonders if Australia is, in fact, now behind or ahead of the curve.

After scanning the horizon in her state and country for so long, and taking 2019 like a bullet, 2022 has renewed her faith. 'It's kept hope alive,' she says, 'and that hope is that Australia, far more than any other Western country, has a real chance to show what modern democracy looks like.'

ACKNOWLEDGEMENTS

I would like to thank two genius editors: Katrina Strickland, who first pushed me down this path, and Richard Walsh, who not only commissioned this book but descended into the trenches with me to turn it around in under three months. Without his generosity, guidance and good humour it would never have happened. Particular thanks, too, to Elizabeth Weiss and her formidable team—Angela Handley, Nicola Young and Allegra Bonetto—for their support, patience and consummate professionalism.

Huge thanks to all the people who really know stuff and helped bring a rookie up to speed. Their names are on every page, but particular thanks to Cathy McGowan, Simon Holmes à Court, Lachlan Harris, John Daley and Margo Kingston.

The community-backed independents movement is a story with 20,000-plus characters. No account can be definitive. With that in mind, I would like to thank all those who moved mountains, changed the landscape and then sat down with me to share their experiences, particularly Kirsty Gold, Tina Jackson, Lyndell Droga, Ann Capling, Kristen Lock, Mark Kelly,

Ranya Alkadamani, Sue Barrett, Louise Hislop, Tony Fairweather, Jacqui Scruby, Matt Murfitt, Suzy Bessell, Trine Barter, Meredith King, Denise Shrivell and Charlie Caruso.

And finally, thanks to my first and best reader, John Ireland.